WHAT'S ON YOUR MIND?

Your Success Begins With Your Thinking

by

Thomas Weeks, III

Harrison House
Tulsa, Oklahoma

Editorial development by ASarah Publications (www.asarah.com)

10 09 08 07 06   10 9 8 7 6 5 4 3 2 1

What's On Your Mind?
Your Success Begins With Your Thinking
ISBN 13: 978-1-57794-748-6
ISBN 10: 1-57794-748-7
Copyright © 2006 by Thomas Weeks, III
Thomas Weeks, III Ministries
P.O. Box 60866
Washington, DC 20039

Published by Harrison House, Inc.
P.O. Box 35035
Tulsa, Oklahoma 74153

CONTENTS

The Protocol of Prosperity

Abundance, prosperity—true success in the form of joy, happiness, and peace—is a realm that involves more than finances, although we should not ignore that aspect. True prosperity is a result, rather than a primary goal in itself. It results from forming a relationship with God through His Son and growing in relationship with this God of goodness, love, and abundance by learning to think in line with the way He thinks.

God does bless His people with abundant life both now and in eternity, but He does this within a protocol that is not to be tampered with. I discovered that God established a synchronization of the specific principles in Philippians 4:6-9 to bring us into a protocol of releasing true biblical prosperity, the abundance He has already ordained for us. This protocol of prosperity is centered in knowing the God of peace and learning to live from that place of peace He has for us.

The "door" God provided for us to go through into the restoration of the vital, living, breathing relationship with Him, full of the life and joy that He originally created for mankind to have in fellowship with Him, is Jesus (see John 10:9). Jesus' statement we read in verse 10, "…I am come that they might have life, and that they might have it more abundantly," is His promise of prosperity in the general sense, not just regarding financial abundance. When we receive the Way the God of peace has provided for us to form a relationship with Him (see John 14:6), and we go through the Door, we are ready to learn the protocol for moving into the true prosperity God has ordained for us.

In this commonly known passage of Philippians 4:6-9 (below), the Apostle Paul identifies key principles that govern what I term "the protocol of prosperity." I use the word *protocol* because there are procedures that we must accept in our spirit, as we do in the natural realm, as being true and workable in our lives.

> *Do not fret or have any anxiety about anything, but in every circumstance and in everything, by prayer and petition (definite requests), with thanksgiving, continue to make your wants known to God.*
>
> *And God's peace [shall be yours, that tranquil state of a soul assured of its salvation through Christ, and so fearing nothing from God and being content with its earthly lot of whatever sort that is, that peace] which transcends all understanding shall garrison and mount guard over your hearts and minds in Christ Jesus.*
>
> *For the rest, brethren, whatever is true, whatever is worthy of reverence and is honorable and seemly ["honest" KJV], whatever is just, whatever is pure, whatever is lovely and lovable, whatever is kind and winsome and gracious ["of good report" KJV], if there is any virtue and excellence, if there is anything worthy of praise, think on and weigh and take account of these things [fix your minds on them].*
>
> *Practice what you have learned and received and heard and seen in me, and model your way of living on it, and the God of peace (of untroubled, undisturbed well-being) will be with you (AMP, emphasis mine).*

"Protocol" refers to procedures we live by that work. Just as we know there are laws in place that tell us driving 75 mph in a 45 mph zone will get us ticketed, there are also laws (protocol) in the spiritual realm that we must accept and live by to bring into our life on earth God's desires for our abundant well-being.

People tend to look at finances to determine whether someone is prospering. Even though bank accounts, homes, and cars are measurable tools, financial prosperity alone does not provide the answers we are seeking.

Those answers are found in the well-being that comes from relationship with God, the Source of prosperity and all things good.

We usually prosper in many ways before we reach our goals of financial security. If we base our opinion of prosperity strictly on the amount of money we have accumulated, we can be deceived into thinking that God is not prospering us. My point is that we were not created to have money as the focal point of our thinking. The principles in Philippians 4:6-9 extend far beyond the financial realm.

The Path to Peace

God births our prosperity through our thinking. We know from Proverbs 23:7 that as we think in our heart, we are. The Apostle Paul understood this. When He wrote the passage in Philippians 4:6-9, some people in the church were living with anxieties and emotions about their spiritual life and the things they saw happening around them. Paul recognized that too many believers were living in a place of anxiety instead of walking the path of peace that leads to the place of eternal assignment.

The protocol Paul began laying out for the believers would put them in position to walk in God's abundance and fulfill their eternal destinies. He taught them to think in line with who God is, with His ways of doing things, and with His principles. These types of thoughts would change their mindsets.

Paul instructed the Philippians not to be anxious ("careful" KJV) for anything. In so many words he was saying, "Don't be so emotional—let me tell you how to get rid of those controlling emotions." He explained how to approach God in the right state of mind, with confidence in Him—"in every thing by prayer and supplication with thanksgiving"—when they made their requests to Him. He was teaching them to exercise patience and allow God's peace to guard their hearts and minds through Christ Jesus. As they waited for the answer, they were to keep their minds on the thoughts that would allow them to live in the untroubled, undisturbed well-being of the God of peace who was with them.

Emergency-Based or Peace-of-God-Based Living

Many people are driven to God by their anxieties; when instead, God desires for us to seek Him by assignment and experience supernatural peace and that divine release of greatness within, an inkling, of the eternal magnitude of their destiny. I have found that these two approaches by people in their relationship with God represent two groups of people in the church today.

The people in the first group are in a constant state of turmoil, worried about everything that comes their way. They have not grasped the concept from Proverbs 23:7 that as we think in our heart, we are. Rather than heed Paul's teaching that gives them direction for the way out of their emotional state, they continue to live from their emotions, fears, and worries.

The people in the second group have read the Apostle Paul's words in Philippians 4:6-9, believe, and act on them. These people pray their way out of all anxieties and worries. They enjoy the peace of God in their lives because they refuse to live with constant worry and anxiety. These proactive believers are walking in that not-to-be-tampered-with protocol of prosperity in order to move into the true biblical prosperity God intends. They are not waiting for an "emergency" to arise in order to begin thinking about biblical prosperity.

Perceptions, Precepts, and What's On Your Mind

In the Old Testament we see three levels described upon which truth is built. These levels, of course, carry into the New Testament, and in them we see the thought of Proverbs 23:7 reflected: As we think in our heart, we are. The first level is *perception*, viewing something in the way God views it. In Psalm 27:11 we read that David said, "Teach me thy way, O LORD...." When we know how God views something, we can base our thoughts and actions on His viewpoint. This gives us the right perception.

The second level of truth is comprised of God's *precepts* and *statutes*, or guidelines (rules), He has set in place for us to follow. As we learn how

God wants something handled, we find it much easier to follow His guidelines, or rules, for our lives when we know what they are! David spoke of keeping God's precepts throughout Psalm 119 (see AMP).

The third level is comprised of God's *laws*. God established two important laws in the Old Testament (which in the New Testament Paul expanded in the light of Jesus) that came into play in the commandments God gave Moses:

1. The law of righteousness, and

2. The law of death.

We read in Romans 8:1-2 that Paul speaks of these two laws, stating that each has its rewards.

> *There is therefore now no condemnation to them which are in Christ Jesus, who walk not after the flesh, but after the Spirit. For the law of the Spirit of life in Christ Jesus hath made me free from the law of sin and death.*

To be concise, the law of righteousness brings the reward of eternal life with Christ, while the law of death brings the "reward" of an eternity in hell. As we think in our inner man, this is who we will become: slaves to our flesh or servants of righteousness. As sons and daughters of God, we need to be knowledgeable of the spiritual laws and the way God works through them and remain determined to think on the things God's Word tells us to keep on our minds.

Why don't you stop for a few moments, re-read the virtues listed in Philippians 4:8-9, and ask yourself if you are acknowledging these virtues? Are you letting God work them into your life? *Thinking* becomes our primary point of reference. The person you are right now is a direct result of what has been on your mind, but above all remember that God wants you—all of us—to grow to the place of entering a deeper realm of relationship with Him, to become so well-grounded in who He is and in who we are to Him that we live in His untroubled and undisturbed peace in every area of our lives.

Your Thoughts, Your Now, Your Future

As you learn to "think on and weigh and take account of these things," the virtues of God listed in Philippians 4:8-9, the "protocol of prosperity" will bless your life abundantly. Building your relationship with God and changing your thoughts to agree with His thoughts will serve to shape your future.

It is important to grasp that heeding Paul's instructions in this passage begins to take effect at the point we begin, not just in the present. For example, people who understood and heeded Paul's instructions ten years ago would probably have a much better mindset than they currently possess. I know that I would. More importantly, if we grasp these principles now, we will be in a much better posture to receive and activate God's blessings, favor, and prosperity ten years from now. We can be much further ahead in the things of God than we have ever been or ever expected to be.

I write this humbly, because I have often wished I had known more people in the past who could have taught me the importance of the types of thoughts we have on our minds. Now that I have discovered the principles Paul teaches in this passage and applied them to my life, I am determined to share with everyone who is seeking God's true prosperity this major aspect of our relationship with God that Jesus provides in this protocol of prosperity.

When I was growing up in church, one of the most important things I remember being taught was to look toward heaven. We sang the old song "I'll Fly Away"[1] over and over again, clapping and stomping the floor as we sang. Those songs birthed a spirit of praise in us and also brought real joy in our lives. Yet because most of those people were working on a daily job that didn't pay very much and living from paycheck to paycheck, this approach to life put them in a mode of simply existing. We comforted ourselves with those songs of promise that one sweet day, by and by, life would be better. I was young, but I knew those people believed they had to die and go to heaven in order to have a better life. We didn't understand the significance, the importance, of the types of thoughts God intends for us to have on our minds.

Do Your and God's "Philosophies" Agree?

For the last several decades the church has begun to change its *philosophy*. I am using this word carefully (in a broad sense) about life in general. If you adopt a philosophy that opens you up to more of what God has available, you will walk in more of what He has for you, but if you adopt a philosophy that limits you, you are hindering everything that God wants to do in your life.

Theologically speaking, as Christians we know about salvation, some of us about speaking in tongues as well as confessions or statements in line with God's Word that we release from our mouths, but every church adopts its own "philosophy" as to why the particular church does certain things while not allowing other things. My meaning, in capsule form, of "philosophy," for lack of a better word in this sense, would be that it consists of our daily thoughts toward righteousness (or unrighteousness), our value systems, and our understanding of the plans God has for our lives.

I have never been "high" on drugs, but people tell me that when they are puffing on a "weed" or sniffing a substance, they reach deeper inside of themselves, pursuing thoughts and philosophies that they had not comprehended until then. As a result, their thoughts and perceptions are usually based on the experiences they had and the conclusions they reached during that "high." Whether their conclusions were right or wrong, these thoughts became their philosophy or the thing they thought about most. This, in turn, led them to communicate with other people in ways and on levels that were previously unknown to them. My point is this: Relationships open up to us based on our thinking and perception about people and belief systems.

This leads us back to the central core, or epicenter, of *What's On Your Mind?* What you allow to exist in your thoughts will determine whether you are going to grow closer in your relationship with God, progressing to something greater in Him, in the pattern given in the Old and New Testaments, or whether you are going to stagnate spiritually, instead heading down the path to destruction. The thoughts you allow in your mind—either by renewing your mind to God and His Word in relationship with Him, or by conforming your thoughts to the world's way of thinking when that way conflicts with God's way—will determine whether you will walk according to the law of righteousness after the Spirit or according to the law of sin and death after the flesh.

If your thoughts are based on an inaccurate philosophy, even one you acquired in church, and those thoughts tell you there is nothing greater for you, then you are already hindering everything that God wants to do in your life. God always wants to take you to your next dimension of relationship, and in doing so He often changes your surroundings. He does this to change how you view things.

Incidentally, this is one reason why you should never judge someone else, because one day God may put you on that same level. You may reach that level and go through a process similar to the one the person you were judgmental toward experienced. From understanding what the person was walking through, dealing with, and feeling, you will see how important it is for other believers to pray for, encourage, and follow the leading of the Holy Spirit in determining if there is something else they should do to help. Thoughts dedicated to judging someone will block insight that God may be trying to give by instructing how to pray for or help bear the other person's burden.

If you judge another person's actions, you are telling God that you are not ready to grow to that level of thinking. Here's another point to consider. Never judge a person who is being blessed more than you are—you may be judged when you arrive at the same level.

Free From Self-Imposed Limitations

My goal in writing this book is for you to uncover any thoughts and erroneous philosophies you have held that, instead, have held *you* captive. My desire is for you to become free by building your relationship with God through learning how to replace any thoughts imprisoning you with His thoughts in His Word about you and your life, instead.

As you walk with me through this book and through this process, you may be astonished to learn how some thoughts have limited you in ways you hadn't realized and how they have shaped you into the person you are today. If your mind—so worthy of greater thoughts for so long—has been imprisoned until this point, you will see those dungeon doors lift, and you will begin to transform into the person who is fulfilling the desire that God placed in your heart.

The honest situation is that many of us Christians have selective amnesia. We may try not to remember how we acted at a certain time (as a result of faulty thinking), but our hearts will always remind us. Let's say you were upset about something trivial and acted in a manner unbecoming to your image as a Christian, but now you can't erase those thoughts that you imagined you had buried long ago. Thoughts about that incident occasionally come to mind when something reminds you of it, especially when you see someone you have wronged. Instead of living from a place of untroubled and undisturbed peace in that area, those old feelings return and you are in a constant struggle to keep your emotions under control. That part of you is living in and reacting out of the past.

The devil uses those things to accuse us, telling us that because of the things we have done in the past, we have no future. He wants to hinder our forward progress to try to stop us from fulfilling the future God has for us. If we succumb to those distracting, accusatory thoughts, we *will* let him limit us.

This book will walk you through the process of opening those dungeon doors and freeing you to leave in the past, where they belong, any thoughts that are slowing you down or stopping you from moving into position for all God has for your life.

Based on the scenario above, we can see far more than the obvious reasons why Paul instructs us to forget the things that are behind (Phil. 3:13) and the reason the next point is extremely important: We, each one of us, must watch ourselves so that we do not live out actions that we have already scripted for ourselves from our past experiences. Our thinking can keep us deadlocked in the past. All too easily we can lose the progressive forward movements that we must rely upon to bring us the biblical rewards we are seeking.

God Births His Desires From Our Thinking

Once you understand and believe that your thoughts are the birthing place of what you receive from God, that your thinking is the place where He begins to orchestrate your destiny, you will always protect the types of thoughts you have on your mind and your thinking processes as well. You will guard your thinking with everything that is in you. As you read this book, keep Proverbs 4:23 *on your mind*: "Keep thy heart with all diligence; for out of it are the issues of life." A closer look at the word *heart* in this verse reveals it actually means "the inner man, the mind, the will...under-standing...."[2] Don't live from the script you wrote for yourself in the past.

God-Ordained Thinking

The majority of the many people who live on that "emergency-based" (as I term it) level Paul brought to light (in v. 6) have ignored the prompt-ings of the Lord for years and years. People who live from one emergency to another have ignored His instructions; but let trouble come, and they run to Him in a split second crying, "Oh, God, You have to help me. I need a miracle, and I need it now, Lord!"

Hear me on this: People who live in an emergency mode almost never grow into thinking God's thoughts. They won't grow in relationship with God because they are living according to the flesh rather than according to the principles of the Spirit. They move from emergency to emergency rather than from a place of peace into true prosperity.

This book will walk you through the process of building your founda-tion of thought life on "these things" Paul teaches in Philippians 4:6-9 in order to live a God-ordained- (Prince-of-Peace-) based life of abundance and fulfilled purpose, rather than a walk-according-to-the-flesh-based existence of living from one emergency to the next.

We will look at Paul's text which tells us how to live above anxiety—how to let God's peace guard our hearts—as we wait upon God for the answers we seek. Verse 6 begins the simple outline Paul gives us:

1. Pray.

2. Pray with supplication: Put your definite requests before God. What are you asking Him to do?

3. Let your requests be made known to God with thanksgiving.

4. Stop worrying—God heard you!

5. Rest in that peace of God that passes all understanding.

We will walk through building and enhancing our relationship with God by thinking on and practicing the things in verse 8: whatsoever things are true, honest, just, pure, lovely, of good report, of virtue, and of praise. As we mature in Christ and think, speak, and do everything from the basis of the foundation that results from thinking on these virtues, we move in the abundance God has already ordained to be released in our lives and in the lives of others in whom we invest ourselves.

So as you move forward in this book, also look forward to the transformation that comes from renewing your mind to the Word of God and the life that comes from keeping God's thoughts on your mind.

CHAPTER 1

Whatsoever Is *True*: Separating Spiritual Truth From Natural Fact

If your thoughts were played over an audio system, would people recognize that you are a Christian? What are you thinking about right now? Are you an optimist or a pessimist? Do negative thoughts control the way you think, or are your thoughts focused toward heavenly things and building a productive and prosperous future? Remember, the things that are *on your mind* become the parameter or guide of how you live on a daily basis. They determine your now and your future.

By following the pattern in our thinking (and as a result, in our living) that God lays out for us in Philippians 4:6-9, we will become all that God has destined us to be and live *a settled,* peaceful life. The question is whether we will let God work the spiritual protocol into our minds so that ordered thinking will manifest the unique, incomparable fruits of virtue in every area of our lives.

I had been praying and seeking the Lord for quite some time for more of His sons and daughters to become knowledgeable in building their foundation of thought life on theses virtues. He revealed to me a deeper meaning for each virtue by showing me the word for each as an acronym.

The principles work synergistically to bring about the abundance God has already ordained in our lives, so let's begin thinking on these virtues by looking at them one by one through the acronym God gave me for each, beginning with the spiritual virtue of whatsoever is "true."

This acronym begins with "Tested Thinking" that gives you the confidence of already knowing what the outcome will be so that in the end you won't have a result that is totally wrong for you. With *Tested Thinking* you think on what is true rather than fact.

- **T** ested Thinking (to differentiate between "fact" and "truth"), *leads to a*

- **R** eward System, *of lives blessed with dividends, from embracing the truth, that leads to*

- **U** ndeniable Favor, *amazing atmosphere of God working out our experiences by manifestation of His divine favor that releases*

- **E** mpowerment of Tested Thinking, *blessing others and imparting a "mantle" to them, then moving to our next level*

Tested Thinking

The first letter in our acronym is "**T**" for "**Tested Thinking**." When we speak of something being *true* we must understand that "truth" is not constituted by simply feeling something may be right, even if it has been spoken of as being "fact." Every day we hear things on television or read news in magazines and on the Internet that are conveyed to us as "fact." Let me be clear: Just hearing a piece of information does not necessarily make it a "fact" that is true.

Directed by Truth Rather Than Fact

A piece of "information" can be true, or it could be false. For example, I live in the Washington, D.C., area where it is normally hot during the month of August. That is a fact. However, the truth of the matter is that some days are cooler than normal. Now if I relied on the fact (that August days are usually hot) I might get up one morning, put on a pair of shorts and a T-shirt, dash out the door to go for a short run, only to turn around and go right back in the door. Why? The fact may have changed: instead of being 85 degrees outside it was only 60, very atypical for that time of year; but nevertheless, it is true!

So the facts (statistics for the weather outlook) are not necessarily true. Facts can be true according to the season, but truth is always true, *regardless of the time or season.* You need to be careful to not allow people to direct your life with facts, because facts always move you into your feelings.

How can *Tested Thinking* help you to determine truth? After much prayer and study I have come to this conclusion: *Tested Thinking* leads us into an understanding and belief that what God has set before us at this point to consider and act upon is attached to a law. As a result, we can refer to and look back at that law, knowing that it is going to bring us to the place God has for us, and we will live in His untroubled, undisturbed well-being in every phase along the way to that place. With *Tested Thinking* you have a means to determine what is "fact" and what is "truth."

Let me illustrate. Suppose you are a single mother, living in a tiny efficiency apartment with two small babies. Knowing you need more space, you begin to look at one-bedroom apartments. The fact is: You need more room. Another fact is: One more bedroom is not going to meet your needs—you need at least three bedrooms. "But," you say, "I can't afford more than one bedroom, so what do I do?"

Let me share a secret I have learned: Show God that you are willing to work with what you have now, and later He will trust you with something greater. Maybe you should try to do a little redecorating in your small efficiency apartment. Hang a picture, change things around a little, or see if there is a way to put a few things in storage. Meanwhile, save your money until you are able to afford the home you desire.

I would rather live in a small apartment and have money in the bank than live in a large home I cannot afford. Above all, don't do anything just to impress people. God never does anything to impress anyone. He will help you to do the same, because His goal is to build your character and establish your foundation in Him.

When you make decisions that demonstrate your belief that what God said is *true* and follow through by living in line with that decision, you are deepening your relationship with God. He will manifest His favor in your life in a way that *undeniably* attests to Him having worked things out for you.

Let's look in detail at how the single mother kept "whatsoever is true" on her mind and applied it through *Tested Thinking*. *Fact:* She needs more room. *Truth:* Even a slightly larger place wouldn't give her the room she needs. *Truth:* At this time, she couldn't even afford a slightly larger place. *Truth:* She needs to stay where she is.

The law that is attached to the truth she is acting on is one referred to many times in the Bible: Those who are faithful will be blessed. One example is in Matthew 25:21: "His lord said unto him, Well done, thou good and faithful servant: thou hast been faithful over a few things, I will make thee ruler over many things: enter thou into the joy of thy lord." As the single mother is faithful in utilizing and appreciating what God has given her in the place where she is now, God's favor will manifest in her life to work things out and point *undeniably* to Him as the reason, empowering her to reach someone else with that testimony.

The Process of Building a Truth-Based Thought Life

Tested Thinking means there are no overnight wonders. You have to go through a process, little by little, precept upon precept, in each area of your life, or character flaws will pop up one day that you did not even know were there. They will hinder your progress, revealing that you skipped the process God meant for your learning. I would rather make progress a little bit at a time, instead of rushing into something that in the end is totally wrong for me. Parking spaces are a good example. Driving around waiting for a good space to open up is time consuming, but taking a space that is too small can be costly and frustrating if someone hits the side of your new car. Learn to wait for what you want.

Tested Thinking is important in our business transactions, as well as our personal lives. Think back to the last time you went shopping for a new car. How many times have you heard something like this? "If you don't buy this car today, we cannot promise you it will still be available when you return.

We are not sure when we are going to get another car that is this same color, with the same interior, the same equipment, and all the extras this car has on it."

Salespeople, God bless them, try to work on your emotions so that you feel you will never get another chance to take advantage of this outstanding deal! What you must learn is that if you don't get *this* car, there will be another car lot just down the road that may have an even better price on the car you want.

If you apply *Tested Thinking* you will realize that in a few months, all the cars will go on sale. The car you are ready to pay $15,000 for today will sell for $12,500 several months from now. I don't know about you, but $2,500 in the bank sounds pretty good to me. This is the time to *Test* your *Thinking*, "Do I really need this car now? Why do I need it? Am I buying a car because I want to impress somebody?"

Remember, prosperity has nothing to do with *things*, money, or other material *possessions*; it has to do with God's ability to trust you. Think about it. Can He trust you with greater goals now than you had before?

God's laws are so true that even the weather is more predictable today because scientists and weathermen understand the laws of nature. They understand what is going to happen when cold weather starts coming down from Canada towards Seattle, and winds coming off the Pacific Ocean meet it. When a system is making its way across the Midwest and is met by another system coming up from the Gulf of Mexico, they are equipped to predict the next move this combined system will make. Meteorologists understand there are certain natural laws. For instance, because they have studied those laws, they know that hurricane season occurs at a certain time each year and that tornado season will occur in the midsection of the country each spring.

An Expected Outcome

Many people do not really listen to the weather reports; they just wake up and look outside to see what is happening. They judge the weather by what they see. *Is it raining outside? Will I need a coat today? How warm will it be today?* The problem with this type of thinking is they are living from facts rather than truth. Yes, it may be raining, but in an hour the sun may be shining. So, what are the facts? They may change from moment to moment.

Now, let me deal with spiritual fact versus truth. When you read the Old Testament, you can see that it paints a vivid picture of the Law (Ten Commandments). The Law is based on God's precepts and statutes. The precepts (rules for moral conduct) are the building blocks for the statutes. The statutes (established rules) are the building blocks for the Law (established rules expected to be observed.) The established rules expected to be observed include such laws as the law of righteousness and the law of death as well as the Law, the Ten Commandments. God never made a law without first thinking of mankind. Every law was designed with His love for humanity in mind. Basing your life on God's truth will take you where you need to go and (the end result will show you) where you want to go.

Let me go into *Tested Thinking* a little further. When you apply *Tested Thinking,* you know what the outcome will be because you have thought the situation through to the end result. Luke 14:28–30 says, "For which of you, intending to build a tower, sitteth not down first, and counteth the cost, whether he have sufficient to finish it? Lest haply, after he hath laid the foundation, and is not able to finish it, all that behold it begin to mock him, Saying, This man began to build, and was not able to finish."

Things remain uncertain if you have not thought through what will happen if you do things one way versus another. That is why mentorship and the examples given by other mature believers are so important in teaching us how to make quality decisions. We need someone to teach us the next level of thinking, someone who will explain to us the cause and effect, the *whys*, the *hows*, the pitfalls, the struggles, and the successes they have experienced. Mentors in the church must show a representative picture of their struggles as well as their successes in giving their testimonies because a lack of honesty will result in their students going through similar problems that follow faulty thinking.

Back in the day when brothers and sisters in the church used to stand up and testify by saying things like: "This is where my struggle was; this is where I went wrong; this is what I needed to do; this is how I came back to God; and this is how I survived," these testimonies brought a level of empowerment and mentorship to others. However, we do not see a lot of people overcoming their problems today, because today people often fake one another out, trying to sound like they have it all together.

It will take maturity to recognize and admit that this current trend in the church of thinking that by continuing to mask our testimonies, we will begin to see different results, won't work. The trend, the action itself, must change to change the outcome. I have heard it said that the definition of insanity is doing the same thing over and over, expecting different results. To change the type of results we have been achieving in the Kingdom, we simply must change our thinking.

It's similar to this: Would you put five dollars of gas in your car and expect it to last as long as fifteen dollars would? You already know how far five dollars of gas will take you, so if you act as though it's actually fifteen-dollars' worth, there will be a problem down the road. Right when you hit that five-dollar-and-fifty-cent mark, you will be stuck trying to figure out what is wrong with your car. The truth of the matter is you went beyond the T-factor, *Tested Thinking*.

The Proverbs 23:7 concept of "...as he thinketh in his heart, so is he..." is phenomenal. I see it this way: If a man (meaning "mankind") understands the effects of what he is thinking, he can begin to test what he is going to receive. Let me prove this to you. *Do you grasp the idea that thoughts are already things?* You couldn't think about something if it weren't already a "thing." If you hear the word "vacation," your thoughts immediately go to beaches, hotels, good food, lazy days, and sleeping late. Do you believe that you are going to be able to take a vacation, or do you think that vacations are only for rich folk or special people? How you label a thing in your thinking is the way you are going to see it manifest in your life. You can see pictures of vacations all the time, but if you don't start thinking differently from the way you always have, you won't leave town for the beach anytime soon.

Changing Your Perception to Change Your Behavior

One day I was listening to the news on the radio while I was driving to the office, and just as I turned right, I saw a police officer signaling me to pull over. I had been driving this route for several months and hadn't looked down at my speedometer to check my speed. Well, he stopped me, pulled me over to the curb, and as he looked in the car, saw I was dressed for the office. "License and registration," was all he said. I gave him my license, but when I opened up my glove compartment I could not find my registration.

Have you ever had one of those days when it seems like everything is going wrong? I went though my entire glove compartment trying to find that registration. I had just had the car in the shop to have some work done on it, so I was sure they must have neglected to put the registration back in the car. Now I'm sitting there in my car, certain the officer was thinking I had stolen the car and was going to arrest me.

The officer looked at me and said, "Do you know why I stopped you?" I replied, "I think there must be a very good reason, but no, I don't know exactly what it is." He said, "You were doing 42 mph in a 35 mph zone." I answered, "That's very possible, because I was trying to get to the office, and I was afraid I was going to be late. My mind was on something else, and I guess wasn't paying attention to my speedometer."

He looked at me and he looked at the car, then he walked away. I thought he was going to write up a ticket, but when he came back, he said, "I'm just going to give you a warning today."

Since that day my perception has changed—I know I had better look at that speedometer, or I could have another experience like the one I had that day. It would not have benefited me at all for him to just give me a warning if the next time I took that route I drove too fast again. My perception had to change in order for my behavior to change. My thinking had to be tested. This type of experience will be similar for anyone who wants to grow to his or her next level in God. If you want to walk in the promise of undisturbed and untroubled well-being, then get ready. Your thinking is going to be tested throughout your life. So make the decision to start right now, and begin "thinking on" *whatsoever* is "true."

Reward System

The second letter in our acronym is "**R**" for "**Reward System**," because embracing truth always leads to rewards. I was praying some time ago and began to ask the Lord about our rewards for the things we have done on earth. I asked about His timing, and how it affected our destiny. He dropped a phrase into my spirit that I have never forgotten. "Do not separate God's timing from His eternalness." My first thought was, *How could time and eternity ever be combined in the same thought?* He said, "I am the First and the Last; I am the Beginning and the End. Time starts with Me, and it ends with Me. I am not separate from time. Never think I do not work in time. I am the One who initiated it. I am the One who conceived it as a point of reference for the things I have done in your life."

Tested Thinking determines how you choose to think about a thing, how you believe God's Word on a matter, and how you wait for the thing you are praying about to manifest. This yields eternal rewards. God is so "eternally time" that when He starts a thing, He has already ended it before He starts it. He has already seen the end from the beginning, because He is eternal. He is only waiting for your Tested Thinking to line up with His thoughts, so that He can manifest what has already been done. David said it this way, "Let the words of my mouth, and the meditation of my heart, be acceptable in thy sight, O LORD, my strength, and my redeemer" (Ps. 19:14).

Wise Choices Bring Rewards

As we learn to *test* what we receive from God, we discover the divine *Reward System* that begins to bless our lives with the dividends of Tested Thinking. Have you noticed that on some television channels there is a little scrolling bar at the bottom, which lists the abbreviation codes for various companies and the percentage of gain or loss they realized that day? As you test your thinking and come up with the correct "code" to identify the source and truth of every thought, you can reap the dividends that will invariably come at the "end of the day." In other words, you will receive measurable results from embracing truth.

Jeremiah 29:11 tells us the Lord's thoughts toward *us* when He declares, "For I know the thoughts that I think toward you, saith the LORD, thoughts of peace, and not of evil, to give you an expected end."

God knows His thoughts toward you—He knows what He has already planned for your life. Therefore, He will reward you according to your Tested Thinking and the actions you take as a result. Think of it this way. Through your thinking you can determine the type of reward you will receive. When you follow the pattern of Tested Thinking that God has demonstrated, start obeying His precepts (planned thoughts, as spoken through Jeremiah), and are living according to the statutes that He has established, He will cause the rewards of obeying His eternal law to bless your life.

The reward system includes both progress and pain. It is up to you to choose the level of progress and limitations of pain, the limits of what you are willing to sacrifice—such as time or activities or areas where you would normally spend money—in order to press through to receive the dividends, the end results, that your Tested Thinking will yield. Our struggle begins when we try to qualify our spiritual growth by how much we have acquired in the natural realm. Proverbs 19:1 says, "Better is the poor that walketh in his integrity, than he that is perverse in his lips, and is a fool."

I was having a conversation with a friend recently about how much we travel. He relayed to me that he had learned to pack in the Army, using every little "cubby hole" he could find to include more items, even stuffing things into his shoes to save space. By the time you pack everything in its proper space, you can travel with one bag for a three- or four-day trip (instead of using three or four bags). By thinking through the process in advance you can find a system that works for you, which in turn will reward you with less weight to wheel through the airport along with saving you extra time while waiting on your baggage at your destination. God's natural laws will tell you that it is better to have a little of something than to have a whole lot of nothing, and that it's definitely better to test your thinking to yield the fruit of divine rewards.

Valuing What God Gives Us

People who drive an extremely reliable make of automobile (such as Honda, for example) know the car as a rule will last at least ten years when taken care of according to the manufacturer's instructions. If the owners simply perform routine maintenance on the car like having the oil changed regularly, keeping air in the tires at the suggested level, and so on, they can reap great results. The car will provide good, sturdy transportation for years if maintained properly.

On the other hand, people who drive a smaller, less reliable car and load it with twenty-two-inch rims, a big sound system, and put fancy stickers all over it to make it a really "fabulous" set of wheels will more than likely have that car for no more than two or three years.

Why? First of all, very possibly it will be stolen. If not, the owner is probably the type of person who thinks he or she has to prove the car is the best on the road by "taking curves" or road racing whenever the opportunity presents itself and more than likely will wreck it.

How do I know this? The thinking of a person who drives this kind of car is flawed and demonstrates a level of immaturity. The person is more concerned about what is on the surface (immediate gratification) than about what is under the hood. An individual more concerned about shopping for a better constructed, although less flashy, automobile is motivated by the capacity for it to function at optimum levels for a much longer period of time.

My point again is this: Tested Thinking will *reward* you for making wise choices. You may drive a car that doesn't shine quite as much as a higher-priced BMW or Lexus or drive as fast as a car like a Jaguar, but it is your "high-dollar" car and you should value it as such. Some of us aren't blessed in as great a measure as available because we do not value what He has already given us. We have not cleared "materialism" off our plate yet. When God blesses us with something, we must learn how to take care of it and how to use it for His honor and glory. Then the reward will come.

At every level, God is going to measure your progress, because He wants to see how your character is growing. Learn to be happy with two sets of earrings, one watch, five dresses, three blouses, and only two pair of jeans. Make every piece of this wardrobe work for you throughout the week. Here's a tip: You can do more with less if you wisely buy good quality items that will last for a while instead of thirty pair of cheap shoes, fifteen outfits, costume jewelry that comes apart almost immediately, and handbags that will be all scratched up after a week.

By the time you spend your hard-earned money on thirty pair of cheap sunglasses that break the first day you wear them, you could have bought one good brand-name pair that will last much longer. It is better to hold on to that mainstream-brand watch and wait until you are able to upgrade it than to go for super "bling, bling" but totally fake one! Cheap imitations never last.

There is a factual mindset in Western culture that says, "More is more" when actually the opposite is true. Less is more. If you ever look at a fashion magazine such as *Vogue*, you would see and agree that *less* is more elegant. Look at the people who go to finer restaurants or plays. They don't have five rings on every finger. Hear me on this: Don't stack up rings that look like the ones you used to get out of cereal boxes on your fingers; get a ring that means something to you. Wear it, and be happy.

The "less is more" philosophy is important in illustrating our divine reward system. We should never flaunt style or fads, because this will demonstrate to the world that God's reward system is superficial, temporary. Often people look at believers to choose whether they want to serve the type of God we say He is, the One who provides us with everything we need. Whether we realize it or not, someone is looking at our lifestyle of how we portray the Christian life. That person should decide that he or she wants more out of life than a few popcorn rings and "bling, bling" jewelry. If people looking at us to consider whether they are interested in knowing the God we serve see a God who can give only the temporary gain that the world already offers rather than the eternal rewards of God, why on that initial basis would they be attracted to choose to receive and serve Him?

It is better to apply Tested Thinking and wait for what you really want than to settle for that which is not God's best for you. Our divine reward system is based on our progress in life as we make decisions based on Tested Thinking, not on what we accumulate.

Undeniable Favor

The fourth letter of our acronym for "true" is "U," which stands for **Undeniable Favor**. Why? Because *Tested Thinking* leads to a *Reward System*, and because of this you will be able to testify that it is **undeniable** that the hand of God has been at work in your life. Challenging situations invariably come into our lives that only God can remedy, so that we can see the **undeniable** hand of God at work! When I have come through a difficult situation, truth tells me that the only way it worked out for me was that God did it, in spite of who I am or what I have done. No person or spiritual principality can convince me that God has not favored or rewarded me.

God's work in our lives is beautifully illustrated in the story of the prodigal son (Luke 15:11–24). In this story, God reminds each of us who our Father is, what His House represents, and that we are entitled to an inheritance, *simply because He loves us*. It is *undeniable* that I have a Father who can bless me with all the blessings of heaven whenever He so desires. If I were to share my entire testimony with you, it would bear witness in your heart that God has clearly and always been at work in my life. Through all of the struggles, tests, heartaches, and ups and downs, my life proves out His faithfulness.

Hebrews 10:37 tells us, "...he that shall come will come, and will not tarry...." Coupled with this, the old saying is also true that, "God is never early, but He is never late." God has promised that He will always be undeniably our Savior and Deliverer. He will work out all things for our good. Here's why, according to John 8:36, "If the Son therefore shall make you free, ye shall be free indeed."

A Higher Perspective

Let me explain to you why, as a truth-filled believer, you may become frustrated with people who are satisfied with staying on an elementary level. When you have been set free from the level you once knew, and God has placed you on another level, you cannot settle for living according to a lower eternal mindset. As a result, you many find that people around you do not understand you anymore, so they backbite and cause problems in your life because they fail to realize that you are no longer on the same level with them. You have moved to a higher perspective. Your thinking has changed, your rewards are manifesting, and you are glorifying God in your life. God is granting you favor and you are reaping the rewards of Tested Thinking according to Proverbs 16:3, "Commit thy works unto the LORD, and thy thoughts shall be established."

If you walked through life without ever going through a situation that felt as though the Lord was not working in your life, to later come through with the testimony that it was undeniable that His hand had been orchestrating the outcome for your good all that time, your growth as a Christian would be slow indeed. At times, God allows us to walk through scenarios that appear to be so negative we "feel" (emotional thinking) all is lost. Our sensual thinking tells us that we will never make it through this one! Imagine, if you will, experiencing a job loss or a cut in pay, which leaves you wondering if you are going to lose your home. Then a new opportunity comes "out of the blue" that would allow you to refinance your home, with a payment $400 per month less than before.

That's a savings of $4,800 annually, and over the course of twenty years the savings would come to $81,600. Bearing this in mind, would it have been worth going through the process to come out $81,600 ahead? Your initial perception of a negative situation could not compare to the Tested Thinking God birthed in you by walking through the process.

God's Undeniable Work

Now you have a solid testimony of God's undeniable work in your life. That is why you must never let the enemy lie to you again about the truth of God's love, your reward system in Christ, or His undeniable hand of mercy. God wants you to use the testimony you gain to mentor others through the necessary steps to prosperity.

I hear people say quite often, "But Bishop Weeks, you are well-known and successful; you've written books; you speak on television and travel everywhere—I know you could not possibly understand my problems." If people heard the truth of my story they would know that I do understand. There was a time I wanted to commit suicide—yes, I wanted to end it all. I even thought about driving my car over a cliff. This is the kind of information no one wants to stand and tell an audience, but the truth of the matter is, we need to tell our testimony to others. This lets them know that we understand how they may be feeling, and even more importantly, encourages them when they are going through tough times that God is able to deliver them.

Our trust in God grows as we see Him doing things for us that are undeniably Him at work. When we gain a testimony, just one time, that God "came through for us" we can testify undeniably to the goodness of the Lord like the psalmist did in the following verse: "I had fainted, unless I had

believed to see the goodness of the LORD in the land of the living"
(Ps. 27:13).

Believe me, I am not speaking from a background of "having it all."
Yes, I grew up in a very "Yuppie" family, but I went through some tough
times. It was as if God was saying, "Listen, before you can pastor a church
you must be able to understand what it feels like to be evicted and how
repossession can wreak havoc in your emotions. You will have experienced
seeing your credit in such a mess (from wanting to possess everything at
once) that it will take much discipline to recover your good standing."

You go through a process that will bring you to the place of being more
understanding of what other people are feeling so that you do not judge
them. That way, you will instinctively know how to pray for and encourage
others and know how to walk beside them when they are going through a
trial. By coming through life's challenges into a life of undeniable favor
with God, you will become more giving toward people in need. You will not
hesitate to drop a $20 bill in their pocket to help them along until they can
receive a paycheck. You know what they are going through because you
have been there. Most importantly, you know that God will undeniably be
there to work things out in their lives.

Empowerment

The final letter in our acronym is "**E**," which represents **Empowerment**, because God will use truth to empower you. As I have already begun
to reveal, because of the experiences you have gone through that only God
could deliver you from, God has undeniably prepared you to bless someone
who is currently in a similar circumstance. Peter walked on water, but when
he started to sink he was close enough for Jesus to reach out and pull him
up out of the water. What I am trying to tell you is this: When God reveals
truth to your spirit get ready to declare, "Jesus is walking on water again."

When Peter came through his earthly trial of denying Christ when He
was being tried and crucified, he came through this undeniable experience
not possessing silver or gold, but knowing where God's hand of power
could be found (see Acts 3:1-11). He said to the man that was lame,

16

"...Silver and gold have I none, but such as I have give I thee..." (v. 6). In saying this, he was encouraging him, "I know what it is to fall and to have a hand reach out and deliver me. Believe in Jesus Christ, take my hand, and you will rise up from your affliction."

The *fact* is that nobody can walk on water, but Peter discovered the truth, so he walked in that truth until facts started to pull him under—then Jesus reached out to Peter and prevented him from drowning in the threatening waves. This reveals the truth of Tested Thinking. Jesus knew from the beginning of time that He had authority over the depths of the sea, because the Father had called those elements into submission. Then the eternal rewards sprouted up as the earth came into the order God was declaring into existence through the law of the spirit of life which, with every step of the process, overcame the law of death. This reveals our reward system: that which declares an undeniable experience with God in turn allows us to empower someone else with the knowledge we have gained.

Passing That Level of Empowerment Along to Others

You can be assured the truth is firmly established in your life when you can pass it on to another person. When Peter needed help, he didn't need silver or gold; he didn't need a meal or a car. He needed a supernaturally empowered hand to pull him up and into walking in truth. Only truth can walk on top of circumstances that, according to *facts*, cannot exist. After this undeniable experience, Peter was later able to discern what the lame man at the Beautiful Gate needed. He was able to tell him that Jesus had changed the way he perceived life and that, above all else, he wanted to pass that level of empowerment on to others.

When God places a spiritual mantle upon you, He does not empower you for your satisfaction only. He intends for you to pass it on to someone else. And when the truth in you touches another person's life and it begins to bear the same results, you know that your works are wrought in God. The principles that brought you through your dilemma start empowering others as they are healed or brought out of their situation. In Peter's story, not only did the lame man get up; he leaped and ran, praising God everywhere he went. This man had gained a testimony! So I ask you today, are you using your testimony to reach someone else?

Don't forget—Peter had denied Christ three times not long before, yet God had undeniably empowered him so that he could empower someone else. This is the key. A few years ago I read a book that brought me into praying for two, three, then four hours a day, when something came to me. This is what I believe Jesus was saying to His disciples when He asked them why they could not "tarry" with Him for an hour.

Although it has been widely taught that Jesus was disappointed when the three disciples could not stay awake to pray with Him in the Garden of Gethsemane, it came to me that perhaps Jesus was asking them why they couldn't even take twenty minutes each (which would have totaled an hour) to intercede with Him. Jesus realized it was late and they must have been tired, but if they had prayed just twenty minutes each it could have yielded the results of a full hour of prayer. Jesus did not need their prayers as much as He needed them to share in the experience with Him, before they took up the mantle of discipleship.

Because the disciples kept falling asleep, Jesus identified their area of weakness—they had a lot of faith *in* Him, but tiny faith in the power of prayer. Earlier that evening, Jesus told Peter that He had prayed for His faith not to fail (Luke 22:31–32), because his faith was vitally connected to his thinking. In essence, Jesus was praying that Peter's thoughts would line up with truth so that his faith would not fail when trouble came—because a man becomes whatever he "thinketh." The faith you stand on leads you to believe who you are in Christ, and that is the truth God accepts.

Peter ultimately came to the realization that he had to release his old mantle—the experience of walking on water. This meant he had to pray in order to let God build something new in and through him. He went daily to the House of Prayer, because he knew from painful experience that lack of prayer was one of his weaknesses. Peter was not weak in believing; he was weak in intercession. Hear me: You may be able to believe for yourself, but can you intercede for anybody else? If you can't help someone through the vehicle of prayer, then you have a spiritual issue that needs to be corrected. As Christians we should ask ourselves, "Do I think it is all about me?" We should pray until we have received an overflow of spiritual mantles that we can pour out to others who, in turn, will pass them on to yet others. This synergy will create a dynamic and ever-increasing flow of prayer and intercession around the world.

As Peter was being strengthened in one area, he had to release another. You must reach the place that when God speaks to you, you realize that there is someone you need to mentor, or to share with about what God has done for you. There is someone waiting on the other side of your undeniable experience with God who needs to hear your testimony. Perhaps the people around Peter were whispering, "Did you hear that Peter walked on water with Jesus?" Let's get real. Do you think the lame man didn't know who Peter was? If the Pharisees and Sadducees knew of his testimony, then those who gathered at the Beautiful Gate also knew. Do you not think that many had already testified throughout the city and beyond about the miracle of Peter walking with Jesus on the water? *That lame man had an understanding of truth—he knew that healing was possible—but he needed someone who would testify of the Source of the healing power—Jesus.* So it is important for you to keep your mind on the truth that God has allowed you to experience, and always be ready to share that truth with someone else.

Moving to the Next Level

Simply knowing the truth is not enough. It is imperative that you start operating in the level of truth you know. If not, you will hold onto mantles that you are supposed to transfer to someone else, and you will never reach for the next level of thinking. Peter's next mantle was evangelism, and because he let go of what he had known before to step into a new level, his ministry was amazingly effective—so much so that when his shadow fell on people they were instantly healed. Hear me. God wants every believer to pass our experience on, to empower other people's lives, so that they can start experiencing the rewards and empowerment of Tested Thinking for themselves.

There is a level of empowerment you will reach that will not allow you to remain silent. You will constantly be looking for someone who needs to hear about your experience to pass on tested thinking, reward systems, undeniable favor, and empowerment. You will not reach your next level until you leave the old level behind. You will not move into your next dimension until you are willing to help another person reach the level God has ordained for that person to reach. Follow the instruction of Philippians 2:5, "Let this mind be in you, which was also in Christ Jesus." You will know that you are operating in the mind of Christ when you begin to do things the way He did.

Embrace whatsoever is true in your life. Rebuke those things that are not rooted in truth—things that do not promote Tested Thinking, do not bring biblical rewards, or will not lead to an undeniably abundant life for you and others. Jesus said in John 10:10, "The thief cometh not, but for to steal, and to kill, and to destroy: I am come that they might have life, and that they might have it more abundantly."

As you grow in God keep this in mind: If something does not yield an undeniable experience with the God who is actively at work in your life, and it does not empower you to bless someone else's life in the future, *then it is not truth.* You will only reap abundant prosperity as truth rewards your right thinking in God.

CHAPTER 2

Whatsoever Is *Honest*: The Distinction Between Truth and Honesty

To enjoy an undisturbed and untroubled life in God, strive to be honest. You might respond to that statement by saying, "I *am* honest!" There is much more to honesty than telling the truth. I am referring to such things as being true to the heartfelt desire God put in you and concentrating on doing things that are true to the person God made you to be and become. Haphazardly doing things simply because they are good ideas or because other people feel they would be good things for you to do is not honest dedication to God's defining purpose for you.

In Philippians 4:8, Paul makes a clear distinction between truth and honesty while weighing the importance of each: "For the rest, brethren, whatever is **true**, whatever is worthy of reverence and is honorable and seemly [**honest** KJV] …think on and weigh and take account of these things [fix your minds on them]." He listed truth and honesty separately because each has a unique meaning. If we test our thinking about these things, we must recognize that *whatsoever is true* comes before *whatsoever is honest*. Truth establishes the foundation for honesty. As we embrace truth, we are able to "think on" those things that are honest, because truth allows us to identify what *is* honest.

A few words that describe things that are *honest* include "honorable," "upright," fair—"showing fairness," "sincere," "genuine," "respectable," and "truthful."[1] From a biblical perspective, one of the words used to define *honest* is "august."[2] This describes anything that inspires reverence, admiration, and supreme dignity—things that reflect the preeminence of God. If you were to play back the thoughts and images that have passed through your mind during the last twenty-four to forty-eight hours, could you identify *whatsoever is honest?* Let's go to the acronym to reveal the deeper meaning:

- **H** **eartfelt Desire**, *knowing God's desire that He has placed in our hearts makes us*

- **O** **pen to Rebuke**, *from the right sources, willing to grow in what He desires, which births a spirit of*

- **N** **o Harm Intended**, *correct motivations and actions toward others, that develops*

- **E** **arnest Passion to Get It Right**, *consistently rising to the standard, which births a*

- **S** **teadfast Pursuit of Greatness**, *understanding of and consistency in covenant, and*

- **T** **rusting God Always,** *a deeper trust in God and greater honesty in our lives*

To be a person whom God can use, it is important to understand that everything you do must be from the heart of God within you, not because something sounds like a good idea or because you want to try a popular fad or because someone you know is doing it. Even if something is the "in" thing right now, if what you want to do is not in line with your godly character, the godly nature that is in you, your inner being when you receive Jesus, then you are very likely doing something that is not of God.

This turns what should be honest into something that is rooted in *dishonesty*, which is defined as "a disposition to lie, cheat, or steal…a dishonest act; fraud."[3] The thief who comes to steal, kill, and destroy in a believer's life (see John 10:10) is the enemy of our soul, Satan. This verse describing his nature helps reveal why he launches outright attacks against *whatsoever is honest* in our lives. He starts by attacking the heartfelt desire we have from God.

Heartfelt Desire

A key to following God's desire in your heart is in being able to distinguish it from a wish that someone else has for you. When you begin building your foundation of thought life on Philippians 4:6-9, you start recognizing God's desires in your heart. As you walk in whatsoever is *honest*, your thoughts turn toward a deep heartfelt desire God has placed in you that leads you in fulfilling that defining purpose He has for your life.

Honesty encompasses so much more than just telling the truth because, for example, you can tell the truth and still not be honest. Honesty is living in truth, and many times honest living is not convenient or comfortable. For instance, if somebody asks if you are hungry, you could respond "Yes." Then when the person asks what you would like to eat, you might respond that you really do not care. That is not a true statement, because you know what you want, but either you do not have money available to pay for it, or you think the other person might not be able to afford it. Deep down, you really want something specific, but you choose not to tell that person what you want. In order to be completely honest, you have to be honest in everything.

In a situation like this when someone asks you what you would like to eat, you might respond by saying something discreet such as you do have a taste for a particular food or to eat at a particular restaurant, but doing so that day isn't something you are really prepared for financially or budget-wise. That way you are being completely honest, but not stating it in a way that sounds as though you are asking the other person to take you out for a meal, or are being manipulative. You are being honest in a polite way, and in turn, the other person is able to make the decision to either invest or not invest in your desire without feeling put on the spot, *because you were honest*. Of course, if the person is a good friend, you could simply say if you could afford it, you would have this or that meal.

Honest Decisions Rooted in Truth

Let's deal with the thought behind the above example a little bit more, because the more we talk about honesty, the more we must explore our own heart, and the more we discover in ourselves, the more we realize that a surprising amount of the time many of us are not honest...*even* with ourselves.

If you do something because you are trying to fit into a group or a club, God may look at you and ask why you turned away from what you feel comfortable doing, in the sense of doing something only to please people. That's why Paul said to the Galatians in the first verse of the third chapter, "O foolish Galatians, who hath bewitched you, that ye should not obey the truth, before whose eyes Jesus Christ hath been evidently set forth, crucified among you?" In other words, some people had become fascinated in their thinking to the degree that they turned from walking honestly with the God of Glory and tried to fit in a place they did not belong. They were happy in the presence of God until someone or something "messed up their mind," and they walked away from Him.

Has this ever happened to you? If so, can you trace your thoughts back to that time and identify who or what bewitched you? Who took you to a place that made you think it was not important to please God anymore? Who made you feel that you no longer had to read your Bible or study, or that you could just come to God only when you need Him? Some people clearly do not understand that God desires for us to have His best. When you walk in the truth of this, it means you have to be honest with yourself and realize that you can no longer play games with God. You know too much...God has placed too much of His desire in your heart for you to waste what He has invested in you. So again I ask, *What's on your mind?*

It is vital for you to understand your daily life from God's perspective, not your own, and not someone else's idea of what your life should be. Do not let people speak into your spirit if it is going to "bewitch" you. Hear me. Do not be guilty of doing something just because "the preacher" or an evangelist told you it was the right thing to do. Someone you know to be a prophet may have prophesied great things for you, but you should do something that contributes to the direction of your life only because God has put it in your heart.

If your words and actions do not come from the heart of God, you will never live an honest life before Him. This is why God wants to make sure that you learn how to be passionate for His will and to have a heartfelt desire for the things that He desires: When the spirit of prosperity (God's Spirit) is planted in your heart, He will always give you the ability and the integrity to produce, create, and birth it out.

Now, stay with me as I follow a line of thought to build a different foundation for the word *honest*. In the first chapter we dealt with manifesting truth through *tested thinking*, *reward systems*, and *undeniable experiences* with God. We concluded by looking at *empowerment*. With this in mind, let's talk about making honest decisions that are rooted in truth rather than in our emotions.

Emotion-Based Decisions

Nowadays it is a little easier to broach this subject because people have become a bit more conscious of the way they behave emotionally. For example, many who are going through the process of Tested Thinking in the area of their diet are beginning to understand they do not eat only because they are hungry. Many times they eat because they are emotionally lacking in some area. When our emotions drive our eating habits, we no longer know how to accurately judge our hunger. Therefore, we judge ourselves based on our emotions.

Have you ever noticed that sometimes when you open your mail and see a bill, you immediately want to go eat? When your car payment comes due, suddenly your thoughts turn to pizza? The reality is that you are craving pizza because your emotions desire something to immediately appease your anxieties, and as a result, your emotions are not allowing you to live from the integrity of honesty. You would not be experiencing these counterproductive emotions if you had enough money already in the bank for the car payment.

Whenever you are unhappy about wanting something you cannot have, your emotions try to substitute this perceived lack with an immediate feeling of gratification (such as eating, for example). Your emotions *dishonestly* tell you that eating this or that "comfort food" will make up the difference for what you are not able to afford right now. So the emotional eating becomes your initial substitute for what you are not able to possess, but that behavior will ultimately lead to disastrous results. Not only will it not bring in the funds nor give you the discipline to manage your funds properly, you will gain unnecessary weight in the process. However, if you choose to live honestly with what you may or may not possess, you would realize that you can have almost anything you want if you discipline yourself to obtain it.

Open to Rebuke

Living honestly from heartfelt desire also involves the second letter in our acronym, "O," the necessity of being **Open to Rebuke**. One of the greatest concerns you should have is guarding against allowing people into your space who will try to control the matters of your heart. Once you open your mouth, you give people permission to start speaking to your heart. So you need to be careful what you say, because some people will take what you say and turn it for their benefit. Those who do not live from the vantage point of truth and honesty will try to use your emotions to gain control of your life.

From the Right Sources

If you are honest, however, you will be open to correction and rebuke from the right sources. A true sign of honesty (and a first principle of correction) is allowing someone you know and trust to tell you what you really do not want to hear, especially if you know in your heart that you deserve to hear it. Understand this: Where there is no honest rebuke in your relationship with someone who speaks into your life, you are being restrained, held back, and held captive from obtaining God's desires. However, you must be sure that you are around people who are willing to speak honestly into your life.

Another principle of correction is to always have someone in your life who has more materially than you have. You need friends around you who are not thinking about what you have, because they do not *need you* to be happy. They will speak into your life with sincerity, because they are not afraid of losing your friendship or what you can do for them. On the other hand, people who need you will try to manipulate you. If they need your food, or perhaps your car to take them places, they will try to manipulate you to get you to be exactly who they need you to be. When you open yourself up to these people, you will find that a spirit of correction soon turns into a spirit of control.

Once you let people begin to set goals for you, and you start striving to reach the goals they have set (when God has not planted them in your heart), then there is no way you can judge the soundness of your decisions. Make sure you know what God has placed in your heart. Whatever it is, know that you have thought it through (tested your thinking), so that when another person tries to tell you what you should do, you can stand on faith and declare what God has said to you.

It's dangerous for you to take other people's opinions on what you should do and apply them to your spirit if God did not put those things in your heart. You are allowing other people to control your life or manipulate you to their advantage. You are not making honest decisions based on what God has for you, which limits what He wants to do in your life.

Another danger sign that you are succumbing to other people's desires for you is if you become disappointed or depressed when someone who counsels you either forgets about what he or she had encouraged you to do or fails to appreciate your accomplishments. This is why you have to learn how to know and act from the *heartfelt* desire God has placed in you to make up your mind: "*I am not doing this for anybody else. I am doing it because God has put it in my heart.*"

When you are confident about God's desire within you, you will not allow yourself to be controlled or negatively influenced by anyone who is not speaking from a point of biblically based truth and honesty to you. And you won't be disappointed when no one seems to notice your efforts. When your grandmother says, "Baby, if I were you, I would think about getting married right about now...," don't rush into marriage just because Grandma said it. If getting married is not in your heart at this moment, then don't. Otherwise, you will end up getting hurt.

I will reiterate this again because it is so important: Do not ever do something simply because someone else feels it would be good for you to pursue. Wait until it is passionately and deeply rooted in your heart; that's when you will know without a doubt it is right for you. When God has placed a desire in your heart, you can't sleep at night, you are not hungry, and your thoughts are totally toward doing what He has placed in your spirit. Your heart has a way of speaking to you—it will let you know when you are on track. Learn to say what David said in Psalm 19:14, "Let the words of my mouth, and the meditation of my heart, be acceptable in thy sight, O Lord, my strength, and my redeemer."

Be quiet before the Lord until He reveals the desires of your heart. He will show you and confirm what is acceptable to Him.

True to Yourself Before God

Now notice that David said *meditation of my heart.* To me this means my heart is "thinking" while my mind is thinking. In other words, my heart keeps my thoughts in check. It is my divine "measuring stick" that invariably determines whether or not I am being truthful and honest with myself. At all times, I want to make sure that I am not destroying the integrity of who I am by living a lie. Shakespeare said, "to thine own self be true."[4]

Don't try to be someone else; be true to yourself before God. If you do not like baseball, then don't buy season tickets simply to befriend somebody. Tell that person, "Listen, I do not like baseball." If you like baseball, however, then buy season tickets, even if you go by yourself. You can enjoy baseball alone! Sit next to somebody who has season tickets, and make friends because you enjoy the same things, but do not continue doing something if your heart is not in it.

So many times we get comfortable with people who think like we do, and then we are challenged by trying to bring their thinking up to our level of thinking. It is a struggle trying to bring people up to your level of thinking, especially when they refuse to budge. They are not ready to deal with honesty, because honesty opens you up to rebuke and correction. They have not arrived at the understanding that, "Open rebuke is better than secret love" (Prov. 27:5).

You must be honest with yourself about how you accept rebuke and correction. God can trust you more when you are open to rebuke, and as a result, He can take you to higher and higher levels as you follow Him openly and honestly. Rebuke is not necessarily open and public. It can be that way at times, but most of the time someone who is mentoring you should most often give you a correction or rebuke in a quiet, private setting where you can respond with openness and repentance.

In May of 1997 I was assistant pastor of my father's church, and was making a decent salary. My father was in his fifties, and retiring was the last thing on his mind. I had begun to feel the call to pastor my own church in the Washington, D.C., area. My friends were not only against the idea, but I kept hearing things like, "Man, you are crazy! Your father has this big church with two services, you are the assistant pastor, so just wait until he retires and the church will be all yours anyway."

I was getting counsel from every side telling me to stay where I was, but deep inside I knew that God was saying clearly, "Washington, D.C." That same month I received a call from Bishop T. D. Jakes, inviting me to dinner in Dallas, so I flew down to visit with him. When Bishop Jakes came into the room and walked up to where I was, I began our conversation with some questions, because I knew that we had the same type of thinking (we were born just one day apart). I knew that he would have the answers to my questions.

About twelve years ago I met him while picking him up at the airport to preach at our first church revival meeting. I asked him questions as we drove, and he gave me a variety of insightful answers before we reached the church. The things he shared with me were relevant and real for that time in my life, but now (at dinner in Dallas) I needed his wisdom for some current issues I was dealing with.

His advice to me that night was clear and concise. He did not lay hands on me, or pray for me, or tell me to fast until I received an answer. His words were full of reality. First, my father was still a relatively young man with no intentions of leaving his church. Most importantly, God's voice was clear—*go to Washington, D.C., to start a church.* What could be clearer than that?

Bishop Jakes reminded me that a pattern had already been established in my family. My grandfather had gone to Boston to start a church, where my father had served as an assistant pastor for him. My father left my grandfather's church and went to Wilmington, Delaware, to start his own church. Now God was following the same pattern, calling me to step out on my own by faith, to start my own church. The answer was obvious, but it took some wise counsel to help me see that God was again following the history of His dealings with our family. Had I not listened and followed Bishop's advice, I could still be an assistant pastor in Delaware, miserable because I had not heeded God's call.

It is not always easy to listen to the advice and correction of other people in your life. It was not easy to go out on my own to start a church from scratch. It takes a lot of openness to correction and rebuke to get to the place where you are able to stand on your own faith and build what God has told you to build. You can never grow in God until your spirit is open to correction and rebuke. Your openness and willingness to obey will affect those around you as well. Anyone running from God's call will try to encourage you to stay where you are, because it will ease his or her conscience, which is full of disobedience. Standing strong in your faith toward God will speak louder than any words you could say.

No Harm Intended

When you have grown to a level of honesty and openness, you will do all things in harmony with the word for which the next letter of our acronym, "**N**," stands: **No Harm Intended**. There will always be occasions when we offend people or wound their spirits, however unintentionally. When this happens, be honest and open, assuring the people that the action or deed was done with no harm intended. Let them know that although you may have "stepped over the line" into their space or brought up a sensitive issue, your intention was never to hurt them.

Be honest with yourself and look deep into your heart. You will know if you are being totally honest and are telling the whole truth about the mishap, or if perhaps you actually meant what you said or did. You may have known at the time that you said the wrong thing. If you are honest with people, they can feel it from your spirit through your sincerity.

There is something convicting about saying, "I am really sorry!" when the person you are speaking to is still upset. Relationships are delicate and precious—too important to let careless words destroy them. You may have to stress to the other person that you are not trying to destroy your relationship, but are merely striving to improve it. Let him or her know your thoughts come from an honest heart.

Accepting People for Who They Are

When you maintain an attitude of *no harm intended* you will accept people for who they are and not who you expect them to be. If a relationship makes you uneasy because of your fear of being hurt, you will usually try to protect yourself, which will cause you to view the other person with suspicion. When that happens, you will become judgmental which will eventually destroy the relationship. Understand there is a difference between judging someone and giving wise counsel. If the person is not open to rebuke or correction your words will be like a ball bouncing off a brick wall.

When you are constantly protecting your heart, it is hard to create strong friendships that are built on trust and respect. You must come to the place where your spirit is both trustworthy and trusting. Do not ever be afraid to say, "I am sorry." As you grow in spiritual maturity this becomes easier and easier to do, but, oh, what a struggle it is for "baby" Christians!

Easily Recognized Sincerity

Applying the principle of *no harm intended* in your life will give you a sincerity that will be easily recognized by everyone. Have you ever stood in line at a movie theatre or a play when someone jumps in front of you in line, without even giving a backward glance? To top it off, you know this is going to be a sold-out performance and there are only ten minutes left until starting time. It takes a lot of honest sincerity to tell that person you were first in line and ask him or her to go back, without starting a confrontation. On the other hand, have you ever been that person who stepped in front of someone in order to be first at the counter? Were you able to honestly say, "I am sorry, I know you were here first"? Can you honestly say there was *no harm intended* or would you do it again, just to be sure you got your ticket?

This can happen in any area of life. Recently, when I was driving my car and my wife was with me, I needed to move into the right lane and ahead of a car full of people to make a right turn before the traffic light changed. I said to my wife as I rolled down her window, "Honey, ask them if I can go ahead of them. I do not want them to think I don't have the courtesy to consider their feelings." I could have simply kept my turn signal flashing and pushed ahead, honking my horn as I went by! But the attitude of honesty and *no harm intended* was stronger than my need to make that turn in a hurry. Get my point?

Now, I am sure that you have faced similar situations when you wanted to push your way to the front or get what you wanted without considering someone else. Regardless of what the situation may have been, you had to make a decision as to how you would handle it. What did you do? Did you want to run someone off the road? Be honest with yourself. Did you act with *no harm intended?* This virtue has to be deep in your spirit in order to come out at the right time, so practice acting in an honest, *no-harm-intended* manner.

Not too long ago I was sitting at a stoplight when a young person pulled alongside of me in a little sports car, obviously wanting to race. I knew that I had the power to race with him—I could have punched that accelerator and left him sitting there— but I knew that would awaken a spirit of competition in him that could someday result in his harm or even death. After a split second of temptation, I chose to let the challenge go by and show him *no harm intended.* Did I help him? I don't know, but I do know this: God has given everyone the same amount of time each day so that we can choose to invest in others. Most of the time we never know the results of our efforts, but what's most important is that we know in our spirit we are walking in obedience to God.

Earnest Passion to Get It Right

After understanding how to live by and communicate *no harm intended*, next we move to desiring to have an Earnest Passion to get things done right. If I am living an honest lifestyle, I will want to make sure I'm doing things right before God! If I do not know how, I need to start praying for the passion to do it and for the answers to how. We, none of us, have the answers to every problem we face, but we have the ability to pray for God to supply all the right answers then listen and watch for them. If we are honest about our motives, God will give us the necessary desire and passion to correct a matter.

Honesty says, "I can never go back to my old, shoddy ways. I must get it right!" That's when you begin to seek out people who have the ability to either show you a new way of doing something, or introduce you to a new process or system so that you can get it right. When you arrive at the place of "*Earnest Passion to Get It Right*," you will be willing to sacrifice yourself to help someone else for unselfish reasons.

I will never forget the time my dad sent me to the airport in Washington, D.C., to pick up a minister and drive him to Philadelphia, so that my dad could fly home to speak in his own church. My mother had a quality car with a five-speed engine that my brother and I liked, so we took that car for the trip. As we were crossing the bridge at Aberdeen, there was a powerful little sports car right ahead of us. (I have never forgotten that car.) We were traveling at least 90 mph, catching up to the sports car.

When I got on the bridge I knew I was just about ready to pass him. Just as I caught up with him, he did the strangest thing. I was still doing 90 plus when he pulled off the road and began to increase the space between us. I will never forget that image. My brother and I watched him thinking, *What happened? He just pulled off.* That situation stuck with me for years. I promised myself I would never let anybody beat me racing again.

From that time on I made sure every car I bought would do 130 mph plus, or I wouldn't buy it. The Lord finally had to deal with me about the matter. He told me I should choose to either act like a teenager and race up and down the roads, or to grow up and be honest with myself. He reminded me that life is too valuable to end it wrapped around a tree or hanging off a cliff, just because someone provoked me to race. To this day I still have to "pray for" my foot (for self-control, that is)—it gets pretty heavy sometimes! Come on now. Be honest. You may have prayed that same prayer, right?

Heeding the Integrity of Your Heart

My Lexus has the most power of any car I have known. If you drop down to third gear and punch it, you will get whiplash in your back. The other day I was starting to speed up when the car in front of me sped up as well. Now, they did it on the wrong day. (I *really* needed to "pray" for my foot that day!) I knew what to do, but my wife looked over at me, wondering if I was speeding. My ego told me to "go for it," but my common sense reminded me that if I killed Prophetess Bynum I would have a hard time explaining it to the world.

You have to be honest with yourself at a time like that. I decided to do the wise thing and slow it down to about 45 mph and let the other car go on. Since I am planning to live a good while longer, racing cars down the highway will not do. *What would you have done in a similar situation?* The integrity of your heart must always be, *Lord, I do not want to use something You have blessed me with to offend or to inflict harm on another person.*

I have heard it said that truth is stranger than fiction. It is also more humorous because it is real. My wife and I were vacationing in Martha's Vineyard, eating breakfast at our favorite restaurant. Since we were still going through our "early marriage adjustments" at that time, trying to fit my schedule and her schedule into married life, I said something that I should not have said. The subject should have not been brought up at that time, but I brought it up, and I know she had a right to be upset the moment my words came out of my mouth.

I must say she conducted herself like the lady she is, quietly getting up and leaving the restaurant. She could have said a lot of things, but very wisely, she simply left. I knew she was angry, and as it is often said, the best defense is a good offense, so I got angry. Actually, I became furious.

I settled the check, went out and got in the car, started it, and pulled forward to where she was.

She was holding her cell phone like she was ready to call someone, but I said, "Come on, now, and get in the car. Let's go back to the hotel." She looked at me like she could have hit me and told me to go on—she would walk. Of course, I did the wrong thing—I rolled up the window and started off. I had barely moved a few feet when I heard an awful thump. I thought, *Surely she didn't throw that cell phone at my car!*

I jumped out of the car, and yes, there was her cell phone in three pieces. Nothing was broken, and my car didn't have a scratch on it, but this situation was far from over. She got into the back seat (refusing to sit by me) and proceeded to tell me what I had done wrong (as if I wasn't already regretting it). Then I heard her call and talk to a friend, "Girl, I want to get off this island right now...."

I was driving and trying to decide what I should do next. I kept telling her to get off the phone and she kept getting louder. She finally told me to stop and let her out. I stopped the car, let her out, and pulled the car down a little way (not far, mind you). I stopped the car again, got out, and walked toward her, trying to show her I was the man. That's when she reached down and grabbed a rock—a big one. I knew it was time to get honest; this girl had grown up on the West Side of Chicago. My first step was to pray. Then I did what any husband would do—I disarmed her.

It was good for us to have that moment, humorous as it sounds, because it allowed us to move to a new level of honesty. I was able to tell her why I had said what I did in the restaurant. I told her the reason why I had acted the way I did. Now, we were dealing with *us*. When two people come together, there is a level of truth both discern instantly; other levels of truth take years to begin to understand.

We must be open to *honesty*, as well as to *correction* and *rebuke*, even if we do not agree with what the other person is saying. We never know the full extent of another person's struggles—in his or her early or adolescent years or later in single or married life. We must maintain the attitude of *no harm intended* and keep an *earnest passion* to get things right in order to take into account the needs of the other person.

Seeing From the Other Person's Background

Having an *earnest passion* to get it right is essential. This requires that you get inside the heart of the other person to see what he or she has been through. Not only will this give you more sensitivity, it will convince you that there are more important things in life than arguing. Share your emotions, sit down, and talk things out.

It is not easy being married to Prophetess Bynum. She is such a wonderful person that people feel the need to shield and protect her, but there are also those people who would like to control her life. Some people did not want her to marry me, because it changed their perception of who she is. I had to admit to her that I had a difficult time dealing with people who might hurt her in any way. In turn, she shared there were things about me that she didn't like. (Just imagine!) She is a wonderful wife, yet she has been called to the nations. It would be extremely difficult for her to sit down, be a First Lady in our church, and be content staying in one spot when God has called her to other assignments.

I had to be honest with my congregation and tell them she was not able to be there every Sunday. It's part of who she is. How could I marry her because of who she is and what I saw in her, and then try to make her over into someone else? That would not reflect *honesty, openness, no harm intended,* or an *earnest passion to get it right.* At the end of the day, what is most important to both Juanita and me is that we are pleasing the Lord and each other.

Steadfast Pursuit of Greatness

The next letter of our "honest" acronym is "S" for **Steadfast Pursuit of Greatness.** One of the issues that challenges most of us is being consistent in our steadfastness. We all have areas in our lives we would describe as being "off and on." Sometimes we do something well, and at other times it just seems to be too much trouble to make the effort. In each of those areas, we need to be honest with ourselves and admit that we have a problem being consistent.

Consistency in Steadfastness

One morning my wife and I had a discussion about this very thing. I have certain things that I do regularly, and that day I had not done all of them. It is very irritating to me having to admit I just did not do the things I know I needed to do, even though the opportunity was there. Human nature, being what it is, leads to a well-known response. When you are angry with yourself, you usually try to change someone close to you to make yourself look better! It is always best to change yourself before trying to change everyone around you. If you are not honest with yourself, you will create a monstrosity of myths. There are no shortcuts to consistency or steadfastness.

As an example, let's use eating lunch. You may get busy and forget to eat, or perhaps your car was in the shop and it was easier to skip lunch rather than take a taxi somewhere to eat. The change in your personality or disposition is usually not too noticeable until about 2:00 in the afternoon when you start getting a little grumpy. Someone suggests going next door for coffee or tea, and the first thing you reach for is the sugar. Now, you know you shouldn't do that! It is only going to make you feel worse, but you open the packet and pour it in your cup anyway. About 4:00 that afternoon, you realize that because you reverted back to old habits, too much sugar has taken you "out of sorts" again. In this situation you were not honest with yourself, and you certainly were not steadfast in your habits.

When you fail at being steadfast in any area of your life, you soon see a decline in the growth you had worked so hard to achieve. People on some diets know that some allow a "cheat day" when you can eat anything you want all day. I might be able to cheat a little on one meal, but if I cheat all day my steadfastness will be sadly lacking. I must discipline myself in every area of my life. When I am not steadfast, I find it much easier next time to give in to my craving for Tiramisu or submit to my urge to sleep an extra hour, whatever it was I had worked so hard to control. The key is consistency. We must make a covenant with steadfastness through consistency—because steadfastness brings rejoicing, and rejoicing unlocks the incredible favor of God.

Trusting God Always

The final letter of our acronym is paramount, "T," for **Trusting God Always** and seals the other five letters. To live in total peace, you need to be able to trust God in spite of your situation, in spite of what others may tell you, or in spite of how something might feel. Your trust must be in God alone in order for honesty to exist completely in your life. You must be able to say without reservation, "God, I trust You. I believe You. If You say, 'This is the way,' then I will do it Your way, Lord." Remember, it's better to have little with greatness in your spirit than to have much with nothing of value in your spirit (see Prov. 16:8).

The more I see people in the house of God struggling to be happy in Him, the more I ask the question: *Why are you struggling so hard to be happy?* God meant for us to live the abundant life—joy and happiness are part of that life. So, what is the problem? Why are so few Christians truly happy?

Obviously, the problem is not with God, so it must be within us. If you were to ask most people this question, you would get a surprising answer.

"I was much happier back in my younger years, making $16,000 a year and living in a little two-bedroom home, than I am now, making $60,000 and struggling to pay for an expensive, much larger home that we do not need since our children are gone."

The answer here is obvious. When your heart begins to desire material possessions more than an intimate relationship with God, you are beginning a downhill slide into depression and unhappiness. I am not saying that acquiring possessions is wrong, I am emphasizing that its place in your life is a matter of the heart. God wants you to be honest with him and equally honest with yourself. If you think you need a larger home, look at why you need it. Is your family growing and you need more rooms in your house, or are you trying to impress someone? Until you are true to yourself, you will never be able to be honest with God.

Heartfelt Honesty—Kind and Fair

When you can be happy with what God has given you, and you are willing to wait for "more" in God's timing, you will find yourself thinking more of other people's needs than your own. You will spend more time before His throne in prayer for others. This is when you come to realize that your *honest* actions are *heartfelt*. When you stay in His presence, you are no longer resistant to correction and rebuke. You act with no harm intended. In your dealings with other people you are now part of the "fix" rather than the problem.

The more you learn to trust God in everything, the more you will let down your walls, become more vulnerable, and begin to trust other people. We all have a tendency to protect ourselves from harm, especially from intentional hurts, but as we learn to trust others more readily, we will also look inward to measure how we are treating other people. Through this process, we gradually expose our own flaws: our tempers, our attitudes, and so on. With *earnest passion to get it right*, we try to be more consistent in our *honest* efforts to deal with others in a kind and fair manner.

Proverbs 3:3–4 says:

>*Let not mercy and kindness [shutting out all hatred and selfishness] and truth [shutting out all deliberate hypocrisy or falsehood] forsake you; bind them about your neck, write them upon the tablet of your heart. So shall you find favor, good understanding, and high esteem in the sight [or judgment] of God and man (AMP).*

God desires honesty from us, not just when we need something from Him, but at every moment of our lives.

Proverbs 3:5–6 goes on to add:

>*Lean on, trust in, and be confident in the Lord with all your heart and mind and do not rely on your own insight or understanding. In all your ways know, recognize, and acknowledge Him, and He will direct and make straight and plain your paths (AMP).*

God deeply desires that you extend your trust and honesty toward Him as your Fellow Traveler on life's pathways: "Be not wise in your own eyes; reverently fear and worship the Lord and turn [entirely] away from evil. It shall be health to your nerves and sinews, and marrow and moistening to your bones" (vv. 7–8 AMP).

If you want something fresh and new in your life, you must learn how to be honest. Look into your heart and acknowledge: *Have you been telling God the truth lately?* Have you been sharing with Him what He really wants to hear, or are you filtering the truth that God wants to reveal through your life? To you, this may be a minor issue; but to God it is profound, because He already sees in your heart the things that you refuse to acknowledge. This takes me back to why David spoke the words recorded in Psalm 19:14: "Let the words of my mouth, and the meditation of my heart, be acceptable in thy sight, O LORD, my strength, and my redeemer."

Again, one principle I have learned is the more I trust *God*, the more open and honest I am *with God and man.* If I cannot trust God to lead my life, I will be doomed to a degraded state of never trusting people, viewing them as enemies who are dishonest and untrustworthy. Without trusting in the Lord, we would always be in a state of trying to protect our own heart and life. It is a *fact* and also *true* that as we learn to trust God more and more, we increasingly see people as being good and not evil.

When you learn to trust God completely, it will allow Him to steadfastly lead and encourage you in the passionate pursuit to always get it right. This will bring you to the place that you will make sure you do not harm anyone, and if for some reason a mishap occurs, you will be quick to apologize.

If you want to enjoy an undisturbed and untroubled life in God, strive to be honest. Do things from *heartfelt desire*. *Be open to correction and rebuke*. Live your life with *no harm intended*. Do everything with *earnest passion*. Be *steadfast* in all your endeavors. *Trust God always*. Let a reflection of God's glory be seen in you.

CHAPTER 3

Whatsoever Is *Just*: Trusting the One Who Is Just

Whatsoever is just may not always *seem* to be fair; nevertheless, it is always right. God is just, and actions we take based on *whatsoever is just* will bring the results we need. As basing our decisions and actions on *whatsoever is true* will bring the results that take us where we want to go, basing our actions on *whatsoever is just* will bring the results that are right for us (which we will see eventually, if not immediately).

In order to grow in our relationship with God, we must trust Him: We must trust that what He has said is true and that He deals fairly with us. Think about it. It is actually quite difficult to spend time (and grow in a relationship) with someone if you do not believe the person's words. If you do not trust the person or the person does not trust you or believe anything you say, it is nearly impossible to develop a lasting friendship. Neither do we usually count as true friends, people who are judgmental of our past and are unwilling to accept that we have changed, who will not accept our forgiveness and acknowledge that we are sincere in being sorry for things we have done. It is equally difficult to have a relationship with God if we do not believe His words.

If we want to be called a "friend" of God, we must learn to trust in the integrity of His character. God is perfect. He is fair. His Word tells us He is just.

> *Tell ye, and bring them near; yea, let them take counsel together: who hath declared this from ancient time? who hath told it from that time? have not I the LORD? and there is no God else beside me; a just God and a Saviour; there is none beside me (Isa. 45:21, emphasis mine).*

The word "just," referring to God in the verse above, is translated from a Hebrew word which includes the meanings, "lawful, righteous...right, correct."[1] If we truly believe God is just—lawful, righteous, right, and correct—we will not question one iota whether or not He is trustworthy.

Sometimes people improperly try to test God when they do not trust Him. For example, they may want to see evidence in the natural realm that He is moving before they take a step in the direction He is leading them. They really do not believe He is perfect in every way and cannot fail them. If I had a relationship like that with God, it would be like going home to sit down at my mother's table and wondering if the food she puts on the table is good. I do not wonder about the food or sniff it to see if it is good because I know her talent for cooking. I have experienced her cooking and baking for many years and am beyond questioning her abilities in the kitchen. I trust my mother's cooking because of the many meals I have eaten at her table. Our trust in God works the same way.

A History of Trust

Trusting God builds from a history of believing Him, seeing Him do what He said He would do in the past, both in our lives and in the Bible. After many years of trusting Him, we should be convinced beyond any doubt that He is absolutely just. Each time we experience His mercy and forgiveness, we are more likely to trust Him the next time.

If we think that God is not fair in His dealings with us, the reason is we lack understanding of His plans and intentions towards us. By continuing to read His Word and practice keeping His thoughts on our minds, we grow in our understanding of His good intentions towards us. His Word shows us that He corrects us, His children, as the loving Father to keep us walking in the direction He has planned for us.[2] His Word also teaches us not to be ignorant of Satan's devices (2 Cor. 2:11). If we hold an inaccurate philosophy, we may attribute an action or circumstance to God that actually had at its source a device of Satan or was a consequence of a poor human choice.

God's intentions towards us are so good that He sent Jesus to justify us. Isaiah 45:21 also points prophetically to the coming Messiah: "...a just God and a Saviour; there is none beside me." God is just and Savior of all. He is available as Savior of all to anyone who will receive Him through Jesus.

Some people believe God from what they have experienced with little to no knowledge of His Word or words spoken about Him. Other people believe God because of something they first read, or perhaps heard, but not from what they have experienced. Many believers have separated the two, but in reality, experience and knowledge of Him and His Word work hand in hand to build a history of trust in Him.

No matter what a person's background or perspective of Christ may be, no matter what picture a person has formed of Him, this is the place the principle of God's being *just* enters the picture: God says we are justified through Jesus. Whether or not a person believes it, whether or not a person believes it *and* accepts it by receiving Jesus and His provision for us to form a relationship with God by making us upright, righteous, and virtuous in God's eyes, the principle is the same because God says in His Word that He is just; He is right. His Word also says that He cannot lie (see Titus 1:2; Num. 23:19) and that He doesn't change (Mal. 3:6). Because God is just, He never deals unfairly with us. He is consistent in His dealings with us. He is steadfast in character and in His methods of training us for our growth.

Whatsoever is just according to God's justice is right because God is never wrong. In everything we must recognize that we can always trust God, because He is never wrong.

Justified

As God is just, Jesus is just. Jesus is just in His judgment because He does nothing in Himself, but seeks the will of the Father (see John 5:30). Jesus' life on earth is the example we have of being just because everything He thought, felt, and did conformed to the will of the Father. There was perfect harmony between Jesus' nature and His acts.

We are *justified,* made "righteous" in God's eyes "just as if" we had never sinned and been separated from fellowship with God depending upon how we receive Jesus and His death on the cross: "Being **justified** freely by his grace through the redemption that is in Christ Jesus" "...by faith."[3] God renders us "upright, righteous, virtuous...," indicative of people "keeping the commands of God,"[4] when we receive "the gift of God,"[5] Jesus' provision for us. Jesus is the perfect Lamb of God—innocent, faultless, and guiltless—there was no need to rectify sin in His heart or life. In His sinless state, He observed and fulfilled every divine law.

Once we receive the justification Jesus provided through His perfect sacrifice on the cross to take our sins upon Himself then rising from the dead to provide the Way back to God for us, God is in us to work effectually so that we become more and more like Jesus.

[Not in your own strength] for it is God Who is all the while effectually at work in you [energizing and creating in you the power and desire], both to will and to work for His good pleasure and satisfaction and delight (Phil. 2:13 AMP).

As we learn to trust Jesus completely and continue building our foundation of thought life on the virtues of Philippians 4:6-9, we will conform more and more to the standard He established as we walk out the will of the Father in our lives. Christ "is the image of God,"[6] "the brightness of his glory,"[7] and when we continue "...to behold [in the Word of God] as in a mirror the glory of the Lord," we "are constantly being transfigured into His very own image in ever increasing splendor and from one degree of glory to another...."[8] We will act from a *just* heart.

God justifies us through Jesus because He foreknows our future, not because He dwells on our past. Knowing this, when the devil accuses us of things in our past, we need to remind him of our future *because of our trust in God.* There will always be someone in our lives who will try to bring up our past, voicing the thoughts we've heard before from the devil, telling us that we have no future because of things we have done. God says in effect, "I do not base your spiritual development on your past; I am looking to your future growth." Romans 8:30 (AMP) tells us, "...whom He called, He also justified (acquitted, made righteous, putting them into right standing with Himself). And those whom He justified, He also glorified [raising them to a heavenly dignity and condition or state of being]."

We know we can trust our future to God because we can trust His past. And we can live in the joy that knowledge brings.

Now, let's go to our acronym. It is based on a joy-centered existence with God, a releasing of that joy He created us to have that comes with trusting that what He has said is true. When this spiritual virtue of thinking on "whatsoever is just" is fully revealed in your life, you will reap powerful benefits.

- **J oy Centered**, *intimacy with God through a history (the Bible and your life) of trust that God will do what He says He will do*

- **U nbiased Decisions**, *always to the benefit of God and others, decisions that bring more joy, which leads to*

- **S teadfast Standards**, *consistency in His character that keeps you*

- **T rue to Yourself**, *standing in truth, forgiving others*

Joy Centered

To build on a heartfelt spiritual experience with God, you put your focus on things you know will bring joy-centered thinking into your life. Believers everywhere love singing, "Jesus, You're the center of my joy..."[9] for the message it contains. It reminds us that no matter what we are going through or how unfair it actually is, Christ is *just* and able to turn it around for His glory and our good (for those of us "who love God" and "are the called according to his purpose").[10]

Even when *whatsoever is just*, God's justice, does not necessarily seem to be fair, we know that it is always right. In the midst of every circumstance, we are able to rejoice in recognizing that we can trust God because He is never wrong. First Thessalonians 5:18 (AMP) tells us, "Thank [God] in everything [no matter what the circumstances may be, be thankful and give thanks], for this is the will of God for you [who are] in Christ Jesus [the Revealer and Mediator of that will]."

God takes pleasure in those He has justified, rejoicing over them with joy.[11] He is a Father who delights in His children. Are you one of His children? If you are, do you realize that God takes pleasure in *you* because you are? *You bring Him joy.* Now, think about it. *What brings you joy?* I am not referring to temporary joy. I am talking about proof-positive, consistent joy—something that is going to last far longer than just a few minutes; it's going to last every minute of your life on earth and into eternity. *If your thoughts and your actions are not joy-centered, you are living in a false reality.* This makes it difficult to fathom why people continually do things that do not bring authentic joy.

If God blessed you on the reality of your present, your future would be bleak indeed. But because of God's grace, you can walk through your present days knowing "...the joy of the LORD is your strength" (Neh. 8:10). In order to grow in the Lord, your thoughts must be joy centered. When joy-centered thinking is not part of your life, it will be difficult for you to communicate intimately with God, for He literally is (or should be) the center of your joy. By centering your thoughts on your joy in Him, you will trust Him to order your steps (see Ps. 119:127-133). Otherwise, your joy will be short-lived. It will stem not from the things of God, but from other, worldly things.

There are times in our lives when we are unhappy and turn our problem over to God to "fix" it, but at the same time we insist on "fixing it" ourselves. We make decisions that we regret, and then run to God so that He can turn our situation into a happy one. Hear me: yes, "we know that all things work together for good to them that love God" and "are the called according to his purpose,"[12] but God is not going to take your "messes" and justify your bad decisions just to keep you happy. Look again at Philippians 2:13: "[Not in your own strength] for it is God Who is all the while effectually at work in you [energizing and creating in you the power and desire], both to will and to work for His good pleasure and satisfaction and delight" (AMP).

If God is not at work inside of you, then a dangerous "time-bomb" called pride is getting ready to explode, and when pride is operating in your life the glory of God cannot shine through you. The spirit of pride makes you become haughty, encouraging you to lift yourself to a higher level than where God has placed you. In no time you can become your own idol, choosing the path of happiness you think you deserve. Anytime you choose a path of happiness that you have planned for yourself, you must accept the consequences of your actions when they do not bring you to a joy-centered life in Christ. So, why not trust in the God who can never fail you to take you where you need to go?

Unbiased Decisions

If you are not living a joy-centered life you will be prone to making wrong decisions. When you are joy-filled, you leave the decision making to God. This leads to the next letter in our acronym, "U," which stands for **Unbiased Decisions.** *Just* thinking will specially equip you to make balanced, unbiased decisions. For example, when you are acting from a *just* heart, you will not make decisions based on how popular the outcome will be. When you are *just*, you will make a decision because it will serve to bring more joy to your life and to the lives of others.

Jesus did not go to the cross simply because He saw a lost and dying world. He knew the reality of our future without a Savior, but Hebrews 12:2 says that He went to the cross "...for the joy that was set before Him...." That joy came from the Father, for He was seeing a dying world not only eternally redeemed, but also having the opportunity to live an abundant life. Jesus made an unbiased decision to go to the cross. His death offered us an opportunity to make our own choices. Yet, we must be careful to make sound decisions from the joy He gives us, which comes only from the perfection of His just nature. Unbiased decisions are not made on the basis of friendship or because we feel pressured to do so; they are wrought in God.

You can know that you have become joy-centered when you begin to make careful, unbiased decisions. With each, you will ask yourself how it will impact the level of your relationship with God and how it will impact others.

Steadfast Standards

Being *joy-centered* in God leads to making *unbiased decisions*, which takes us to the third principle in our study of *whatsoever is just*—**Steadfast Standards.** Your personal standards reflect what you believe, and you cannot have beliefs that are one way today and completely different tomorrow. You must be *steadfast* in your *standards.* Hebrews 13:8 declares, "Jesus Christ the same yesterday, and to day, and for ever." Therefore, His decisions *toward you, for you,* and *in you* can never be biased and they will never change.

The enemy would love to persuade God to turn His back on you when you sin, but nothing in God's character will allow that to happen. God could never be biased against you. If Satan really understood the person you are becoming, he would realize that God is constantly working in your life and that His love for you is eternal. God knows that when you begin to understand who you are in Christ, your whole thinking process will change, impacting how you relate to Him and treat others.

The enemy would also like to turn your neighbor against you. He would love nothing better than to take you into the next step of negatively influencing your thinking toward that person, as well, so that a judgmental process between you could begin to fester. This can happen only if you drop your standards in the Lord, which would hurt everyone involved. When you realize who you are in Christ, you will never want to judge anyone again.

First Corinthians 2:16 says that we have the mind of Christ; that means we should see each other through His eyes. Being judgmental of others hinders your growth and gets in the way of the joy you are seeking for your life. Romans 14:4 asks the question, "Who art thou that judgest another man's servant? to his own master he standeth or falleth...." If you live by *steadfast standards,* you will not judge others; you will take them in prayer to the throne of grace. As God's children, we have not been given the right to judge His servants; we have been given the charge to love them, pray for them, and release them to Him. When we do this, we demonstrate the steadfastness of His character through the consistent reflection of our personal standards, our belief in the instruction of His Word.

God is always consistent in guiding us upward to another level. There are many different levels in the Christian life, because there are so many different experiences, lifestyles, cultures, and areas of ministry. God pours out His blessings on each of us in unique ways. Jesus said in John 14:2, "In my Father's house are many mansions: if it were not so, I would have told you. I go to prepare a place for you." God has prepared a future that is tailor-made for each one of us, both here and in eternity.

God is so fair and unbiased that He will bless a person who is unsaved. Matthew 5:45 tells us, "...for he maketh his sun to rise on the evil and on the good, and sendeth rain on the just and on the unjust." Understand this: Being saved does not pre-qualify you to receive God's blessings. If being saved made you a millionaire in three years, everybody would want to be saved. So if God made decisions according to whether or not we are saved, many of us would have been dead before we ever reached our teenage years. God's steadfast standards have seen to it that He looks beyond what you did in the past, so that He can lead you into the future. God is always faithful in how He judges us; therefore, we can be supernaturally equipped to live according to the same standard.

True to Yourself

Let's review. *Whatsoever is just* involves being *joy-centered in God*, making *unbiased decisions*, and having *steadfast standards,* thus leading to the final letter of our acronym: the letter "**T**," which stands for being **True to Yourself**. Humanity is in a sinful state because Adam was not true to himself. Had Adam been true to himself, he would have told his wife, "Eve, you are going to die if you take a bite of that fruit." Because Adam was not steadfast in his standards, he followed Eve in eating the fruit that brought about their judgment. He chose to agree with his wife's decision, rather than follow the instructions of God. This cost him his home, his relationship with God, and the abundant life God had planned for him and his family. And, of

51

course, this has affected every human being born from that time until the present day on earth.

When you are not true to yourself, you will automatically make wrong decisions, stray from steadfast standards, become judgmental, and wake up one morning to find that your joy is no longer there.

The essence of who you are (and true blessing from God) begins with being true to yourself, the self God made you to be. When you are not true to who you are, you can delay or abort His blessings. God is good, but if you stop walking His path, if you stop listening for His instructions that He wants to give you for you to progress on the path of peace and abundance He has already ordained for you and the others you bring with you, you start walking down the path leading to emergency-based living. When you stop receiving and living daily in the redemption and deliverance Jesus came to earth to provide, you are walking on the path where the effects of the curse and calamities of Adam's disobedience begin.

Now, let me be clear: God is not going to curse you, and no one can force you to do things to curse yourself, that is, force you or draw you in to thinking and speaking in a way that you know is contrary to "these things" of Philippians 4:8-9. No one can force you to do the things that will keep you from walking in all the goodness God has planned for you in life. You are the one who makes the decision that thrusts you into that realm by choosing to become something that you knew you did not want to (or should not) be. When people are not true to themselves, they make decisions based on the momentary facts, not on the truth of their future.

When we fail to make the right decisions, we begin to judge others, because on a subconscious level we want someone else to experience the same pain we are experiencing. We want to identify another person who is as miserable as we are. That way, we can compare our sin or wrong decision with what we see in others who are in error in order to feel justified again. Self-justification brings a sense of false joy, which can never satisfy. True joy can only be found in God. "Thou wilt shew me the path of life: in thy presence is fulness of joy; at thy right hand there are pleasures for ever-more" (Ps. 16:11).

Judging others offers momentary gratification, because to indulge in this behavior we must hide our bad decisions and undisciplined standards. A just person is already joy-centered in God, because his or her thoughts are always focused on Him. We are confident in knowing that we can trust our future because we can trust His past. If, however, we do not trust His past, then we will never trust who we could become. We cannot be true to ourselves.

Jehoshaphat had a problem when he realized three armies were coming against him (see 2 Chron. 20). He knew one thing was true: the people had to unite with one mind if they wanted God to move in their behalf. Being true to ourselves in a context like this may require a time of fasting and prayer or meeting with other believers to discuss God's will in the matter. But above all else, no matter what, we must remember to remain steadfast in our standards, following God's instructions, knowing we can trust Him.

Being true to himself in what God would have him do was firmly planted in Jehoshaphat's spirit. Jehoshaphat knew God's history with Israel. We read in 2 Chronicles 20:3-7 Jehoshaphat's response, revealing his unwavering trust of the future to God. Jehoshaphat then led Judah in seeking the help of the Lord, ready to hear and obey the Lord's instructions.

And Jehoshaphat feared, and set himself to seek the LORD, and proclaimed a fast throughout all Judah. And Judah gathered themselves together, to ask help of the LORD: even out of all the cities of Judah they came to seek the LORD.

And Jehoshaphat stood in the congregation of Judah and Jerusalem, in the house of the LORD, before the new court, And said, O LORD God of our fathers, art not thou God in heaven? and rulest not thou over all the kingdoms of the heathen? and in thine hand is there not power and might, so that none is able to withstand thee? Art not thou our God, who didst drive out the inhabitants of this land before thy people Israel, and gavest it to the seed of Abraham thy friend for ever?

When your joy is centered in God, you won't try to find a shortcut through a difficult process. You will always acknowledge, "Lord, aren't You the One who is in heaven? Aren't You the One who understands? Aren't You the One against whom no Kingdom can stand?"

When God—the just God who causes us to have the right attitude and spirit—is the center of our joy, we will seek Him in times of trouble and find His will in the matter...just like Jehoshaphat did.

God called Abraham His friend, because Abraham put all of his trust in Him. Many people want God's blessings, but they do not want to carry the responsibility of trusting Him. Jehoshaphat became a great king because he acted on the history he knew of God and trusted Him. In 2 Chronicles 20:9–11, we read Jehoshaphat's words to the Lord reflecting his confidence that the Lord will save Judah.

> *If evil comes upon us, the sword of judgment, or pestilence, or famine, we will stand before this house and before You—for Your Name [and the symbol of Your presence] is in this house—and cry to You in our affliction, and You will hear and save. And now behold, the men of Ammon, Moab, and Mount Seir, whom You would not let Israel invade when they came from the land of Egypt, and whom they turned from and did not destroy—Behold, they reward us by coming to drive us out of Your possession which You have given us to inherit (AMP).*

Do you see the principle? If you do not know your history, nor understand how God has intervened in your life, you will let the enemy gain victory over you every time. But when you know and acknowledge God's past history, His blessings will open a path for you and give you strength during situations where the enemy is planning to destroy you. Remember Paul's wisdom as recorded in Philippians 2:13, "[Not in your own strength] for it is God Who is all the while effectually at work in you [energizing and creating in you the power and desire], both to will and to work for His good pleasure and satisfaction and delight" (AMP).

Jehoshaphat knew God's history and the strength with which He could and would move. In 2 Chronicles 20:12 we read that he said to God, "...we have no might to stand against this great company that is coming against us. We do not know what to do, but our eyes are upon You" (AMP).

Second Chronicles 20:14-27 tells us in detail what happened. We see in verses 14-17 that through a member of the congregation, the Spirit of the Lord spoke to King Jehoshaphat and all Judah.

Ye shall not need to fight in this battle: set yourselves, stand ye still, and see the salvation of the LORD with you, O Judah and Jerusalem: fear not, nor be dismayed; to morrow go out against them: for the LORD will be with you (v. 17).

Then Jehoshaphat and all Judah worshipped the Lord, some bowing and falling before Him, some standing up and praising Him with a loud voice. The next morning, they rose early and went forth as Jehoshaphat admonished them to believe in the Lord and believe His prophets. After consulting with the people, Jehoshaphat appointed singers to go before the army, to sing and speak praises to the Lord God of Israel. (See vv. 18-21.)

Verses 22-24 show us the outcome:

And when they began to sing and to praise, the LORD set ambushments against the children of Ammon, Moab, and mount Seir, which were come against Judah; and they were smitten.

...every one helped to destroy another.

And when Judah came toward the watch tower in the wilderness, they looked unto the multitude, and, behold, they were dead bodies fallen to the earth, and none escaped.

In the midst of the praise, God showed His strength. He fought and won the battle for them! Because Jehoshaphat was true to himself, steadfast in his standards of trusting the future to God based on God's past, and following what God would have Him do, the Lord "...made them to rejoice over their enemies" (2 Chron. 20:27).

Let's pause and take an honest survey. What is working inside of you right now to pursue God's best for your life? What energizes you on a daily basis? What is rising up inside of you and becoming your passion? What is driving your inner man that either wakes you up or keeps you asleep when needed? What do you talk about most often? Which desire is burning deeply in your heart? What are the truths or falsehoods of your thinking? When will you wake up with joy without needing anything external to make it happen? *When will you have a day of joy just being you?*

Joy is not dependent on your age, or if you have lost that extra ten pounds you vowed to lose. You can experience joy in the middle of losing your business or while failing to be recognized for an accomplishment. Hear me closely. Being forgotten on your birthday or wishing you had the education you always desired will not affect your joy. Looking back at wrong decisions, credit problems, and friends who have betrayed you can cause untold heartache, but joy is an ever-present reality when your trust is in God.

Be true to the person you are, the "you" that God made according to His marvelous plans. When you finally arrive at the place of being true to yourself, your Father will be there to lead the celebration in honor of your homecoming. Think about the story of the prodigal son in Luke 15:22–24. God will kill the fatted calf for you, give you a ring, cover you with a robe, and celebrate that His child has come home. Ultimate joy can only be found in the presence of the Father.

When you sense there is no growth or fresh direction in your life, you may need to examine your joy, your unbiased decisions, and your steadfast standards to see if you are being true to yourself. Perhaps you are choosing a path to happiness that is of your own making instead of embracing the life God has planned for you before the foundation of the world. You will find the "real you" by being true to yourself, even when others are telling you how you should act and what you should think.

Here is something to consider. When you talk too much about your personal life you are actually creating another "you" that you will not be able to control. How is this possible? Other people will take your words and form opinions that create a totally different person from who you really are. People take "you" as *they* have created you, and before long they will have told so many people about "you" that the "real you" is someone even you do not recognize.

The person that you are today is not necessarily who you are going to be tomorrow. By default, you will begin to change when you learn to be true to the "you" that God has meant for you to become.

On the other hand, you can find the "real you" by examining your failures. How so? When you take a look at the "you" who made the wrong decisions, you will see what choices you made and what happened to allow those failures to happen. Then when you admit and deal with the failures, you will start becoming the "you" that God has planned. He is working in you to help you discover the "real you," the person who is true to His Word and true to yourself. Take a moment to be encouraged by Hebrews 13:20-21, "Now the God of peace...working in you that which is wellpleasing in his sight, through Jesus Christ; to whom be glory for ever and ever...."

For God to begin a new work in you, on any level, you must acknowledge who you are. He wants you to be *joy-centered* in your relationship with Him. He wants you to live in a place of *unbiased decisions* and *steadfast standards*, and He wants you to *be true to yourself.* Here is an important truth about *just* thinking—it will never allow you to judge anyone but yourself.

When the joy of the Lord is in your life you will not want to look at your neighbor's faults. Your *just* character from your relationship with Christ will keep your eyes focused on God. Start today by blessing the Lord and thanking Him for the joy and happiness He has brought into your life. Give thanks in everything, for this is His will for you. Live a *just* life, serve a *just* God, and be true to yourself.

CHAPTER 4

Whatsoever Is *Pure*:
Keeping Your Past Out
of Your Future

If we allow our past to come with us into our future, we won't be excited about the next day, week, month, or year. In Philippians 4:8-9, Paul shows us that our goal and utmost desire should be living our lives in the abundant untroubled, undisturbed peace of Christ. Following the list of virtues Paul states we are to think on, practice, and model our lives on, he states the *result*: "and the God of peace (of untroubled, undisturbed well-being) **will be with you**" (v. 9 AMP). Leaving behind the old to move into the present and the future is part of this.

We have established the importance of not only acknowledging the law governing the "protocol of prosperity," but also seeing ourselves operating in its full extent. We must guard against ever ignoring or shoving aside as unimportant the principles we must learn and practice as part of this law when other priorities inevitably try to crowd them out.

The level of growth to strive for in our lives is the place of allowing the God of peace to bring us into a realm of relationship that will provide a lifestyle of excellence. To be blessed with biblical well-being means much more than just being alive. It is maintaining your quality of life and exemplifying a passion to edify others, to bring them into the same lifestyle of well-being.

Again I am referring to the "protocol of prosperity" to strengthen my point that *what's on your mind* will surely manifest in your life. What you *think on* according to Philippians 4:8–9 will become the parameters and guidelines that order your life on a daily basis. *That is why your life must be virtue focused.*

To keep the principles Paul outlined in Philippians 4:8-9 before us, let's look at the passage again:

> *For the rest, brethren, whatever is true, whatever is worthy of reverence and is honorable and seemly ["honest" KJV], whatever is just, whatever is pure, whatever is lovely and lovable, whatever is kind and winsome and gracious ["of good report" KJV], if there is any virtue and excellence, if there is anything worthy of praise, think on and weigh and take account of these things [fix your minds on them].*
>
> *Practice what you have learned and received and heard and seen in me, and model your way of living on it, and the God of peace (of untroubled, undisturbed well-being) will be with you"* (AMP, emphasis mine).

Untainted by Evil or Guilt

The next virtue Paul instructs us to think on is *purity*, a small word that carries a big punch and has a plethora of meanings! First of all, note that the word from which "pure" in Philippians 4:8 is translated is derived from the same root as the word used most often for "holy" in reference to our relationship with God in the New Testament.[1] So when we *think on* things that are *pure*, we are activating in our mind that which is free from spiritual contamination and untainted by evil or guilt. We are embracing the core of the Father's character according to 1 Peter 1:15–16: "But as the One Who called you is holy, you yourselves also be holy in all your conduct and manner of living. For it is written, You shall be holy, for I am holy" (AMP).

In light of this, let's go to our acronym:

- **P rophetic Purpose**, *living according to the defining purpose God has for you will make you a person of*

- **U** nshakable Intent and Convictions, *firm resolve when you walk in spiritual maturity and develop a*

- **R** ighteous Focus, *consistency before God as you follow the*

- **E** xample of Christ, *to change unrighteous patterns of behavior for a brand-new lifestyle*

Prophetic Purpose

Purity is intimately tied into knowing your purpose. Purity can begin in your life when you understand why God has allowed you to be on earth in the Kingdom at this particular time "for such a time as this" (Est. 4:14).

It is easy to fall into the pattern, or habit, of attending church just to hear your favorite worship song or an outstanding message from your pastor. Our existence here on earth is to exemplify what we have already mastered in our understanding of God's heart, His intent, concerning us and to bring others into the same lifestyle of well-being. When we attend church and bring God glory by truly worshipping Him and by modeling who He is, people see Him. They are blessed by His presence and learn many different facets of who He is and what He is like through the distinctive ways He appears in the different members of the body.

Let go of formality with God and depend upon and trust Him as you can no other to walk out the purpose He has for you. Enter the realm of *prophetic purpose.* He has specific ways for you to relate to the members of the particular body of believers in your church as a part of walking out your prophetic purpose (and they with you). If you haven't already, let Him specifically direct you.

You can understand and live your life to its fullest only when you have captured the essence of where God has *purposed* for you to be *right now.* This is why Paul wrote in Philippians 3:13–14:

> *Brethren, I count not myself to have apprehended: but this one thing I do, forgetting those things which are behind, and reaching forth unto those things which are before, I press toward the mark for the prize of the high calling of God in Christ Jesus.*

Fulfills the Passion God Has Placed in Your Heart

Your life must have at least one defining purpose. You merely exist when you are constantly shifting from pursuing one direction today to something different tomorrow. If you ask most college freshmen what their major is, you will often get the same answer, "I don't know." Perhaps he or she has been studying biology during first semester, but now their thoughts are changing to pursuing a major in pre-law or accounting. It is important to be firmly settled on your goals when you are in college, but it is far more important to understand your life's purpose.

One of the most difficult things in life is staying centered on your purpose. Until you have discovered your own unique path you will aimlessly drift from one thing to another, never reaching your potential in any area. Many believers struggle with this very dilemma in their service for God. One day we are certain that God has called us to do a work in one area, and the next week we are going in a totally different direction. This happens more often than not in the absence of an example (or a mentor) to help in discerning the will of God and making strategic decisions. We often need someone who is more mature in the faith to help us find a purpose that fulfills the passion God placed inside us.

How often do we hear of someone dropping out of college or quitting a good job, or have we done such things, simply from not being satisfied? Satisfaction comes from fulfilled passion, and passion is birthed from purpose, so we cannot stay where we are not supposed to be. We are passionately searching for satisfaction, and we will satisfy that passion in fulfilling what God has for us to do. That comes from walking out our purpose daily.

Those who lack passion because they have not found their purpose often wonder why they even exist. They feel an inward anger toward others who seem to know where they are going and, to top it off, are obviously enjoying the trip! If this describes what you have been dealing with personally, then you must embrace your *prophetic purpose.* If you don't know what your purpose is you must find it. Purpose sets everything in motion in your life. God knew you before He formed you in your mother's womb, and He already had a purpose for you long before you showed up on earth (see Ps. 139:13–17 and Jer. 29:11).

What is the deep, heartfelt desire has God placed in you? What is your passion? Your purpose fulfills the passion for a particular thing that God has placed in your heart. Is the desire one that comes from you and isn't the wish of someone else for you?

There is a "Catch 22" here. If God has already planned your life and your purpose, but you never pursue it, is that purpose truly meant for you? Why would you have a purpose, full of excitement and promise that God has pre-ordained for you, if you choose not to follow it? *Your choice to follow a path that is entirely different will not yield God's best for your life.* I love the way Paul says it as recorded in the *Amplified Bible.*

> *I do not consider, brethren, that I have captured and made it my own [yet]; but one thing I do [it is my one aspiration]: forgetting what lies behind and straining forward to what lies ahead (Phil. 3:13).*

In saying this, Paul was simply being honest about his own experience. He says (paraphrasing), "There is one thing I have to do; I have to forget those things which are behind me." Most people allow their past to come with them into their future. Hear me on this: If you allow this to happen, you will never get excited about the future, and you will duplicate old patterns that you been living for years.

The sad thing about that lifestyle is that most people get upset at sheer existence, because when they look back over the previous three, four, or five years they find they have been doing the same thing over and over again without purpose and without results that provide the satisfaction God created them to have in their lives. Frustrated by living in the mundane, they feel as if their life has almost ended, so they find no reason to change. This is why I love to do new things and think about new things as a consistent pattern of living. I live daily with a focus toward Philippians 3:14:

I press on toward the goal to win the [supreme and heavenly]
prize to which God in Christ Jesus is calling us upward (AMP).

Allow me to paraphrase Paul's words again. He was saying, "I made a
goal, and I set myself to forget those things that are dead and gone. I am
reaching toward those things that are ahead of me, things I see that are
divinely part of my prophetic purpose. I know it, I see it, I understand it, and
I am pursuing it."

Reversing the wording in this Scripture would read, "Upward God is
calling me toward the prize that is a goal." This opens a new train of
thought: What goal could you reach for that you have not yet obtained, that
you know is the prize the Father desires you to have? The answer is found
in Philippians 3:8:

> *Yes, furthermore, I count everything as loss compared to the*
> *possession of the priceless privilege (the overwhelming preciousness,*
> *the surpassing worth, and supreme advantage) of knowing Christ*
> *Jesus my Lord and of progressively becoming more deeply and inti-*
> *mately acquainted with Him [of perceiving and recognizing and*
> *understanding Him more fully and clearly]. For His sake I have lost*
> *everything and consider it all to be mere rubbish (refuse, dregs), in*
> *order that I may win (gain) Christ (the Anointed One.) (AMP).*

Paul is clearly saying that we should count *things to be obtained* as
rubbish. To me this is saying in one sense that if you do not have some
"stuff" you are throwing away, you will not have room to receive other
"stuff" that comes your way. You can always tell where a person is going by
the stuff he or she leaves behind. If you consider your own life and look
back to find nothing is left behind, you are not in the process of moving to
a new place.

Paul says (again I am paraphrasing), "If there is nothing greater, I
would not have given up all of this. I am the chief of Pharisees, I have the
accolades of great accomplishments and rewards; I would never have given
all of that up to go for something less. Let me tell you, church at Philippi;
let me say this to you: 'I would never pursue God unless there was some-

thing greater that lay ahead for me. I willingly gave up everything because the prize I see waiting for me is worth pressing toward.'"

All that had come before in Paul's life, he had done on his own. But the things that were ahead of him were from God. Therein lies a world of difference.

Receiving the Gift then Pressing Ahead

When we get saved, we "get happy" about our salvation and the assurance that we are on our way to heaven, but there is something that happens in our salvation that we don't associate with the experience. We know salvation is by grace, and that it is a gift of God—so we think everything that follows is also a gift. We put on a suit and tie (or if you are a lady, a beautiful dress), and off we go to church, thinking we have it all. That is not how it works.

A life lived for Christ is a life of sacrifice. There are things we must do after we accept His eternal gift. We must be willing to give up "the stuff" that He requires we put on the altar. What matters to God is an attitude that says, "Father, I love You, I need You, and I seek Your will for my life. Nothing can take Your place in my life. Have Your way, Lord. Teach me and guide me into all truth, and I will obey and follow You." That is seeking His prophetic purpose for your life.

Jesus knew His prophetic purpose even while He was growing up in the home of Joseph and Mary. Luke 2:42-49 tells us that at age twelve Jesus stayed behind and taught in the temple, astonishing all who heard him by His understanding and answers. In response to Joseph and Mary when they came back looking for Him, He asked if they didn't know that He must be about His Father's business.

For thirty years He was known as the carpenter's son. He was the Anointed One, called from Mary's womb, but His life did not change until He walked to the river Jordan, stepped into the water, and was baptized by John. *That is how fast things can change in your life.* When you walk to the place where God has ordained for your life to change, you will be submerged in the "waters" of transition and come up knowing that you have found your purpose.

Few people ever arrive at the place where the Father stops everything, opens the windows of heaven, and says, "This is My beloved son [or daughter], in whom I am well pleased, because he [or she] was willing to die to every other purpose in order to pick up My purpose. This, My child, knows what I need, and is willing to die so that someone else might live."

People in the body of Christ forget, or have never actually considered or realized, what Jesus, the Ultimate Sacrifice of the Father, was willing to give up so that we could form a relationship with the Father and experience the joy and satisfaction of fulfilling our prophetic purpose. Jesus gave up everything—an honored place in heaven, loving parents on earth—knowing that His assignment would lead to His death for *us*. He is the epitome of prophetic purpose. He died and rose from the dead to make the Way available for us, so that we are able to fulfill our prophetic purpose.

To whom God would make known what is the riches of the glory of this mystery among the Gentiles; which is Christ in you, the hope of glory (Col. 1:27).

I am not certain whether everyone who claims to be a Christian actually knows Christ in this way. For example, at the point of your salvation when you received Jesus, you received God's Spirit, but you may never have put aside your own purposes for God's purpose and ever experienced the anointing. You may have the Spirit, but you may never experience the anointing. There is an enormous difference. The Spirit is the Truth. He is also the Comforter. On the other hand, the anointing gives you the ability to go beyond your own understanding and do greater works. Jesus talked to His disciples about the Comforter when He said:

And I will pray the Father, and he shall give you another Comforter, that he may abide with you for ever; Even the Spirit of truth; whom the world cannot receive, because it seeth him not, neither knoweth him: but ye know him; for he dwelleth with you, and shall be in you. I will not leave you comfortless: I will come to you.

Yet a little while, and the world seeth me no more; but ye see me: because I live, ye shall live also. At that day ye shall know that I am in my Father, and ye in me, and I in you (John 14:16–20).

You will not see the Christ of Glory in His fullness until you die to your own purposes. There is a difference in knowing about Christ and "winning" Christ. Remember Paul's words in Philippians 3:8? At the cost of everything he had known, he had a burning desire to "win Christ." He counted everything as rubbish and dung compared to the glory of being in His presence and purpose. We should live with that desire in mind. Only Jesus can satisfy; He is our "...hope of glory" (Col. 1:27). Yet Philippians 3:15 tells us that God will remind us when our thinking is not on track with His.

So let those [of us] who are spiritually mature and full-grown have this mind and hold these convictions; and if in any respect you have a different attitude of mind, God will make that clear to you also (AMP).

The important thing to remember is that Paul had a burning desire to "know Christ."[2] Many Christians today know about Christ, but do we really "know" Him intimately? *Do we know Him as the Friend that is closer than a brother?* [3] Every believer knows Jesus as the Lamb of God, the One who took away our sin.[4] We know He is the resurrected Lord who sits at the right hand of the Father, making intercession for us continually[5]—but do we have a relationship with Him, a one-on-one friendship that surpasses all others? When we can truly say that we *know* Him and that we understand His purpose for our life, we will be on our way to experiencing the abundant life and prosperity He has promised.

Unshakable Intent and Convictions

This leads to the second letter of our acronym for *whatsoever is pure*: "U," which stands for **Unshakable Intent and Convictions.** When your convictions are so strong that other people question why you keep praying or fasting when they have long since given up, you are displaying *unshakable intent.* Often, God places a firm resolve in our spirit when He wants to take us further or to another level. When God has placed that intent in you through leading you in your prophetic purpose, you cannot be shaken or moved. No one will be able to change your convictions with new thoughts or persuasions. God will use the *intent of your heart* to bring about His purpose and desire.

Let's look again at Philippians 3:15 which tells us, "...those [of us] who are spiritually mature and full-grown have this mind and hold these convictions..." (AMP).

Do you see this? When you become mature and full-grown in your spiritual walk, you will have strong convictions. Full-grown does not refer to an age or position. It speaks of you reaching the point where you have substituted for everything in your mind that you thought you wanted or had placed value on accomplishing in the past, with, instead, the surpassing worth of knowing Christ Jesus your Lord. Full-grown—having "this mind" or "attitude of mind," as Philippians 3:15 (AMP) refers to as the verse continues—speaks of you placing your highest value on deepening the intimacy of that relationship. It speaks of your firm resolve to seek and fulfill God's prophetic purpose for your life to gain the mind of Christ.

You have given your purposes over to His purpose, His will. It is like Jesus is saying, "When you have given your mind to Me, that is when you have become mature in Me. I am able to minister what I have intended, and my intents cannot be shaken, because now you will not change your mindset."

Pressing Through

There are times we have difficulties being unshakable due to the influence of others. But when we look at this, we must understand it is actually not their opinions that trouble us; it is something in our own spirit we must deal with. At other times we run from God's desires because of the pain involved in bringing about the purpose He is trying to show us. Let me clarify: *That pain* is the result of holding onto the world and what it offers while trying to extend the other hand to God. That simply will not work, because if you can be pulled in two different directions at the same time, your intent is not unshakable. You cannot be unshakable when you are wavering.

Maturity also displays an attitude of forgiveness. It does not argue with God about someone's behavior when he or she treats us badly. I do not change my love for God because someone who professes love for Him hates me. At the cost of all, I must hold onto my convictions, regardless of what others may say or do. In the pain of wounded relationships, my convictions will lead me to say, "I am going to love you because my Father says to love you," and, "Love them that hate you." My convictions say, "Do good to them which hate you; bless them that persecute you. Pray for them that despitefully use you."[6] This is the attitude of a pure heart that is pursuing prophetic purpose.

Focusing Forward

You cannot maintain purity of heart with distractions interrupting your unshakable intentions. If you are going to be strong in your prophetic purpose, you have to avoid the distractions that come your way. God says that we must be spiritually mature, even though we may not be mature in natural years. I'll say it again: Strong convictions come from mature and unshakable intentions.

When I was growing up, many of my contemporaries used to say to me, "Why are you going to morning prayer every day? Why are you pressing into prayer like that?" I told them God was developing something in my prayer life that I could not explain. Whenever I went into prayer, the Lord would tell me, "Do not ask for anything for yourself; pray for something else." When I responded, "What do You mean?" He sent me to a Scripture that says, "Commit thy works unto the LORD, and thy thoughts shall be established" (Prov. 16:3). That was one of the greatest blessings of my prayer life: when I stopped praying for my desires, yet they still came to pass. This is when my faith toward God and convictions became unshakable. It is also when I realized my prayer life was pleasing to Him.

When you are spiritually mature and commit your works to the Lord, you hold fast in focusing your mind and attitude toward the things ahead. You press through the influences and distractions that could pull you a different direction from the one God has for you. You strain forward toward the goal to win the heavenly prize to which God in Christ Jesus is calling you, and God will make you unshakable. As we saw before in Philippians 2:13, it is God who is at work in us to will and to work for His good pleasure.

By allowing God to establish our thoughts, then seeing Him establish a thing without our having to pray for it, we know that we have oneness with Him. We see in Jesus our example of oneness with the Father. Jesus did the Father's will—there was no disobedience with Him. When we submit our will to God's will by giving our desires over to His desires, living each day by seeking His will and obeying Him, we have oneness with Him.

Through that oneness in our prayer life, God establishes His desire in us so that we will *think on* it. In our prayer life, He allows us to see what He desires for us. He does this so that as we see and believe what He has already prepared for us and as we think on it, He starts establishing His desire within us so that our desires become established as His desire. In that oneness and obedience we begin walking in the blessing of the abundant life that Jesus talked about. When our thinking lines up with God's desires, our prayer life is anointed.

God taught me a long time ago that if you have to be on your face for long periods of time hollering and screaming so that people can hear you, you do not have a prayer life. This is not the kind of anointed prayer that comes from thinking that lines up with God's desires. If you are hollering so that God will line up His desires with your desires, hollering will not make God change His mind.

When we pray, we should stand by the conviction that God has already heard us (Isa. 65:24) instead of hollering to try to convince Him or argue with Him. The Bible tells us that the Holy Spirit prays for us in line with God's will, and Jesus is interceding for us (see Rom. 8:26-27; Heb. 7:25).

We know that Jesus prayed for Peter that his faith would fail not (Luke 22:31–32), and we can believe that Jesus is praying that our faith will fail not. You must have an unshakable resolve to be led into prophetic purpose. Here is something that may help you. When I am praying for something that is bigger than my capacity to believe, I pray that God will give me the faith to believe it will happen. I ask Him to give me a resolve that will transition me to a level that I have never seen. I ask Him to stretch me beyond my knowledge and desire: to take me, turn me, focus me, and put me in the place where I can trust Him beyond anything I could ever imagine. If you are having difficulties being unshakable, try praying this way, "Lord, stretch me to believe for the things that You have promised." He is faithful to perform His purpose in you.

Unshakable intentions come with the ability to live your convictions. When your mind is set on fulfilling your prophetic purpose—your intent is unshakable—you have the ability to live your convictions. No one can appreciate a purpose more than somebody who has a strong conviction about it. Luke 12:48 says, "...For unto whomsoever much is given, of him shall be much required...."

You can be given a purpose, yet not have great faith or conviction. Many times, this comes from a lack of spiritual discipline. I can always tell when people are disciplined, because they have the conviction to go with it. Now, hear me, because this is important. *People who are not passionate about their conviction will never become great. Great people have discipline, as well as conviction.*

Righteous Focus

The third letter of our acronym for the virtue of purity is "**R**," which stands for **Righteous Focus**. You must be *righteously focused* on what God has called you to do through your *prophetic purpose*. That means you have *unshaken intention* that comes from righteous standing with God.

We become righteous when we receive Jesus, who justifies us and puts us in right standing with God. However, in the sense of being righteously focused, I am referring to living out righteousness as expressed in Hebrews

12:11 (AMP): "...conformity to God's will in purpose, thought, and action" which results "in right living and right standing with God."

This righteously focused conviction in you comes from, is birthed from, God's purpose for you. You have a firm, unshakable resolve to focus on conforming to His will in thought and action to fulfill His particular purpose for you. Each of us has God-given convictions. They will be similar to those held by other people in some instances but will also differ greatly in other cases.

Your conviction must be strong if you are going to touch other people's lives with Jesus. You must have discipline; you cannot constantly be up and down, this way and then the total opposite, not knowing what God has called you to do and expect God to allow you to touch people's lives to bring them into purpose. If you are not disciplined, God cannot trust you with all that He has for you.

Hebrews 12:11 (AMP) tells us that "discipline...yields a peaceable fruit of righteousness," righteousness in the sense of the meaning described above. James 3:18 tells us, "the fruit of righteousness is sown in peace of them that make peace," or as worded in the *Amplified Bible*, "those who work for and make peace [in themselves and in others..., in a peaceful mind free from fears and agitating passions and moral conflicts]." This describes the goal of the process we are walking through in this book. We are building our foundation of thought life on Philippians 4:6-9 step-by-step, virtue by virtue, to reach that goal Paul shows us should be our utmost desire: living our lives in the untroubled, undisturbed peace of the Prince of Peace. From that place of peace, we walk in our God-ordained life of abundance and fulfilled purpose.

You must be focused enough to be sensitive to the discipline that is needed. If getting up early in the morning doing your regimen is difficult for you, then be focused and disciplined enough to do whatever is necessary. You will notice that great people have the greatest discipline...and the greatest conviction many times comes from people who live long, because greater focus and discipline are needed. They eat the foods that are good for their bodies, like potato skins and orange peels! I was at a restaurant with an older couple once when the woman told me, "Eat the skin." "Eat what?" I asked. "Eat the skin," she replied. I took a lesson from her, because she was past eighty and looked like a fifty-year-old. I knew there must be something in the fruit and vegetable skins that I needed.

That is often the way we do things in church. We eat the "good stuff" and throw away the rest. We want the Holy Spirit, but we do not want to partake of the passion of Christ. We do not want to go to the level in Him where the real nutrients are. We need to receive Christ for all that He is so that we can become everything He has created us to be.

Looking at Philippians 3:16 along with verse 15, which we have been examining in detail, gives us a good description of *righteous focus*:

> *So let those [of us] who are spiritually mature and full-grown have this mind and hold these convictions; and if in any respect you have a different attitude of mind, God will make that clear to you also. Only let us hold true to what we have already attained and walk and order our lives by that (AMP).*

What if you have attained purpose and have convictions and focus, but do not like the path you are on and decide to stop living true to what you have gained? Some people would not want to "order" another three years of what they have been through. As God's children, we should desire the next three years to be better, clearer, easier, less stressful, undisturbed, untroubled, and full of well-being! So if you are true to what you have already attained, but have discovered that is not what you want, then you have to change some of your convictions—you have to get new convictions to change the things you are not happy about as you are walking that path. If you don't do anything, you will get exactly what you had before.

Have you ever gone regularly to a restaurant where you always order the same thing, so that every time you show up the person waiting on your table doesn't even bother to give you a menu? They put you at your "usual" table and start bringing you food, because they already know what you want. They serve you "as usual," giving you the same drink, appetizer, entrée, and dessert you always order. They know what you want because you are consistent in ordering. If you were to change, they might go into shock.

I used to go have breakfast every now and then at a restaurant close to my office. I always had them pile everything possible on my plate—turkey bacon, corned beef hash, eggs with Swiss cheese, potatoes, grits, and toast. With that, I would enjoy a mixture of iced tea and lemonade. Whenever I walked in, the person waiting on my table knew what my order would be. I knew exactly how much this meal would cost to the penny.

Then one day I went back in and said, "Listen, all I want is sliced turkey grilled with eggs and no cheese." The waitress looked at me as if to say, "Are you the same person we have always known?" I had to say several times, "No turkey bacon. No corned beef hash. No mix." The people who worked in the restaurant were shocked when they saw the change in me. I had a new conviction: that I could not eat those foods to maintain my physical well-being. I was on the right path toward accomplishing God's purpose for my life, but I didn't like the idea of walking the path weighing too much for my physical well-being.

For me to change, I knew it had to be my desires causing it to happen, not because somebody else said, "Oh, you have put on a little weight; would you like to change your order?" The waitress absolutely will not come out and say, "You need to lose ten pounds"! She will keep giving you what you order. I knew that I was the one who needed to change the type of breakfast I ordered from the "usual" to bring change—I couldn't blame the restaurant employees for my weight being more than I desired. Did I want to ultimately weigh up to two hundred and fifty pounds? I have a tall frame, but that was not my desire. Thus, I knew I had to change my conviction, and I did.

If you don't like something along the path to fulfilling God's purpose for you, and you can't live your life with the conviction to change some of the ways you are doing things in order to allow God's peace to come into that area, you know that your *focus* has not been pure. You have not been single-minded before God to achieve the peace in every area while fulfilling what He has for you.

It doesn't matter who you are or what your economic status is, what type of education or background you have, or what your marital status may be. If you have purity in your life, you must have *righteous focus* to keep living a virtue-focused life. With these pure intentions you can hold on to what you have already attained, but if you have no principles, or convictions, and no righteous focus—it will be extremely difficult for you to establish who you are, that is, who you are in Christ in the fullness God intends for you.

Let me give you an example. Righteousness has nothing to do with whether or not you speak in tongues. We are all made righteous when we receive Jesus, but walking in "the harvest of righteousness (of conformity to God's will in thought and deed)...," James 3:18 AMP, or "the fruit of righteousness...," KJV, is a fruit of your relationship with God. Not all believers who speak in tongues necessarily walk in demonstration of this kind of righteousness, although many do. There are also many other virtuous believers who live in a more righteous way than those who speak in tongues. Righteousness, in the sense of living in a way that demonstrates righteousness, is a discipline that is developed from listening to the will of the Father concerning our lives. In other words, if I am focused and discipline myself to do the things I know I am to do, this brings me into walking in the peaceable fruit of righteousness of right living with God in "conformity to God's will in purpose, thought, and action..." (Heb. 12:11 AMP), reflecting right standing with Him.

In a similar way as a father, the more time I spend with my daughter, the more I see disciplines forming in her life. One time upon arriving home she opened the door a little early, even though she knows not to do so until I have come around the side of the house. She knew that was important, but at that critical moment she forgot—so I had to remind her. There are other things she knows and does automatically, like putting on her seat belt. I don't even have to ask her to do it. She has held to what she has already been taught, and in doing so she is developing focused disciplines.

Once when we took a trip together, I noticed something she did that revealed her level of discipline to me. She is not supposed to drink any dark cola but is allowed to have Sprite. On the plane with me, she asked for a dark cola. Being the dad that I am, I let her drink it but said if her mother knew that, whoa! She wouldn't like it (and if she didn't know before, I guess she knows now)! Later at the airport when we got off the plane, my daughter went right back to drinking Sprite. That showed me something about her focus; I realized how disciplined she is, even at her early age.

Some people misunderstand when you alter your decisions and choose to do things differently from the way you did them in the past. Remember, you must be true to yourself and the person God made you to be and become by making decisions that line up with the heartfelt desire God put in you. To keep your desires and focus in line with His desire and purpose for you so that your intent remains unshakable and won't change, it is important to decide to make some adjustments. Even though you have the right to change what you desire, you need to change some of your convictions along the way to keep your focus on God's purpose so that you won't stray from it.

Sometimes people just will not understand why you have changed in some areas. There may be times when your reaction to their response is to feel angry; yet and still, you must maintain your discipline and righteous focus. At other times you will have to be firm or diligent. But you still have to return to being the sweet, loving person everybody adores, or you will not show the world your righteous focus.

How many times have you gotten excited about your relationship with God when no one else is around? How many times have you shouted praise to God in your closet? How many times did the elevator door close, and you broke out into a dance before Him? When you come into righteous focus, you understand that walking with God is a lot more than just going to church or hearing a preacher. Righteous focus is an ordered life of devotion to God.

Example of Christ

Let's move on to Philippians 3:17, where Paul is saying, "Brethren, together follow my example and observe those who live after the pattern we have set for you" (AMP). In other words, he was saying, "If you want what I have, brethren, you have to follow my example," which is the fourth letter of our acronym, "**E**," concerning *whatsoever is pure*, to follow Paul as he was following the **Example of Christ**. We read in 1 Corinthians 11:1 (AMP) that Paul said, "Pattern yourselves after me [follow my example], as I imitate and follow Christ (the Messiah)."

Paul was stating a simple truth: You have to either follow or be an example. If you do not have an example in front of you of what you want to be, and if you do not know how to get there, you will not reach the goal. It is as simple as that. Merely looking at something does not give you the correct pattern. Having the conviction to do what it takes to apply that pattern is what gets you to the goal every time.

Many people want to be blessed without following the pattern. Others want to have a lot of money, but they do not understand the proper pattern to obtain it. It is important to understand that having more money does not make you richer. Money does one of two things: It either amplifies your weaknesses, or it develops a discipline in you to learn and know how to manage it. If you give a child an orange crayon, he will mark up whatever you put in front of him. Give him a four-inch brush and a can of orange paint, and the result will be much worse.

That is what happens when we want God to give us a big brush, but we have not been disciplined by example with the crayon. If a child does not know the crayon is supposed to be used on paper and not on the brown furniture or green wall, we can't turn him loose to do what he wants to do. If we give him a paintbrush and a canvas, he still will not understand what to do any more than he did with the crayon. The child will do what he has always done, so we must wait until he is fully mature. We simply do not give a child a four-inch paintbrush at two years of age. What he does with a crayon, he will do with a brush—make a big mess. He must be nurtured and developed.

This is the very reason why many believers have not been blessed to be exactly where they want to be in God. They never found an example to show them how to become a trustworthy vessel—*purposed, unshakable,* and *focused*—so they could become everything God has already revealed in their hearts. In fact, most of us have failed in this critical area. We fail because we let other people, who never had an example, become our example. Then we establish a pattern of behavior after them—good, bad, or indifferent.

We all need to take a close look at our life. If we do not discipline ourselves to become true to the things we really desire, then we need to find people who are already there. Why would we go to the gym to lose a couple of pounds when our workout instructor is heavier than we are? I would not want that instructor to tell me how many reps I have to do. Would we want the person who is telling us to step up on the scales to be eating a fast-food breakfast sandwich right in front of us? We must have a godly example to follow if we are going to *think on* and *do* whatsoever is pure.

I love infomercials, but I really want to know if those models actually developed those winning abs on that particular equipment. I want to see something real. Show me someone that took eight months to develop firm abs; don't tell me that I can get champion abs in six weeks with six minutes a day of exercise! You cannot eat foods like ice cream, cheese, greens, chitterlings, and lots of deep-fried foods and end up with six-pack abs. To tell the truth, this has been happening in the church for years. We have presented an infomercial on how to get saved. We have not shown people the real example.

We have to tell the truth about where we have been. If there were more real people giving real testimonies about the *truth* of salvation, perhaps more people would believe us. Some people look at believers and think that a life like ours would be nice; but they perceive our lives are almost like what people perceive professional wrestling to be: 80 percent acting, 20 percent real, and "fixed" before a match ever begins. Even the unsaved know we cannot follow the wrong example and expect to get the right results.

Why is it that we serve the greatest God, but many of us end up living the poorest lives? I believe the reason is this: The church has gone through a facade of hype without providing real examples. The only way we are going to be pure is when we are able to look at ourselves and say, "I really need to change; I need to become convicted about some things in my life." But if the conviction comes and we are not changed, we are just playing church. We may be saved, we may read our Bible, some of us may speak in tongues, and we may clap our hands, but we will never have the excitement or joy of a pure life. We will never have the passion of prophetic purpose.

Do you know your *prophetic purpose?* Do you have *unshakable intentions* and *righteous focus?* More importantly, who is your *example* in Christ? I have matured to the level of knowing my God-given purpose can sustain me throughout eternity. I believe as a global church we must reach the place where our excitement about our salvation *is* our purpose. Purpose is bigger than any church or preacher, and it is bigger than anything this world could ever give us. Through God you can find the purity of purpose. You can establish a singular pattern that will take you from pain, to purpose, to prosperity.

CHAPTER 5

Whatsoever Is *Lovely*: Loved and Valued by God

For most people, the most appealing thing about living a virtue-centered life according to Philippians 4:8–9 is that the "God of peace" will be with us. To me, that is the loveliest thought of all. I cannot think of anything better.

When thinking about something that is lovely, pleasant images come to the mind and heart. I love how the *Webster's American Family Dictionary* describes this calming word, "having a beauty that appeals to the heart or mind as well as to the eye...."

Before we move on with looking at the virtue of this chapter specifically dedicated to God being with us, allow me to share a quick nugget about the peace of God that will bless your life. The word *peace* is derived from the Greek word *"eirene"* (also transliterated as *"eireenee"*), which from its root has a number of meanings, including this brief list of pleasant thoughts: "tranquility...harmony...safety, prosperity."[1] I don't know about you, but receiving the truth that these promises can be mine is well worth anything that God requires of me in developing strong, solid, biblical virtues.

I do not know anyone who does not want to live in a world that is untroubled and undisturbed, or who does not desire to be surrounded by an atmosphere of well-being. But here is the catch. It is more difficult to maintain peace and live from it as a basis if your body is not well or your mind is troubled. If everything around you is in turmoil, it is also difficult to concentrate on enjoying inner peace as well.

Now, let's move on. The word *lovely* comes after *true, honest, just,* and *pure* in Paul's listing of things we should be "thinking on" in order to possess the peace of God. This is quite fitting when we consider the things we have been learning about each of those first four virtues we are training ourselves to keep on our minds. When we have mastered the first disciplines, *whatsoever is lovely* can begin.

"Lovely" is an especially descriptive word because of its relationship to things we value or to which we give our attention. When we love something or someone, we often describe that person or thing as being lovely. You cannot love something and not value or give attention to it. Any parents who have a child they love, value the care that they give that child. During infancy, a loving mother or father pays close attention to the temperature of the milk or formula and the type of food that is introduced into the baby's diet. A caring adult would not give a piece of celery to an infant, because he or she knows it could cause the baby to choke. When we love a child, we value that child too much to take such a chance.

When you love and value your child you will give that child attention. Sometimes we hear people say that a child who has been loved and acknowledged is "spoiled," but hear me on this—do not misconstrue that meaning. You do not give birth to a child just to let God's special creation grow up on his or her own without the benefit of love and attention; you desire the absolute best for your child. The bottom line is that we value and pay attention to *whatsoever* we love, which also relates to the meaning of *lovely*.

Now, let's look at this virtue from the perspective that God loves and values us as His children. We should never dismiss this fact or take it lightly. God values His time with us and His attentiveness to us. He has given His angels charge over us, to keep us from harm (see Ps. 91:11-12). God values us so much that He gives us "new mercies" every morning (take a look at Lam. 3:22-23). He freely gives us rich benefits that fulfill our lives every day (Ps. 103:2). God demonstrates His love toward us by making sure goodness and mercy follow us all the days of our life (Ps. 23:6). God has carefully invested His time, love, and attention in us. We can have full assurance of this when we read Hebrews 13:5–6:

Let your character or moral disposition be free from love of money [including greed, avarice, lust, and craving for earthly possessions] and be satisfied with your present [circumstances and with what you have]; for He [God] Himself has said, I will not in any way fail you nor give you up nor leave you without support. [I will] not, [I will] not, [I will] not in any degree leave you helpless nor forsake nor let [you] down (relax My hold on you)! [Assuredly not!]

So we take comfort and are encouraged and confidently and boldly say, The Lord is my Helper; I will not be seized with alarm [I will not fear or dread or be terrified]. What can man do to me? (AMP).

With this realization firmly in our hearts, let us begin by instilling in our minds a few key principles that can be found in the acronym for *lovely*. There are many important truths revealed in this biblical text from which we can feast as we seek after God's peace. Now, let's go to the acronym:

- **L** et This Mind Be in You, *allows you to become*

- **O** f No Reputation, *which gives you*

- **V** ictory Over Pride, *through which God will gladly*

- **E** xalt *you, releasing the flow of His*

- **L** ordship, *as you continue to give Him the*

- **Y** ...Glory *He is due!*

Let This Mind Be in You

The letter "L" stands for **Let This Mind Be in You**. Take a careful look at Philippians 2:5-8:

Let this same attitude and purpose and [humble] mind be in you which was in Christ Jesus: [Let Him be your example in humility:]

Who, although being essentially one with God and in the form of God [possessing the fullness of the attributes which make God God], did not think this equality with God was a thing to be eagerly grasped or retained,

*But stripped Himself [of all privileges and rightful dignity], so
as to assume the guise of a servant (slave), in that He became like
men and was born a human being.*

*And after He had appeared in human form, He abased and
humbled Himself [still further] and carried His obedience to the
extreme of death, even the death of the cross! (AMP).*

Our Lord's mindset that we are looking at here is one of humility.
Understanding the mindset of Christ is vital; because when we begin to
understand His love for us, we realize that everything He does has purpose.
Everything He does is from a humble mindset. Christ is our ultimate
example of humility—so we must let His mind be in us. Let's look at this
from the opposite perspective: If we do not maintain the mindset of
Christ—whether we are a pastor, nursery worker, or church attendee—we
will not have that same spirit of humility.

A Mindset of Humility

Humility is one of those issues in Christiandom about which everyone
has an opinion. Pastors spend a lot of time trying to teach about humility,
and churches are constantly dealing with people who do not understand the
role humility plays in their lives. Allow me to set the record straight. *If you
are going to be used of God, your mind must adopt His mindset—you must
have an attitude of humility.* This way, when He gives you correction you
will be open to His guidance. If you do not possess a spirit of humility,
divine correction will be of no effect in you, and you will not get *the
Father's results* in what you do for the Kingdom.

It is essential to have the mind of Christ when you counsel others or are
simply talking to them about the Lord. It is obvious when you are not being
"real," or you have a proud and haughty spirit. When there is no humility in
your life, people will identify you as a "fake." They will pick up on the fact
that you are trying to be something you are not. For example, it is hard to
maintain a friendship with people who are always trying to impress you
about things they have done or places they have been, especially if you
know the things they are telling you are not true. As God's creations birthed

in *whatsoever is true*, we have an innate desire for our friends to be open and honest; we seek humility in the framework of friendships.

Think of when a comedian puts on different masks to portray different characters. When we try to "fake it" to impress others, we can end up with ten or fifteen different "characters" we use trying to impress others. Finally, we start forgetting which "fake" identity is supposed to be played out with which friend, and then we are in a world of hurt! No one can keep true friends when they have that attitude. We must have the mind of Christ and humility in our relationships.

Another aspect that reflects the mindset of humility of Christ can be found in the theology of salvation. Salvation is not simply a "one-stop moment" in your life. It is also an everyday experience that has to be lived out through the character birthed from your "transformed" mindset. Unless you have an open mind to God from learning to think in the way He thinks and operating in the mind of Christ, you will not "en-*joy*" the salvation He has given you. Remember the reason why Jesus went to the Cross: "...Jesus the author and finisher of our faith; who *for the joy that was set before him* endured the cross, despising the shame, and is set down at the right hand of the throne of God" (Heb. 12:2, *emphasis mine*). Jesus freely chose to go to the Cross, because He was filled with joy He had received directly from the Father in seeing a dying world have the opportunity to be eternally redeemed and abundant in life; He received the Father's mindset and in obedience walked in that vision. In turn, we must realize that life is full of choices, so we must let the same mindset be in us that was in Christ Jesus, and we will make the right choices for the right reasons.

Think about it. You had to make the right choice to receive Jesus and be saved. Love is a choice, although we do not often think of it this way. We are free to either love or to hate, to accept love or to reject it. Our human nature is to love only when it is returned, because we need love. *What if God decided that He needed to have your love in order to continue being God on your behalf?* He could have refused to love humanity when we turned our backs on Him; but instead, He chose to love us, for the simple pleasure of giving love to His children. *Do you have that kind of mindset?*

A mature (tested) mind says, *I will love, even if that love is never returned. At least I will have the joy of showing others what true, unconditional love is all about.*

Making Wise Choices

It is essential that we make wise choices. One crucial choice is your selection of a marriage partner. You may think you love someone just because he or she is *lovely* only to your natural eye, but that is not a sound reason for choosing a lifetime partner—it is not rooted in the humble mindset of Christ. When you base your love on "cuteness," that love will eventually fade. So it is always better to be virtue-centered when making choices in dating and in marriage.

Always start by discovering the inner person and then looking at the outer person. Do not manage your love life the other way around. The choices you make could lead you down a path that you will eventually regret. Remember, love is a choice, not a feeling.

Embracing humility (from Christ's example) will clarify your value system. You will stop making decisions based on what the "in thing" might be and start being directed by that which Christ would approve. You will cease to do things because everyone else is doing them and will start taking action because it is the right thing to do. This is the essence of doing things according to the right pattern in the spirit of 1 Corinthians, chapters 12 through 14, which concludes with Paul's exhortation, "But all things should be done with regard to decency and propriety and in an orderly fashion" (1 Cor. 14:40 AMP). When you possess the mind of Christ and make the right choices, there are supernatural results. Love will be returned to you in many unexpected ways.

One of the long-term benefits of humility is that it teaches you to be *honest* with yourself. We sometimes want to sidestep issues in our lives; things we would rather ignore or minimize. But as we learn to possess the mindset of Christ (and the humility that accompanies it), we will begin to make *true*, *honest*, *just*, and *pure* choices by looking deeply into the desires of our hearts and discovering who we really are in Him. Hear me. Humility allows you to identify your true feelings, give honest answers to your inner questions, and start making decisions that are based on truth—not denial or fantasy. This is when God will begin establishing a standard, a pattern that is empowered by a renewed state of mind.

The reality of your lifestyle today is based on choices you made in the past. So it follows that what you choose today will affect your lifestyle either immediately or in the future. *If you want to change your lifestyle, you must counteract the poor choices you have made in the past.* You cannot change something to make it right if you do not identify what made it wrong in the first place. Poor choices stem from the emotional realm, whether you are aimlessly following the opinions of others or are compensating for lack in another area.

For example, many times we buy things from a desire to feel loved and appreciated, not because we truly need them. When the ill-thought-out purchase does not give us the immediate gratification we desire, we end up feeling cheated, both financially and emotionally. Men often buy new cars as an ego builder. They want to show their friends that they are earning enough money to afford a certain type of vehicle. Perhaps they like music and want to show off a new, state-of-the-art sound system, because it gives a man the satisfaction of "being somebody."

Women act in a similar way when they redecorate their homes or buy new furniture. They want their children to be the best dressed in their school. Again, a desire to be loved and appreciated drives this type of thinking. A host of poor choices throughout history have been made simply because people were trying to find true love and appreciation. So once we identify that we have made a poor decision and discover the unhappiness that results from making that choice, we need to start over and go in a different direction. One of the best things in life is to live with your virtuous choices and experience true abundance and happiness. Proverbs 10:22 says, "The blessing of the Lord—it makes [truly] rich, and He adds no sorrow with it [neither does toiling increase it]" (AMP).

Keeping this humble mindset will allow you to make the right choices, because you will be free from hype, fads, or the foolishness of "non-integral" thinking that is not *virtue based*. When you "think on" *whatsoever* God desires, you stop looking for "quick fixes" (those things you did not have the strength of character to "fix" on your own in the past). Some people go to church, and even accept the Lord as Savior, because they want God to "fix" their problems. A preacher may have even told them God would automatically "fix" everything if they just accepted Jesus into their heart. If this is what you have heard, I am sorry to tell you—it is simply not *true*.

Salvation is not given to relieve your responsibility to address practical areas that may be lacking. Coming to God is not a "quick fix" for all your problems, because if it were, everyone would get saved! Instead of fixing all our issues and putting out fires, God desires for us to build our character and establish our foundation in Him. Through learning how to replace any thoughts that are hindering us with His thoughts and by receiving His virtues and making wise choices, we can "fix" most of those problems. This is accomplished by His grace by letting the mind of Christ be *in us*.

God is interested in our spiritual growth, because He wants to move us to the place where we wake up each morning with His peace shining from within us. Wouldn't it be wonderful to go about life as usual for a week and end the week saying, "You know, God, I do not have a problem perplexing me this week. Thank You for the peace that is ruling and reigning in my heart. Thank You for the virtuous character that You are helping me to develop, and for the love and appreciation that only You can give me. Because of You, all the choices I am making now are being formed in me through renewing my mind to the mind of Christ and operating in it."

Having the mind of Christ will humble you, and having strength with humility is the perfect balance for godly character.

Of No Reputation

The second letter, "**O**," of our acronym for *whatsoever is lovely* also comes from Philippians 2. Let's return to the text:

*Let this same attitude and purpose and [humble] mind be in you
which was in Christ Jesus: [Let Him be your example in humility:]*

*Who, although being essentially one with God and in the form
of God [possessing the fullness of the attributes which make God
God], did not think this equality with God was a thing to be eagerly
grasped or retained (Phil. 2:5–6 AMP).*

*But made himself of no reputation, and took upon him the form of
a servant, and was made in the likeness of men (Phil. 2:7 KJV).*

To continue our development in "thinking on" things that are lovely, we must willingly become "Of No Reputation."

Jesus was essentially one with God. He was in the form of God, possessing the fullness of the attributes that make God who He is—yet He was willing to give it all up in order to do the Father's will. Jesus did not think this equality with God was a thing to be grasped or retained. In other words, He was not trying to use His eternal attributes to make Himself popular. From before time began, Jesus (the Son) always had an intimate relationship with the Father. Being one with the Father is how He displayed that relationship to the world. Jesus understood His earthly role. Though He was one with the Father and they shared the same purpose, the assignment Jesus had to fulfill was His own. Therefore, He had to strip himself, in the wording of the *Amplified Bible*, of all heavenly privileges and "rightful dignity" to take on the form of a servant.

*But stripped Himself [of all privileges and rightful dignity], so
as to assume the guise of a servant (slave), in that He became like
men and was born a human being (Phil. 2:7 AMP).*

For example, you may display all of the attributes of a policeman—the blue uniform, the same model and color of car, as well as the strength needed to place someone under arrest. However, having the power to do these things by virtue of displaying the attributes does not necessarily mean you have authority. There is process. You must apply for the position and go through processing in order to be hired, go through training, and take an oath of service to receive an officer's badge. If you have not done this, you are a false authority; you are not a real policeman.

There are people who appear to have an anointing, but in reality, they do not have any spiritual authority. The inner working of their spirit man does not line up with the Word. As a result, their lifestyle does not measure up to the level they desire to portray. To put it in not so delicate terms, they are spiritual "wanna-be's." Personally, I am satisfied to be what God desires for me to be, and I have no desire to be anything else. I have no desire to become a "wanna-be." There is too much I am focused toward to fulfill my eternal purpose. The same is true for you, as you are reading and absorbing the teaching in this book, to fulfill God's eternal purpose for you. He created you to be a unique and special vessel in His Kingdom. So I encourage you with all that is in me—become what He has created you to be.

Let's look at the addition of verse 8 to verse 7 as we move forward in our text. Paul says:

> *But stripped Himself [of all privileges and rightful dignity], so as to assume the guise of a servant (slave), in that He became like men and was born a human being.*
>
> *And after He had appeared in human form, He abased and humbled Himself [still further] and carried His obedience to the extreme of death, even the death of the cross!" (Phil. 2:7–8 AMP).*

Jesus was born into the world as a human being; He stripped Himself of everything He had in Glory so that He could come to earth and die, yet He was still equal with God in the spiritual realm.

You will never reach your highest level with the Father until you strip off your own plans for yourself—what you think you could have found satisfaction in—and are willing to become *whatsoever* He desires. God may assign you to ministry in a place you would never have chosen to go, perhaps in a homeless shelter. If you are not willing to go to that shelter, or to a prison, in order to help the hurting, then you do not yet possess a true spirit of humility. Proverbs 3:27 tells us, "Withhold not good from them to whom it is due, when it is in the power of thine hand to do it." That means anybody, anyplace, at any time under God's direction.

God has created us to be a blessing to others, but many believers are more interested in waiting to get a title or to make a name for themselves. Hear me: Any of us who have this mindset will not be able to do much of anything that is worthwhile for God. He wants us to start moving into our destiny assignment right now, and that doesn't mean we have to become so super-spiritual that we are "spooky."

We can be a blessing to someone right where we are, just the way we are. Jesus, who is one with the Father, came to earth, yet stripped Himself of His privileges and rightful dignity, making himself *of no reputation* to bring salvation to mankind. Jesus demonstrated to us that if we willingly "strip ourselves" of reputation and the things man has to offer, any of us can reflect all of the attributes of God. If you are someone who didn't think that God could reflect Himself in you in this way, take heart because you are still walking in human form, but you can be filled to the brim with the Spirit of God and be a blessing to anybody, anyplace, at any time under God's direction.

As for me, I am seeking my Father's reward. I want to possess all of the peace that He desires to give me. I long for the strength and power to do what He has called me to do. And I will not abuse that power; I will use it for His glory. Yet I know that to walk in His peace, power, and strength, it will require me to strip away my reputation and everything this world offers. As believers and children of God, if we are not willing to follow Christ's example, we will not have all the rewards the Father has laid up for us. Like Paul's example, as recorded in Philippians 3:10, my deepest desire—more than anything else I have known or experienced—is to *know Christ*.

Shed the Images Others Have of You

When Jesus gives you an assignment, it is meant especially for you. But in fulfilling an assignment from God, we must be careful, because people will label us according to our assignment. For example, through being faithful to our call, we build a reputation for doing certain things in ministry.

That is all well and good. However, sometimes an established reputation can be dangerous, because it limits us to being viewed only in a certain way.

Jesus returned to His hometown of Nazareth, and the people asked:

> *Is not this the carpenter's Son? Is not His mother called Mary? And are not His brothers James and Joseph and Simon and Judas? And do not all His sisters live here among us? Where then did this Man get all this? And they took offense at Him [they were repelled and hindered from acknowledging His authority, and caused to stumble]. But Jesus said to them, A prophet is not without honor except in his own country and in his own house. And He did not do many works of power there, because of their unbelief (their lack of faith in the divine mission of Jesus) (Matt. 13:55–58 AMP).*

Once people "label" your reputation they automatically assume that you have chosen that assignment "forever and ever, Amen." That is dangerous because your old reputation can lock you into a place where you cannot expand your ministry for God. If this response limited Jesus in His hometown, it can also happen to you. Unless you free yourself from being labeled, you will become content in a certain ministry or place and will hear the voice of God less and less in your spirit. You will miss His instructions when He is trying to lead you to another level.

I am sure that for thirty years people were telling Jesus of Nazareth He was a good carpenter, and that He should stay in Nazareth. What they did not realize was that He already knew His assignment—He was born to save the world from sin. Even though he had built a reputation in the city, He was willing to let it go in order to carry out His eternal assignment. People may tell you that you are going to be a great doctor or a talented musician. If you do not know what God is calling (or assigning) you to do, you may follow others' suggestions, as well as try many other things, and more than likely will fail in all of them because they were not your purpose or assignment. Allow me to stress this point again: Do not let others control the destiny that God has for you.

Jesus made Himself *of no reputation*. In other words, He freed Himself *to become* what the Father had destined for Him to be. He was absolutely focused on fulfilling His assigned purpose. It would be tragic if you possessed more gifts than anyone recognized, but because you had established a reputation with your dominant gift, you decided to bury the other ones. For example, let's say that Mrs. Jones makes the best coconut cake that was ever brought to a church potluck dinner. She is known for that cake, and everyone requests that cake for every occasion. So she tells her husband that she will not make any more sweet potato pies because she makes such wonderful coconut cakes. What a waste of talent.

Are you wasting God-given talents because of your reputation? Follow your assignment to the place God has created for you. If you make a tasty sweet potato pie, do not limit yourself to just taking coconut cake to the potluck, so to speak. Jesus made Himself *of no reputation* to follow God's plan for His life. Follow His example, and shed the images others have of you. Do what the Father has placed in your heart. Strength and power will come as you pursue your God-given destiny.

Victory Over Pride

This leads to the next letter in our acronym, "**V**," which declares that obedience to God will give you **Victory Over Pride**. If you are struggling with pride, start by asking yourself if you are being obedient to God. If you do not obey God, you will never have victory over pride. Obedience will bring you into new levels of victory throughout your spiritual life, but when you abandon the principles of God you are in trouble. The moment you stop being obedient to the Spirit of the Lord is the very moment pride will begin to rule your life. Pride puts a wedge between you and God. The blessings of the Lord come through obedience, because that is when God can trust you with the responsibility to maintain the blessings He has given you.

Read closely and take this to heart: When you leave your own dreams behind and begin to live for the benefit of others, *your life will change* in a good way. You will find you are living in the peace of God—because you are practicing His principle of love.

Another aspect of victory over pride is that it will cause you to stop thinking other people are not as smart or as talented as you are. Perhaps you feel that a person is not able to do a job as well as you can do it so you take over the task, leaving that person feeling less important and incapable. Jesus knew His own abilities and powers, but He shed them all to die on the Cross for the sin of the world. After He took on human form, He still had to give up more. He willingly let go of all the joys living a long life afford: marriage, having children, and so on. In making the supreme sacrifice, Jesus gave up everything in heaven and all that He could have become in natural flesh on earth. Jesus demonstrated complete victory over pride, because He knew He was one with God, His Father.

No one looks forward to dying. So just imagine the emotions that Jesus was experiencing in the Garden of Gethsemane when He struggled with His imminent death—the most cruel form of execution known to man at that time—knowing how excruciating it would be to accomplish what He came to do. Beyond the unimaginable pain and suffering, His death was public. That is real victory over pride...*that is true love.*

When we try to mix humility and pride, it creates what we call an oxymoron, a combination of two things that don't mix or are incongruous. An example of this would be trying to mix oil and water. A person who displays true humility is modest, respectful of others, and does not draw attention to what he or she does. A prideful person has a haughty spirit. This type of individual wants recognition for everything, and often believes that he or she is better than most other people. It is impossible to have the mind of Christ and harbor a spirit of pride at the same time. Jesus lived and died with a spirit of humility. He is our ultimate example. So when we face trials and difficulties, we must remember Christ and choose humility rather than pride. In our walk with God it is of primary importance that we remember our need for *victory over pride.*

I want to emphasize here that gaining victory over pride is not something that we do when the situation arises. It is a decision that is made and empowered in prayer before God. Along with meditating on His Word, prayer is how the mind of Christ is imparted to us in our relationship with our loving Heavenly Father. Therefore, we must be determined through prayer to be people of integrity, humility, and love—otherwise when we go through trials, we will not have the *victory over pride* God desires.

Think about it. When Jesus looks at you, do you think He smiles and nods to the Father because He already knows you will obey Him in a given situation? In Galatians 2:20 Paul tells us:

> *I am crucified with Christ: nevertheless I live; yet not I, but Christ liveth in me: and the life which I now live in the flesh I live by the faith of the Son of God, who loved me, and gave himself for me.*

Are you living a lifestyle through which others can see the virtues of Christ and say that of you? Is Christ living in you? If you can answer a resounding "yes" then give God praise that you are letting the mind be in you which was also in Christ Jesus. You are beginning to do things the way He did. Whatever the enemy thought he had buried in your life has been supernaturally resurrected by God's power. The life our enemy was trying to destroy is taking on a new level in the anointing. When you achieve victory over pride, you go beyond the crucifixion to joyful celebration!

Exalt

This brings us to the exciting part, because Jesus was willing to stoop so low in going to the Cross that, as Philippians 2:9 tells us, "...God has highly exalted Him and has freely bestowed on Him the name that is above every name" (AMP).

God is looking for obedient children who are willing to stoop down, take up their cross, and follow Jesus. In return, they will experience the fourth letter in our acronym for *whatsoever is lovely*, "**E**," which stands for **Exalt**. Notice the Scripture says Jesus was "highly exalted" because He willingly humbled Himself. Now, think about pride and answer this question: *When God bestows His blessings upon your life, do you desire just a few blessings, or do you want to be richly, greatly, and highly blessed?*

When God exalted Jesus, He gave Him *a Name that is above every name*. That is why Jesus is the only Way you can be saved. "Whosoever" comes to God must come through the Name of Jesus. *There is no other name above His.* We cannot come into the presence of God except through Jesus. Every prayer must be prayed in His Name, because He was "highly exalted" by the Father. *The Name of Jesus is powerful*—it sends the demons of hell running in fear every time! You never have to fight your own battles again, because Jesus is as close as the mention of His Name.

I do not know about you, but that makes me want to praise and exalt our King. Many people think if they go to church, sing hymns, and give a little "tip" when the offering plate comes around that God is obligated to bless them. But hear me, unless you have called on the Name of His Son, Jesus, God will not be obligated to bless you or even acknowledge your presence. You have no authority or power until you humble yourself under His mighty hand, admit that you are a sinner, and call on Jesus to save you.

When you accept the salvation that only Jesus can offer, everything that comes against you to harm or offend you now has to come through Jesus before it can reach you. Isaiah 54:17 says, "No weapon that is formed against thee shall prosper; and every tongue that shall rise against thee in judgment thou shalt condemn. This is the heritage of the servants of the LORD, and their righteousness is of me, saith the LORD." The Bible tells us that we can know if we are in a place to be exalted as children of God.

The Spirit itself beareth witness with our spirit, that we are the children of God: And if children, then heirs; heirs of God, and joint-heirs with Christ; if so be that we suffer with him, that we may be also glorified together. For I reckon that the sufferings of this present time are not worthy to be compared with the glory which shall be revealed in us (Rom. 8:16–18).

We know that the Lord moves powerfully for us. We looked at the example of the Lord God fighting the battle for Jehoshaphat and Judah when in the midst of their praise He showed His strength. All that was left of the three armies coming against Judah were their dead bodies after the Lord set ambushments and the armies destroyed each other. We looked at the healing of the man lame from birth when Peter said to him, "...In the name of Jesus Christ of Nazareth rise up and walk." It is a fact that in life no one will be completely free from pain and suffering, but as believers in Christ we can rest in the fact that He has not only conquered death, but He gives us the power to withstand and overcome trials and troubles. If we are in Christ, the battle belongs to the Lord.

Philippians 4:19 tells us, "But my God shall supply all your need according to his riches in glory by Christ Jesus." When the enemy tries to use people to harm you, often God will use these same people to bring the blessing He has prepared for you. "Wait on the LORD, and keep his way, and he shall exalt thee to inherit the land: when the wicked are cut off, thou shalt see it" (Ps. 37:34). So do not curse your enemies; they could be carrying the key to your next level.

Never let the enemy block what the Lord has already blessed. Do not let the enemy hinder what the Lord has already healed. In other words, *when God wants to use you, be sure you are ready to be used.* He has created you for a distinct purpose and He will exalt you in due season, when it is time for your purpose to be fulfilled.

Lordship

Speaking of purpose, let's move on to Philippians 2:10, "That in (at) the name of Jesus every knee should (must) bow, in heaven and on earth and under the earth..." (AMP). After God exalts you, you should begin to walk in the authority He has given you. This speaks of **Lordship**, our fifth letter, "L," of the acronym. It is essential that you grasp this truth in your spirit: *Lordship is the key that God uses to test your capacity to serve Him.* It is in *this* practice, and in *this* posture and understanding that you will learn to recognize your capacity to walk in *lordship* on the earth. Because of the Name of Jesus, you can function in His *lordship* in the spiritual realm. That means when you are in Christ, submitted to Him in loving obedience, everything must bow to the authority that is in you.

If you are hearing, obeying, and declaring what Christ reveals to your spirit, everything that has been created by the Father—above the earth, on the earth, and under the earth—has been placed under His authority in your life (see Phil. 2:10). When you are operating in *lordship*, things that are devoid of spiritual life can be resurrected by your voice. This is when you can stand in prayer believing for something that has been long dead and gone and declare, "Come forth," just as Jesus did when He stood at the gravesite of Lazarus (see John 11:43).

True authority and greatness that reflects the magnitude and strength of God is always based on the eternal value of *lordship*. Lordship is a discipline you must learn to manage and master by growing into the full capacity of the assignment God has given you.

The Old Testament prophet, Ezekiel, spoke to the dry bones in obedience to the Lord and they came to life from the midst of the valley (read Ezek. 37:1–10). In kind, God has vested you with power to resurrect what the enemy has scattered. Under the direction of the Lord, you can speak to things that the enemy thinks have dried up and withered away, and life will spring forth once again. The Lord's desire is for you to have access to His all-encompassing authority, yet you must humbly submit to Him and allow Him to renew your mind daily with His virtues. Then when He speaks prophetically in your spirit to do something that is part of His purpose for you, humble obedience will unlock the flow of His lordship.

Y...Glory

Let's continue by reading Philippians 2:11, "And every tongue [frankly and openly] confess and acknowledge that Jesus Christ is Lord, to the glory of God the Father" (AMP). Our last letter in our acronym for *lovely* is "**Y**," which I have taken license to creatively relate to **Glor...y**, meaning *Give Him Glory*. When you *let this mind be in you* that was in Christ Jesus, making yourself *of no reputation*, gaining *victory over pride*, being *exalted* to your true purpose, and functioning in His *lordship*, your life should consistently bring increasingly greater glory to the Father. Bringing glory to the Father adds inestimable value to our lives. Remember, I began this chapter expressing that we give love and attention to the things we value. Since God loves you, values you, and showers His love and attention on you, He only asks that in return you give Him the *glory* for what He has done (and will continue to do) in your life.

For every believer, *thinking on* and enjoying what is lovely should mean that we can always see glory being given to our Father. If He is not being glorified in a situation, then true love has no part in it—because if our Father is not pleased with something we are allowing in our lives, then why do we love it? God cannot be pleased or excited about anything that does not give Him the glory He deserves. Why do believers spend so much time and effort burning with desire over things that will not bring glory to God? God does not *need* our love; He *desires* our love. With or without our love, God will still be God, the One who expects and deserves glory from everything we do.

If you love God, you will show forth the virtuous character that will bring Him glory. Let me be plain: You cannot say that you love God, lift your hands in worship and praise, and at the same time, *not* show forth the virtuous character that will bring Him glory. We have been created to exemplify the character of Christ because, as Christians, we have the mind of Christ[2] to bring God the glory He so richly deserves. We must make ourselves *of no reputation*; we need to gain *victory over pride,* and we must acknowledge that God alone exalts us and establishes us in walking in the authority He has given us—His lordship. He desires only for us to give Him all the glory that is due. In giving Him glory, we are acknowledging that He is the Source of love and all things good in our life, and He is the One who deserves the praise, not us. It helps us keep the mindset of humility.

If your desire is not to bring Him glory, then you will not accept His choices for you as being "lovely." They will become painful and hard to understand. Yes, salvation is complete and absolutely free, but there is much growth required after coming to Christ. Living a virtuous life according to Philippians 4:8–9 will cost you—it will cost you in time, energy, and growth of character as you learn to walk in the light God is giving you.

Giving Him glory is like a two-sided coin. You give Him the glory, and in turn, He gives you the love and attention you have always needed. You give Him the love and attention He so deserves, and He gives you the desires of your heart.

One of the *loveliest* things about being saved is waking up each morning and knowing that God has given you another opportunity to bring Him glory. This should be your reason for living—not obtaining houses, cars, jobs, money, or "stuff." God blesses you richly every day; His mercies are new every morning,[3] so why not *give Him the glory* that is due Him? Remember, He grants you "new mercies" every day because He is testing the value of your spirit: *Do you have the capacity to bring Him more glory?*

When you live daily giving Him glory, you will begin to experience His peace in new and greater ways. You will experience renewed strength and power as you, "Let this mind be in you, which was also in Christ Jesus."[4]

Think on things that are *lovely*. Do not live with a negative outlook, seeing the glass as being half empty rather than *half full*. Learn to see the beauty in the priceless virtues God has given you to enjoy.

CHAPTER 6

Whatsoever Is of *Good Report*: Points of Remembrance, a Pattern of Increase

It makes me want to praise the Lord when I consider how He has built the "protocol of prosperity" into the virtuous lifestyle. In doing so, He has made sure that we understand prosperity is not based on outward things. You might have money in the bank, but still be poor in spirit. You could be wealthy in material possessions, but not have a creative mind or a generous heart. And if you have an abundance of finances, yet have no idea how to take care of these monetary resources, you will be poor before long. However, when you begin to embrace whatsoever is true, honest, just, pure, and lovely, you will have the ability to create resources over and over again. Now, that is a good report! If you possess "right thinking" you will experience abundance in Christ, but again, if your thinking is not correct you could take *abundance* and turn it into *nothing*.

Take a look at your life and you will see either a pattern of *increase* or a pattern of *less than*. Remember the principle we can draw from Proverbs 23:7: "For as he thinketh in his heart, so is he...." When the Lord brought this verse to my attention He said to me, "In order for things to change, you have to check [be accountable for] what you are thinking about." Then He led me to the fourth chapter of the Book of Philippians. As we study what it is to "think on" *whatsoever is of good report*, we are going to discover ten ways to walk in "good report," just as we have already "checked ourselves" in what we are thinking on in order to live according to the first five virtues. This will enable us to focus on the area that immediately applies to begin prioritizing the areas we will give our attention to in our progress.

Too many of us live much like the cartoon character that walks around with the little, dark cloud raining on his head. God never intended for us to live our lives that way. Jesus died to make us free from the everyday cares of this world. Although we live in the world, the cares and anxieties of the world should not be living in us. Right before giving our list of virtues, to review, Paul tells us in Philippians 4:6–7:

> *Do not fret or have any anxiety about anything, but in every circumstance and in everything, by prayer and petition (definite requests), with thanksgiving, continue to make your wants known to God.*
>
> *And God's peace [shall be yours, that tranquil state of a soul assured of its salvation through Christ, and so fearing nothing from God and being content with its earthly lot of whatever sort that is, that peace] which transcends all understanding shall garrison and mount guard over your hearts and minds in Christ Jesus"* (AMP).

The first truth about *whatsoever is of good report* (as well as of the other five virtues) is that it stems from a prayerful heart to God. We are able to walk in virtue when we spend time in the presence of the Virtuous One. This raises our level of thinking to the degree that we begin to live in a consistent state of rejoicing in the things of the Lord. We wake up each day eternally grateful to God for who He is and what He has done on our behalf—and then we say it out loud. We declare a *good report* of what God has done. Thinking on things that are of good report also speaks of what we allow entrance into our spirit. Do you stay in the company of those who are scornful, or do you keep company with people that have a *good report* (praise) in their mouth? Psalm 1:1–3 says:

> *Blessed is the man that walketh not in the counsel of the ungodly, nor standeth in the way of sinners, nor sitteth in the seat of the scornful.*
>
> *But his delight is in the law of the LORD; and in his law doth he meditate day and night. And he shall be like a tree planted by the*

rivers of water, that bringeth forth his fruit in his season; his leaf
also shall not wither; and whatsoever he doeth shall prosper.

Do you see this? The believer who keeps his or her mind focused on *whatsoever is of good report* will prosper in "whatsoever he [or she] doeth"! When you live a virtue-directed life, like a tree planted by rivers of water, you will possess the ability to continually create the resources you need from the posture of abundant prosperity in God.

Trials and troubles will sometimes come, but you do not have to carry around a heavy bag of "garbage" (negative reports) that should be taken to the dump. First Peter 5:7 says you should be, "Casting all your care upon him; for he careth for you." God does not want you to live according to your emotions or to constantly be jumping from one emergency into the next. Our thinking should be fixed firmly on God; planted by the rivers of water. We can choose to live from the knowledge of God's Word, which is the ultimate Good Report, or we can live according to negative reports in a constant state of worry and concern. *Which lifestyle will you choose?*

The parameters of our thinking come primarily from our cultural background and our education. If we consider this according to the principle of "as he thinketh...so is he," a person who thinks from a poverty mentality by accepting the fact he or she was born into a poor environment will most likely always be poor. On the other hand, a person who understands the "protocol of prosperity" will not give up until he or she is consistently meeting his or her goals as part of prophetic purpose.

What makes the difference between the two perspectives? As we study the virtue of Good Report, we will see yet another level that God will move us to, taking us from an outward experience of taking on the care of the things happening around us to the experience of seeking Him intimately, discovering His will, and standing firmly on the good report of His Word. We move to this level of walking in God's will with the resources we need to fulfill what He has for us to do by spending time in His presence. The more we grow in knowing Him, the more we turn our thoughts to rejoicing in who He is and, with a grateful heart, give Him the glory He so richly deserves.

- **G** odly Worship, *leads to*
- **O** utward Celebration, *which helps you to*
- **O** vercome Confidence in the Flesh, *which empowers you to*
- **D** enounce Outward Distractions, *which gives you understanding of*
- **R** ighteousness of God by Faith, *that unlocks His*
- **E** ternal Faith, *which undergirds your*
- **P** rogressive Intimacy with God, *making you more*
- **O** ...Conformable to His Image, *bringing you into*
- **R** esurrection Living, *that is experienced only as you become a*
- **T** ruth Seeker, *one who continually lives to pursue truth, Jesus, and become more like Him.*

Godly Worship

Starting with the first letter of the acronym, "**G**," which stands for **Godly Worship**, let's look back at our text in Philippians 3. In verse 3 we read that Paul tells the church there:

> *For we [Christians] are the true circumcision, who worship God in spirit and by the Spirit of God and exult and glory and pride ourselves in Jesus Christ, and put no confidence or dependence [on what we are] in the flesh and on outward privileges and physical advantages and external appearances (AMP).*

Paul was saying (as discussed before): Our *godly worship* is not based on external things, such as music, preaching, or feelings. It can be experienced only from the realm of the Spirit. *Godly worship* becomes the framework from which we consistently receive divine information from God. This is why changing the way we think is vital.

If your mind isn't changed and renewed toward the things of God, it doesn't matter how much you are in church—attending every service won't bring you into closer relationship with God. The only thing that brings you into a closer, more intimate relationship with Him is your mindset and desire for God. It is possible to have "more of church" and "less of God," if your thinking is directed toward empty "religion" and not directed toward knowing Him. If you don't avoid religious thinking, you will develop a religious mindset basing your spiritual development and maturity more on outward appearance than on inner growth. As a result, you will never pursue the greater development of your inner being.

This mindset of desire for God is emphasized in Colossians 3:1–2: "If ye then be risen with Christ, seek those things which are above, where Christ sitteth on the right hand of God. Set your affection on things above, not on things on the earth."

Think about it. *Where have you set your affections? What do you think about most? Do these things fall into the category of being a good report?* When you receive the mind of Christ, your mind will be fixed on the things of God, and worship will not be something you do only at church. *Godly worship* will become your lifestyle.

Often we put worship in a box by thinking of it only in terms of hearing the church choir sing or joining in with the congregation during praise and worship. While these things are good, consider how limiting it is to worship God only in this way. So many believers are accustomed to coming to church once or twice a week, singing several songs and then sitting down, thinking they have participated in a worship service. That is not worship; it is singing about God. True *godly worship* is an attitude that approaches the God you adore in acknowledgement of who He is and of His worthiness to be who He has been from before the foundation of the world. This true godly worship can be done 24/7.

Let me clarify. God does not *need* your worship; He *desires* it. He would still be God without it. In our congregation we sometimes use the phrase, "God is God, all by Himself." In saying this, we are acknowledging that God already has created a heavenly host. We sometimes fail to remember there are angels around His throne day and night praising and worshipping Him. We read about this in Revelation 7:11–12:

> *And all the angels were standing round the throne and round the elders [of the heavenly Sanhedrin] and the four living creatures, and they fell prostrate before the throne and worshiped God.*
>
> *Amen! (So be it!) they cried. Blessing and glory and majesty and splendor and wisdom and thanks and honor and power and might [be ascribed] to our God to the ages and ages (forever and ever, throughout the eternities of the eternities)! Amen! (So be it!)" (AMP).*

This means no matter what time of day you are worshipping God, there are twenty-four elders and thousands upon thousands of angels worshipping along with you. What an awesome thought!

Then why does your worship matter? Why is it important to God? Allow me to give you a simple answer. *God is holy, and He is deserving of all our praise and worship.* We worship God because of who He is. And He longs to receive our worship because of His great love for us. Let these Scripture verses speak to your spirit: "But the hour cometh, and now is, when the true worshippers shall worship the Father in spirit and in truth: for the Father seeketh such to worship him" (John 4:23). "Exalt ye the LORD our God, and worship at his footstool; for he is holy" (Ps. 99:5).

Do you want to be a true worshipper? Do you want to lift true godly worship to His throne? Then do not let anyone tell you that your worship does not matter to God. It does. Your true godly worship matters to Him, whether it comes in the form of music, praise, meditation, or prayer. Your worship is based on and birthed out of your whole attitude towards God. That is why we have to rise above the poverty mentality that we must go to church to worship; because, if the truth is told, many people take part in worship at church only if it suits their attitude at the moment. Worship cannot be based on the state of your emotions. It must be based on a *good report*: the unchangeable understanding you gain from God's Word and from spending time in His presence, building your relationship with Him as the God who will forever be God in your life.

Godly worship connects you to the divine Power Source. Think of the generator backup power source most companies have for use in case the power goes out so that they do not lose their ability to continue working. The companies thought about the potential threat ahead of time and planned for such an event. Spiritually speaking, if your "power" goes out, you already have a backup resource, because the divine Power Source is on all the time. When you experience sickness or loss, you need to know how to restore the power to your life. That Source is already on, and you can find that power in godly worship. Timothy wrote, "For God hath not given us the spirit of fear; but of power, and of love, and of a sound mind" (2 Tim. 1:7).

In godly worship, you receive divine information that is always a *good report*. When you receive information from God that some people might see as being a bad report, you interpret it through the wisdom God gives you that hinges on seeing it from His perspective. Practically speaking, what constitutes a *good report* is being able to see certain things come out of a situation that are beneficial. What one person would see as bad when looking at a situation, another person looking at the same situation could see good things to come out of it.

One example in an extreme instance would be looking at the effects of the hurricane season in Florida in 2003. The destruction was overwhelming and tragic, and there have been more unimaginably devastating conditions from hurricanes since then. At the same time, because there was such devastation, there would be rebuilding efforts. To those so deeply affected, this example of a "good report" may have seemed of minor comfort during those times, but the outcome would have been even more tragic if viewed from a perspective of complete hopelessness.

When tragedy strikes and you stand the test by walking through and finishing victoriously, you are building your trust even more in God's past and your confidence in trusting your future, including finishing victoriously through any other trials, to Him. There are times when things in your life will be torn down or torn off. While walking through the experience, you can see a *good report*. In place of the old things, you know that God will be able to bring things that are new, more positive, and more appropriate for the season you are in.

The reason you cannot truly worship from a religious perspective is that true worship rises from your spirit to touch the heart of God in spirit and in truth. You must come to the place of understanding that when your attitude is not right before God—even if you look like you are worshipping in your actions, even if you are singing all the right words—if your heart is far from God, you are not worshipping Him. God can cause even the rocks to cry out in praise. Just as Moses was able to get water out of a rock,[1] God can receive praise from a rock if His people are not willing to praise Him. Listen to this, "And he answered and said unto them, I tell you that, if these should hold their peace, the stones would immediately cry out" (Luke 19:40).

Many people worship from the emotional realm. Our emotions tell us that God is worthy of our praise, but worship does not come from our emotions. Many people think that rejoicing because of something God has done on their behalf is worship, and of course it is good to give Him praise and honor for it, but as far as it being true worship, this is simply not so. That kind of rejoicing is based on how you feel toward God at the moment. *Worship rises from the depths of your spirit regardless of how you feel or what God has done.* If God is truly sitting on the throne of your heart, nothing should take the place of who He is right now in your life.

Remember that God is seeking those who will worship Him in spirit and in truth (John 4:23). Some people praise God with all their heart on Sunday, but it is all emotion. If you can praise God Sunday, but not on Thursday, there is something wrong with your praise and your worship, because it is coming from the wrong perspective. When the enemy sees this "on again, off again" pattern in how you worship God, he knows that he can hinder it even more by throwing a difficult situation into your life. He knows it is beyond what you can handle on your own, but that you will not pray about it and handle it spiritually the way you should, because you lack understanding about true *godly worship.*

I have found there are two levels of worship. *The first level is worshipping from your knowledge about worship.* We all possess knowledge *about* worship, but merely knowing about it does not engage our spirit. Therefore, if the enemy can keep you from knowing who you are in Christ, then you will base your worship on human knowledge or insight, which will put your perspective of worship in a box. This is level when you can become "religious" about worshipping God and remain in a state of turmoil about your problems. But when you know who God is, and who you are in Him, you will never fret about your future. When you have this revelation knowledge, Satan can never stop your worship and praise, because you are operating in spirit and in truth. Hosea 4:6 warns, "My people are destroyed for lack of knowledge...." Do not let human knowledge destroy your godly worship.

The second level is receiving divine wisdom through worship. Through knowledge you can understand the facts about worship, but wisdom takes it to another level. Wisdom adds insight to your foundational understanding. When you are living with mere human knowledge of worship, the way you handle yourself (and the things you do not know) can kill your future. Gaining wisdom in worship will teach you to seek after the things you do not know, so that you can change your actions. Obtaining a good report is based on the quality of your worship, so do not let your worship be bound by your inability to see what God has for you. The angels understand worship; in fact, all of heaven understands how vital worship is.

God has an "expected end" for you; His thoughts for you are *good* (see Jer. 29:11). If you believe this, your worship should spring out of a grateful heart, praising God for His great plans for you. Pause a moment and reference that if God has thought about you (which He has), if He foreknew what He was thinking (which He did), and if He called you according to His thoughts (which He did), surely you can take the time to worship Him for all that He has done. Because of Jesus' death on the Cross you now have the privilege of going before His presence in heaven. When you exercise that privilege, God is blessed by your love for Him. He sees the passionate intent of your spirit and begins, in turn, to bless your life exceeding abundantly more than you could ever ask or think (see Eph. 3:20). *Godly worship* is a never-ending circle of love between the Creator and His creation...*you.*

God knows exactly where you are in your walk with Him; He sees your heart in the worship you bring to Him. He sees your faith. He sees when you are lifting your hands in worship simply because of who He is. As your worship grows, your relationship with the Father will grow. You will begin to experience more and more of Him, see amazing answers to your prayers, and watch as things literally start taking shape around you.

Stop right where you are and begin to praise Him. He is worthy of your praise. As you worship and offer up your praises to God, His truth and love will begin to overflow in your heart and spirit. Everything that has been holding you back or keeping you bound will drop off in the presence of His glory.

Acts 16:25–26 describes this happening literally:

> *And at midnight Paul and Silas prayed, and sang praises unto God: and the prisoners heard them. And suddenly there was a great earthquake, so that the foundations of the prison were shaken: and immediately all the doors were opened, and every one's bands were loosed.*

You may never be involved in an earthquake, but your release from the bondage could be just as dramatic as that of Paul and Silas. You see, when you are a true worshipper, you cannot stay bound by the enemy. You must recognize that when people like Paul and Silas prayed, they had to pray from the purity of their worship; in other words, without evil intent, wrath, or doubting.[2] I can imagine what Paul and Silas were praying. Perhaps they were asking God to forgive them of any trespasses. Maybe they prayed that no evil would gain entrance into their spirit. I would not doubt they were praying that God would purify any bitterness or hatred they may have been feeling towards those who had beaten and thrown them into the dungeon. I am almost certain Paul and Silas prayed fervently that nothing would hinder their worship.

The Scripture passage tells us they were praying at midnight, which is the twenty-fourth hour. They probably had not just started praying at that time; they most likely had been praying all day. This reminds me of David's words in Psalm 30:5, "...weeping may endure for a night, but joy cometh in the morning." When you worship and go before the Lord in earnest prayer, you can expect "joy to come in the morning." You can expect a *good report!* The enemy may think he has you locked in a deep, dark place, but *worship is the key* that unlocks every door.

When "morning" came for Paul and Silas, it also came for everyone in that jail. This means your greatest ministry can be released through *godly worship* to people who are still bound by the chains that once held you. Even the enemy will be surprised at what happens when true worship is released. When Paul's jailer awakened to hear the sound of the door opening, he knew that only he had the key to the door. That man believed in the Lord and was saved, because God supernaturally performed a work the jailer thought only could be done in human power. This is how God can use you in the lives of others if you just continue in godly worship until *He* opens the door to their deliverance.

When you come into an understanding of godly worship, the *good report* you give will come to pass!

Outward Celebration

The second letter of our acronym that reveals *whatsoever is of good report* is "**O**," the result of godly worship—**Outward Celebration**. "For we [Christians] are the true circumcision, who worship God in spirit and by the Spirit of God and exult and glory and pride ourselves in Jesus Christ, and put no confidence or dependence [on what we are] in the flesh and on outward privileges and physical advantages and external appearances" (Phil. 3:3 AMP).

When we are weighed down with cares and our countenance is dim, it is difficult to give God true worship (although we may move into worship once we begin focusing on Him). As a result, it will be apparent to others that our worship is not bringing us to an *outward celebration*. The knowledge and wisdom we have received from God in our worship is able to sustain our outward celebrating as we rejoice in what God is bringing to pass. When your worship is real, it is contagious. It will cause others to join in as you rejoice, so that they can ultimately enter into true worship as well. It is a cycle. As you grow in godly worship, you will be able to rejoice continually, no matter what your circumstances may be, and all the more because you know that you are in the will of God. You know that you are walking in prophetic purpose. Godly worship brings you into continual celebration!

At the same time, there may be struggles going on in your daily life, but you can walk through them with an attitude of victory because you know that joy is coming in the morning. Outward celebration keeps you happy, because your spirit bears witness there is an "after this." God always has another level for you as you grow in His purpose. So do not let yourself be limited by what you may be "feeling" right now, because your feeling is a "fact"—it will last only for the moment. The *truth* is that when you understand God (and His dealings with you), it will be easier for you to see the blessings He has yet in store. As you walk in godly worship, you will experience continual outward celebration.

Through growing in your understanding of God, you can start living in a posture of blessing—not one of anxiety, turmoil, and fear. This births the knowledge within you that rejoicing is always toward a Benefactor. Remember Psalm 103:1–5: "Bless the LORD, O my soul: and all that is within me, *bless* his holy name. Bless the LORD, O my soul, and forget not all his benefits: Who forgiveth all thine iniquities; who healeth all thy diseases; Who redeemeth thy life from destruction; who crowneth thee with lovingkindness and tender mercies; Who satisfieth thy mouth with good *things; so that* thy youth is renewed like the eagle's." The greatest benefit of rejoicing is always keeping in mind the faithfulness of God—past, present, and future—because this will keep you grounded in "good report."

When you have come through a life-or-death battle into victory, you will say, "When I pass by this place again, I am going to give God praise. When I get over there, I am going to give Him thanks. And when I come to my destination, I am going to bless His name one more time."

Do not ever forget how God has blessed you. Set up a memorial in your mind, so the enemy will know that he has forever lost influence in that area of your life. He cannot enter an atmosphere of rejoicing. That is why Jacob rose up the morning after wrestling with an angel, put up an altar, and anointed it with oil (see Gen. 28:18). He wanted to remember the exact spot where he fought his battle and prevailed. If God will open the door to Jacob's destiny, He will certainly do the same for you.

Hear me. When you really start understanding who God is, His revelation knowledge will cause you to jump up in the morning and shout, rejoicing: "I thought I was destroyed, I thought I was depressed, but I am praising the Lord this morning, and He will cause this day to be blessed." Stay in an attitude of rejoicing! Set up points of remembrance when God gives you a victory, so that you will continuously bless Him.

There are so many things you can praise God for when you stop to think about it. Focus on the *good report*. There was a time I could afford to put only two dollars' worth of gas in my car. I could not afford a good meal, but I learned to thank God for what I had. Circumstances that appeared to be devastating were actually doors that opened to my destiny. I still keep an old pair of shoes with holes in the bottom simply to remind me that now God has blessed me with shoes that are shiny and new.

What things could you hold onto just to remind the enemy of how good God is to you? Your worship becomes authentic when you keep thanking God for where He has you now compared to where you came from, and when you do that, He will start showing you where He is taking you. Every time I think about where I was and where God has brought me, it gives me strength to press on a little further. *God is so good!* Keep thanking Him for the "good report" that is unfolding in your life. What the devil meant for evil, God has turned around and made it "work together" for your good! (See Gen. 50:20, John 10:10, Rom. 8:28.)

Overcome Confidence in the Flesh

Remember Philippians 3:3, "For we…put no confidence or dependence [on what we are] in the flesh and on outward privileges and physical advantages and external appearances" (AMP). You cannot continue to walk in "good report" if deep down you *think* the power of your flesh has brought *whatsoever is of good report* to pass. If you think you are bringing your destiny to pass, you are giving room for your "flesh" to argue God's sovereignty. This is why after you understand *outward celebration*, you must learn how to master the area that the next letter of our acronym, "**O**," stands for: **Overcome the Confidence of the Flesh.**

I think that I have already made the point well that you must declare to yourself *there is no good work in the flesh.* Therefore, you must start talking to yourself and say, *I will bring this flesh under subjection. I will submit it to God, and it will remain under His control.* When you put confidence in your own thoughts and give credit to what you are able to do on your own, you are adding to the power of your "flesh." Here is the key: The more you decrease confidence in your flesh, the more you will see increase in who you are becoming in God.

Denounce Outward Distractions

Paul ends Philippians 3:3 by emphasizing that we must denounce our "external appearances," which invariably will cause us to be distracted. You must come to the understanding that in order to have a *good report* you must do what the fourth letter in our acronym, "**D**," stands for and demands: **Denounce Outward Distractions.**

Distractions come when you believe that you have outward privileges and that it should be automatic that certain things are extended to you. Privileges that come from God are a measure of grace: *They are not automatic because your stature has increased.* In God's economy, they do not simply happen because of who you are or what your name happens to be. As a person who has increased in godly worship, you must never fail to recognize that certain privileges come by virtue of the favor and grace God has bestowed upon your life. As we remember the things God has done, we begin to trust that He is willing to support His prophetic purpose in our lives.

Once you begin to get distracted, the intensity of your spiritual worship will diminish. Therefore, you must denounce the things that distract you. If you are trying to work from outward privileges, denounce it. I do not consider myself to be a "privileged" person. I am blessed of God. I am not trying to be great or highly educated in my own right, because at one time in my life I thought my education could get me what I wanted. I trusted in my education rather than in God. Whatever you think is going to get you to the place you desire is what you are going to put your trust in. If I think my friends got me to where I am, then I trust my friends more than God. *Outward privileges become a distraction.*

Some people have physical advantages because they are beautiful or handsome, or tall and stately, but do not be fooled. These pleasant physical attractions are no substitute for God's grace and mercy in their lives. The reason that God's favor and grace overtake you is that God is working in you through His virtues to build His character in you. *Never depend on the flesh to take you to the goal.* Learn the difference. You can appreciate the things you have been given in the natural realm, but do not depend on them. Never make temporary, tangible things the source of your blessed life. Once those things change, then your life will no longer be beautiful, good, or happy. "The blessing of the LORD," however, "*maketh rich*, and he addeth no sorrow with it" (Prov. 10:22). The effects of His blessings remain forever.

Righteousness of God by Faith

Paul continues in Philippians 3:9:

> *And that I may [actually] be found and known as in Him, not having any [self-achieved] righteousness that can be called my own, based on my obedience to the Law's demands (ritualistic uprightness and supposed right standing with God thus acquired), but possessing that [genuine righteousness] which comes through faith in Christ (the Anointed One), the [truly] right standing with God, which comes from God by [saving] faith (AMP).*

I want to highlight this first letter of "report" in our acronym. The letter **"R"** opens us to the subject of **Righteousness of God by Faith**. Paul is saying that our right standing with God cannot be based on ritualistic laws that we can check off on a list and say to ourselves, *I was good today; therefore, I am righteous.* Laws vary by interpretation. It is easy to fall into self-righteousness when we have learned certain biblical principles. Yet above this, it is vital for you to intimately know the God who has given the principles. That requires faith in His righteousness, which births authentic righteousness in you.

In the first place, genuine, authentic righteousness comes only from God. As Philippians 3:8-9 (AMP) tells us, we are found in Him (Christ), not by having our own righteousness, "but that which is through the faith of Christ, the righteousness which is of God by faith."

A lot of "good" people with decent principles still do not acknowledge God's worthiness. They do not smoke, drink, or use foul language; they do not gamble or break the law. They live good, clean lives; however, that does not mean they know God. "Good" does not necessarily mean "godly." So although you may do "good" things, you could still fall completely short of achieving a right relationship with God.

In Philippians 3, Paul refers to this principle in his own life. He says (paraphrased), "I had everything that people perceive as being good: my education, affiliations, and all the distractions that come" (vv. 4-6). People may tell you that you are a good person because of the things you have accomplished, but none of those things will give you right standing with God.

Paul shared what righteousness by faith really is: knowing Christ. Not only did Paul count as dung all those things—his accomplishments of the past, all those things Paul formerly looked at as gain, the things others thought of as good in his life—as compared with the excellency of knowing Christ (vv. 7-14), giving up all for the sake of knowing Christ more deeply, but first, he knew those things could not make him righteous. They could not give him right standing with God.

You don't achieve right standing with God through your own righteousness—how good you are or by the good things you've done. No matter how "good" a person is, the only way that person can achieve right standing with

God is through believing in "the gospel of Christ" because "it is the power of God unto salvation to every one that believeth.... For therein is the righteousness of God revealed from faith to faith" (Rom. 1:16-17). Our right standing with God and righteous living stem from faith in God.

When God looks at authentic righteousness (which is evident in the godly worship of a *good report*), He asks, "Do you have the faith to focus on my assignment for you?" The "righteousness which is of God by faith" (as worded in Phil. 3:9 KJV) will cause you to focus on His assignment for you.

Eternal Faith

Because God is eternal, He gives you eternal faith. He knew before the foundation of the world that you would belong to Him, so He set up faith *in you* that would draw you to Him. The letter "E" speaks of eternity, which reveals **Eternal Faith**. Let's take this further. Jesus sent His Spirit (the Comforter) to help you understand all that Jesus gave His life for and to guide you on your path of acquiring a "saving knowledge" of Him.

It is the utmost expression of love that God would take such measures to give you the opportunity to be in relationship with Him and live it to the full. Therefore, your gratitude to God should be so great that to commit sin would be the last thing to cross your mind. I, like Paul, am a prisoner of Christ. I love God so much that I remind myself daily, "...in him we live, and move, and have our being..." (Acts 17:28). The faith of God is ruling in my heart; it is saving me eternally. I was in His plans before I was planted in my mother's womb.

Now, you must make a choice. If you want to advance in a virtuous life of purpose, you must believe that God is *who He says He is*, and that He has given you the "measure of grace" to be saved from your sin. Jesus said to Peter (my paraphrase): "Peter, I know you are going to deny Me, but I have already prayed that your faith will fail not." When I remember those words I know that my faith is not going to fail. It is eternal because I have God's faith. My faith is not based on what I do right now. The "saving faith" of God comes from eternity and strengthens us from the eternal realm.

There are people you gave up on a long time ago, who you thought would never be saved, but they will be. However, they are not going to be saved by *your* faith. We cannot take the glory. They would be in hell right now if it were up to you and *your* faith to save them. The same is true for your salvation experience. I thank God that my salvation did not depend on other people's faith. God gives us faith to believe and become a witness, and He gives us purpose in prayer to believe others will come to God. But if it depended on the faith of human beings, no one would be saved today. After a while, we give up. The flesh will always fail you. Only the faith of God endures forever.

Progressive Intimacy With God

Now let's go to Philippians 3:10:

> *[For my determined purpose is] that I may know Him [that I may progressively become more deeply and intimately acquainted with Him, perceiving and recognizing and understanding the wonders of His Person more strongly and more clearly], and that I may in that same way come to know the power outflowing from His resurrection [which it exerts over believers], and that I may so share His sufferings as to be continually transformed [in spirit into His likeness even] to His death, [in the hope]"* (AMP).

Paul is emphasizing the point of our next letter in the acronym, "**P**," which means we must have **Progressive Intimacy With God**. You cannot just say, "I love God because He is so good," and think that is going to cause you to continue growing in your relationship with Him. As we covered previously, your godly worship is not based on what God does, but who He is. There must be progressiveness in how you relate to God. You can almost hear Paul's heartfelt words about his "determined purpose" to know the Lord. Paul wanted to know on a progressively deeper level the Christ that was willing to die for him.

Many believers today are trying to know God, but without truly knowing His Son, Jesus Christ. In order for us to know God intimately, He sent His Son, not only as the Way to reach Him, but as an example. If we study the pattern by which Jesus lived His life, it will reveal many wonderful things that God deeply desires for us to understand.

Paul wanted to be able to intimately know the One who, without a struggle, publicly and openly, had died on a cross. In his timeless words recorded in Philippians 3:10, Paul was saying (paraphrased), "Wait a minute. I have to find out what kind of power Jesus possessed that, without uttering a word, He would allow people to torture and crucify Him because He knew that He was going to rise up in victory exactly as He had said." It takes a lot of power and revelation knowledge to walk a path where you do good and no evil, and in the end you are rejected. Jesus could have called thousands of angels to rescue Him, but He chose not to do so in order to fulfill His prophetic purpose.

Jesus was ministered to by angels after He declared, "It is written…" to every deceptive tactic of the enemy while being tested in the wilderness for forty days before starting His earthly ministry (Matt. 4:10-11). Jesus stood on that which is eternal (the Word of God), and the angels came from eternity to help Him, because His human flesh was limited. Remember this whenever you are limited in your physical body. Jealously guard the *eternal Word* in your life; God will faithfully release His angels to minister to you (see Heb. 1:13–14).

As you grow in *whatsoever is of good report*, there will come a time when you will have to go much deeper in prayer—like Jesus did in the Garden. As you approach a test you see will be trying (whatever that may be), God has already provided supernatural support for you in prayer, because people often misconceive what you are going through. As a godly worshipper, there will be points in your life where you will have to "die" to your flesh in order to reach your next level. Just remember, as you grow in the Lord—God has placed people around you who are going to mature, so that they can continue being around you as you fulfill His prophetic purpose. So in everything, keep your intimacy with God *progressive*.

O...Conformable

From the foundation of progressive intimacy, Paul speaks of our opportunity to become more **Conformable** into the image of Christ. This represents the next letter in our acronym, which I have creatively applied to the second (not first) letter of this powerful word, the letter "**O**." As you are progressively intimate with the Lord, you learn how to be conformed in your character. Let me break this down. You are transformed by the renewing of your mind. When you begin to be *conformed*, you are manifesting new patterns of behavior because of the revelation knowledge you have been given. When I am transformed by my thinking, then I am able to conform my actions to it. Transformation of thinking without conformity in actions is an oxymoron. It shuts down the prophetic process of God in your life.

If I were to get a speeding ticket, I would tell the officer that I would not speed anymore. If my mind is truly transformed by that experience, my actions will conform according to this transformation. Without conformity, there is no transformation. If I am truly transformed by the renewing of my mind, then I must become conformable, or God's Word is of no effect. Read what Paul says in Romans 12:1–2 (AMP):

> *I appeal to you therefore, brethren, and beg of you in view of [all] the mercies of God, to make a decisive dedication of your bodies [presenting all your members and faculties] as a living sacrifice, holy (devoted, consecrated) and well pleasing to God, which is your reasonable (rational, intelligent) service and spiritual worship.*
>
> *Do not be conformed to this world (this age), [fashioned after and adapted to its external, superficial customs], but be transformed (changed) by the [entire] renewal of your mind [by its new ideals and its new attitude], so that you may prove [for yourselves] what is the good and acceptable and perfect will of God, even the thing which is good and acceptable and perfect [in His sight for you].*

By "thinking on" the virtues in Philippians 4:8–9, your new, transformed mind will cause your body to progressively conform into Christ's image. Most people have a transformed mind while they are in church; but in their day-to-day lifestyle they do not consistently conform to the renewed thought patterns that are being formed. Carrying the label of Christian is a privilege, but if we are not conforming to the Word we are hurting more people than we are restoring. Unless we are conformable, transformation is incomplete.

In the process of conforming you will become a "new image" as you increasingly become more than a conqueror. That is why, when you share your testimony after years of being saved, people will say, "I cannot imagine you went through that...." Bear in mind, sometimes the behavior we must conquer may cause physical, as well as spiritual, discomfort. For example, during a season of my life I was so tired I was "popping vitamins" all the time. I was also drinking four caffeinated soft drinks a day, and I was slipping in other caffeine whenever possible. When people were around me, they might have thought I was really "in the Spirit" when actually I was experiencing the shakes from taking in too much caffeine.

Two things happened when I finally began to conform to what I knew was right before God. First, my body automatically adapted to becoming healthy. It began to say, "This is the way you are supposed to live." Automatically my 18-hour days did not seem to be so difficult. I took all the sugar out of my diet and eliminated almost all fats (except for the healthy Omega 3 variety). Now, I do not have to take so many vitamin supplements. When I go to sleep, my body does not have to come down from a sugar high compounded by an intense sucrose deficiency.

Second, my body automatically began a new cycle. It is like it says, "I can now be up. I can go to sleep and in four and a half hours, I am up." Trust me, once you start living from that realm you will not want to go back. When I get six hours sleep, I am Marathon Man the next day. I am ready to go. When my body conformed to the truth that had transformed my mind, I discovered that I had been cursing myself by doing the wrong things, instead of releasing myself to become all I could be in God.

I am going to emphasize this until Jesus comes back: If you want to be blessed, discipline yourself to get rid of all the stuff that is killing you.

Some people eat the right foods, but they leave the television on all the time. Hear me: Many of our dreams are television inspired because our mind never takes a break. However, your mind does need a break from that type of imagery. If your mind does not receive some silence from sound, it will never be able to have good dreams. Good dreams help you to maintain good report. They can bring closure to negative images in your mind so that new things can be released.

Resurrection Living

As we have studied the insight from the acronym for the word "report," we have looked at *righteousness of God by faith*, *eternal faith*, *progressive intimacy*, and the *opportunity to become conformable*. Now I want to touch on our next letter, "**R**," which stands for **Resurrection Living**. Spiritually speaking, when you start living through the power of Christ's resurrection, you will begin "walking through walls" instead of going through doors (see John 20:19). You will start living a completely different way from what you were accustomed to in the past. People who think they can shut doors on you will discover that you do not need that door anymore. Because of your progressive intimacy with God, He will equip you to create another way in.

Resurrected living allows you to say, "I am no longer obligated to go the way that is conformable to everybody else. I have been conformed to a 'new way' because I have been transformed by the renewing of my mind. Therefore, I no longer view limitations the way I did in the past; this situation is presenting an open door for me. Through Christ, I can create my own responses, both laterally and vertically. I can choose to go up and I can also decide to go down." In the book of Acts, Peter walked out of prison because of the *power of resurrection* (read Acts 12:1–17). Hear me when I tell you: When you have been crucified with Christ, and then come into the power of His resurrection, your life completely changes (see Gal. 2:20).

Wouldn't it be wonderful if by becoming conformable to His image, you were no longer controlled by the limitations of your body? In the spiritual sense, this is absolutely true. When you are conformable and walking in *resurrection life* you can start walking through the obstacles when other people have to find another way around. For you, earthly hindrances will become eternal opportunities.

Truth Seeker

Let's return to Paul's declaration in Philippians 3:10 (AMP):

> *[For my determined purpose is] that I may know Him [that I may progressively become more deeply and intimately acquainted with Him, perceiving and recognizing and understanding the wonders of His Person more strongly and more clearly], and that I may in that same way come to know the power outflowing from His resurrection [which it exerts over believers], and that I may so share His sufferings as to be continually transformed [in spirit into His likeness even] to His death, [in the hope].*

In making this profound statement, Paul is intimating that he wants to be a **Truth Seeker**, from the final letter in our acronym, "**T**," describing *whatsoever is of good report.* When you have been conformed and are *seeking the truth* of living in His likeness, even to the point of His death, you will not settle for mere talk; you will pursue truth at any cost.

If you are going to walk in *good report* you need to learn God's principles in order to apply His virtues in your life, because they are derived from eternal laws contained in His Word. So if you are not walking in them now, seek to grow into whatsoever is *true, honest, just, pure, lovely,* and *of good report.* Make it your prayer to operate consistently in these virtues— celebrate them. The enemy knows that if you are not a truth seeker (someone who operates in progressively new levels of resurrection), you are "fair game" for his attacks.

If you do not seize the opportunity to become *conformable,* or submit to developing *progressive intimacy* with God, or grasp the meaning of *eternal faith*; if you do not walk in the *righteousness of God by faith,* or *denounce distractions,* or have not *overcome putting confidence in the flesh;*

or if your *outward celebration* is dwindling, then you are not truly worshipping, with *godly worship*, that comes from "thinking on" things that are of **good report**—the final virtue listed in Philippians 4:8–9. Here is the key: *You will never have a good report if you do not follow a pattern toward truth*, the first virtue in our text from Philippians. Everything you do must strive toward truth (Jesus), because when you know the truth, you will be forever free (see John 8:36). So if you feel bound by your circumstances, you need to start seeking the truth.

This leads me to Paul's confession in Philippians 3:12, "Not that I have now attained [this ideal], or have already been made perfect, but I press on to lay hold of (grasp) and make my own, that for which Christ Jesus (the Messiah) has laid hold of me and made me His own" (AMP). Our assignment is to be certain that we continue pressing toward or pursuing Christ. Allow me to paraphrase from this verse: "I do not know it all...," Paul was saying, "and I had better not think that I know it all. Once I think I have obtained, I have stopped doing what I was supposed to do." Do you understand this? You can come to a point where you are walking in such spiritual victory that you lose sight of your prophetic purpose. That is why we can never stop pursuing Christ.

If you want to know God intimately you are going to learn that even after attaining resurrection living, you must continue to *seek truth*. Paul expresses it this way (again, in my words), "I do not want to live from the concept of time; I want to live from eternity. In this way, I can really celebrate time." If you live from a time perspective, you always have to wait until somebody confirms what time dictates has happened. *When you live from eternity, you get to celebrate the thing that has not yet been seen.* First Corinthians 2:9 says, "But as it is written, Eye hath not seen, nor ear heard, neither have entered into the heart of man, the things which God hath prepared for them that love him."

Paul could not say that if he had been operating according to the concept of time; he was able to communicate from that level because he was living from the posture of eternity. That is why Paul began to announce that we could live from a level where we can see things that have not been seen, hear things that have not yet been spoken, and celebrate things that have only entered into the hearts of men.

Can you imagine telling the enemy, "You do not know what you are talking about; God has already given me the *good report* for next month this time, and I already have the report for next year at this time. I have been worshipping my God; I live to celebrate Him. I have overcome confidence in the flesh. I denounce every distraction. I am walking righteously by the faith of God. I am celebrating His eternal faith, so I can see my future before it enters the realm of time. My intimacy with God is growing every day, and I am seizing every opportunity to become conformable to His correction in my life. I am thus living in a resurrected life. I will always be the truth seeker that He has called me to be." When you have that bold confession which comes from faithfully living out the virtues of God, how can the enemy even try to deceive you with a bad report?

CHAPTER 7

If There Is Any *Virtue*: Accepting the Truth God Brings You

Now that we have gained understanding about the six virtues listed in Philippians 4:8, let us move on to Paul's summary as he closes this verse, "...if there is any virtue and excellence, if there is anything worthy of praise, think on and weigh and take account of these things [fix your minds on them]" (AMP). The word *virtue* is typically used to describe something that is of the highest moral excellence. In fact, one definition I came across ties in nicely with what we just covered in the previous chapter, "conformity of one's life and conduct to moral and ethical principles; moral excellence ...."[1] Paul instructs us to "think on" these things, because as our minds are *transformed* our lives can be *conformed* into the image of Christ—our ultimate Example of virtue.

Let's explore virtue a little further. Proverbs 31 speaks of the *virtuous* woman, who was of high spiritual and moral caliber, handling every area of her life and household with excellence. She was effective in her marriage, with her children, in business, and also in taking care of the needy. She was a strong, capable woman who knew how to keep her "bubble in the middle" to get maximum results, and everything she touched was blessed.

Another good example of "virtue" is illustrated in Luke 6:19 when Jesus was walking through the crowded streets, "And the whole multitude sought to touch him: for there went *virtue* out of him, and healed them all" (*emphasis mine*). The meaning of this word is from the original Greek word "*dunamis*," and among the meanings of this word are "strength, ability, power, ...the power of performing miracles, moral power...the power and influence which belong to riches...."[2]

When you live a virtue-directed life God will empower you to prevail in spiritual warfare, overcome sickness, disease, and every manner of wickedness. The enemy's plan is to keep you held captive, helpless against all the fiery darts he sends your way. But when your virtuous thinking blocks his deceptive attacks, you will come all the way through to victory. *Virtue is God's pathway to the victorious place where He births your destiny.* And believe me, the enemy will see where you are on that pathway, not because of the church you attend or the things you own, but by the life you are living for God.

Those who are living a life of virtue understand victorious thinking, and this comes by living in obedience to the Holy Spirit. Victorious thinking must be planted deep in your heart. It is a supernatural process. You cannot merely *accept* God's virtues by walking through the church doors, because you will only leave them there as you leave. His process requires you to *receive* them in your mind to *change* your lifestyle...every day of the week. Think about it. You would not expect to walk into a grocery store, without purchasing groceries, and walk back outside to find the back seat of your car filled with food. Neither should you expect to go to church, and walk out with what you need, if you only have a "passing through" level of commitment to God. Just as you must purchase groceries to be able to take them home, you also must "pick up" God's virtues if you expect to "take them home" in your spirit. Let's look at the acronym for the word *virtue:*

- **V** ictorious Thinking, *develops*
- **I** nternal Intercession, *which thrusts you into*
- **R** elentless Pursuit of God, *because you*
- **T** rust in the Touch of God, *which equips you to*
- **U** nderstand Your Uniqueness, *in becoming an*
- **E** xample of Truth, *a son or daughter of God*

Victorious Thinking

Are you in a situation that you think will never end or change? Do you often feel like you are defeated before you ever get started, so you do not even bother trying? If you have not focused on virtuous thoughts (as Paul instructs), you will automatically exempt yourself from virtuous living—which will automatically exempt you from **Victorious Thinking**, the beginning of our acronym. If you are a son or daughter of God and your thoughts are not telling you that you are more than a conqueror (see Rom. 8:37), then something is wrong with your thinking.

In the eighth chapter of Luke there is a story of a woman that we know very little about, although Matthew, Mark, and Luke all mention her, so she evidently played an important role in the ministry of Christ. This woman's experience illustrates what happens when you press in to Jesus, against all odds, to get your deliverance. Talk about victorious thinking! Luke 8:40 says, "Now when Jesus came back [to Galilee], the crowd received and welcomed Him gladly, for they were all waiting and looking for Him" (AMP). This was a distinctive crowd. They had been waiting, probably for a long time, because Jesus had said He was going to return to their city.

Just prior to this, Jesus and His disciples had gone to the country of the Gadarenes, which was close to Galilee. There He had an encounter with a demon-possessed man who had been living in the tombs. Jesus healed him completely, casting the "legion" of devils into a herd of swine...and they promptly ran off a steep place over the lake, and drowned.

The man who had been possessed had been in such a deteriorated condition that he could not help himself. He needed Jesus to heal and deliver him. Here is another victorious thought. When you do not have the power within you to be delivered on your own, God will bring the *virtue*, or the dynamic power, to you so that you can receive it. For example, your thinking may have become so corrupt that you do not know how to help yourself. The man in the story did not know the truth, so God made him free because of what truth he was willing to receive. *Always remember:* When

God brings truth to you it is necessary for you to accept *and* receive it, or you will not be set free.

After that supernatural encounter, the herdsmen ran into the city and told everyone the news of the great miracle that had just taken place. The people ran to see the man who had been completely delivered, but they were so afraid they wanted Jesus to leave their country. Getting back into their boat Jesus and the disciples crossed the lake again, arriving to see the crowd that had gathered.

Now we are almost back to where we started at the beginning of this section about that special woman. As Jesus walked among the people, "...there came a man named Jairus, who had [for a long time] been a director of the synagogue; and falling at the feet of Jesus, he begged Him to come to his house, for he had an only daughter, about twelve years of age, and she was dying. As [Jesus] went, the people pressed together around Him [almost suffocating Him]" (Luke 8:41–42 AMP).

Jairus did not move until he got Jesus' attention. He fell down at Jesus' feet begging for the life of his daughter. I can imagine that Jairus kept reminding Jesus why he was there, even in the midst of a pressing crowd filled with other people pushing through to make requests. But Jairus chose not to leave until he got his answer. It was in the thick of this intense atmosphere that he caught Jesus' attention. This speaks to my heart that when you come to the Lord on behalf of someone else, He will give you the victory!

There is something dynamic that happens in a situation when, suddenly, while God is doing something for one person, others get upset that He is not doing what they desire. Now, hear me. Everyone was anxiously waiting that day; they were all excited at the prospect of what Jesus could do for them. When they did not get their miracle first, they began to throng around Him. I can almost hear their shouts, "Why are You doing *that*, Jesus? Why are You going *over there?* I was here first...." In the economy of God, it is never about who gets to a place first. God focuses His attention on those who understand that He moves according to His purpose. God moves according to the priorities of what He has intended for His people. I submit to you that victorious thinking stems from *heartfelt desire—the place where that which means most to God becomes your top priority.*

Now we are going to discover that special woman I mentioned earlier in Jesus' next divine encounter:

And a woman who had suffered from a flow of blood for twelve years and had spent all her living upon physicians, and could not be healed by anyone,

Came up behind Him and touched the fringe of His garment, and immediately her flow of blood ceased.

And Jesus said, Who is it who touched Me? When all were denying it, Peter and those who were with him said, Master, the multitudes surround You and press You on every side!

But Jesus said, Someone did touch Me; for I perceived that [healing] power has gone forth from Me.

And when the woman saw that she had not escaped notice, she came up trembling, and, falling down before Him, she declared in the presence of all the people for what reason she had touched Him and how she had been instantly cured.

And He said to her, Daughter, your faith (your confidence and trust in Me) has made you well! Go (enter) into peace (untroubled, undisturbed well-being) (Luke 8:43–48 AMP).

This story has great significance because over the course of twelve long years this woman had already exhausted every avenue of assistance. She had spent of all her finances, visited every doctor, and she had no hope that she would ever be healed. Not unlike Jairus, it had become evident to this woman that she had nowhere else to turn. Let me pause here. *When you have lost your job, your money is almost gone, or your health fails, it is easy to lose hope if you do not understand victorious thinking.* Most people rely on their bank account, family, or friends when they need solutions to their problems. What happens when the money is gone, or when your family and friends turn their backs on you?

When you can see no relief on the horizon, yet you are frantically searching for solutions to serious issues, you must have an anchor for your hope, or you will forever be in a hopeless state. This is what makes the woman with the issue of blood so special—she pressed in to Jesus beyond *lost hope*, because for twelve long years she had to live outside of the city, excluded from her family and friends, day in and day out painfully aware that no one and nothing could help her. She is a tremendous example of *victorious thinking*.

One of the unique things about your relationship with God is that *your thinking* in line with His thinking activates what you receive from God and what He already desires to give you. If you are a victorious thinker you will declare beyond any doubt, "God already has it prepared for me; therefore I will not focus on my circumstances or the fact that no one else will help me. God is my Source of help. He has already established it for me. He is ready to hear my cry and deliver me! Victory is mine! I simply have to believe that God means what He says and stand on His faithfulness until the answer comes."

If you still do not realize that God has made you victorious, then you are probably dealing with another serious issue. A primary reason many of us do not have victory in our life is for one simple reason: *disobedience*. Whenever you are disobedient, you cancel out victory. Whenever you choose to not act on what you already know (the truth God has already worked in your life) you have already lost the victory. In other words, God will not trust you with anything more until you start "living" what you are "thinking on." He knows what spiritual level you are on, and as a result, what you should be activating in your life from your belief in Him. When you walk in disobedience, you are defeating yourself. In essence, you are cursing your own life—just like I discovered that I was cursing my body by eating the wrong foods.

You cannot say things like, "All I have left is three dollars..." and expect God to bless you with more, because you have already cursed your source. Learn to declare in faith toward God, "At this moment I have exactly three dollars," and then thank God for blessing you with the rest of what you need. In 2 Kings 4:2 there was a woman who only had one pot of oil; and she would have stayed in debt because she did not recognize the pot was her blessing. The prophet Elisha was able to show her an important principle: *The things you possess, and what you speak about these things, determines what you will receive from God.* That is why it often takes someone saying to you, "You have been rich all this time; you just did not know that your blessing was already in the pot." Hearing this clears your focus. God is able to take whatever you have and multiply it until your "pot" is overflowing.

So many times we miss the value of what God has already put in our life, because we are seeking for something better. If you cannot enjoy what you have right now, how will you celebrate what God gives you in the future? If you are not willing to thank God for a skateboard that you ride for a few blocks to the bus stop, you will not thank Him for a car when He gives it to you. Your thankful attitude will last for about two days, and then you will forget God and His abundant blessings. If you cannot thank God for your one bedroom efficiency apartment with no furniture, you will not thank Him for a three-bedroom house when He gives it to you. *Victorious thinking* always *thanks God right now* for what He is doing in your life, in spite of how it may look to other people.

Always appreciate what God is doing in your life, even if it may seem to be insignificant to others. When you are obedient to God, you will eat the fat (good things) of the land (read Deut. 8:1–10, 28:1–14), though it may take a little more time for your blessings to manifest than you would like. God wants you to learn how to be obedient to His Word. So when you choose to not be victorious, you are choosing disobedience.

The woman with the issue of blood in Luke 8:43–48 exhibited a virtuous, victorious perspective. Even though she had to crawl through a crowd of people that disregarded her, she was intent to touch Jesus. And when she touched the hem of His garment, *virtue* flowed out of Him and blessed her life. In a crowd of people who for twelve long years had cut off all contact with this woman, Jesus turned and spoke directly to her, "...Daughter, your faith (your confidence and trust in Me) has made you well! Go (enter) into peace (untroubled, undisturbed well-being)" (v. 48 AMP). Believing beyond lost hope, this woman did not curse her source. She pressed beyond the feet of those who had scorned her for so many years and touched Jesus, believing Him to restore what she had lost.

It does not matter what the enemy has told you about God. If you want to experience God's manifest presence in your life, you must curse the works of the enemy. Declare to the devil that he has no more influence in your life, now or in the future. The enemy cannot control your decision to live in obedience to God. Do not let the enemy lie to you about God's victory in your life. Hold on to victorious thinking! Philippians 1:6 says, "Being confident of this very thing, that he which hath begun a good work in you will perform it until the day of Jesus Christ." If you maintain your faith in God, victorious living is yours for the asking. So do not complain when people misunderstand your posture in God and try to hinder what He is doing in your life...just celebrate that victorious living is yours.

Now, here is a warning. When you feel that God's work in your life is complete, that is when the enemy will try to destroy what God has begun. Though He has given you victories, do not make the mistake of thinking you have arrived. Remember, God performs the work in you and He is going to bring it to completion. He has placed angels around you to watch over you, and your ultimate victory is yet in store further down the road. Let Him lead you, from victory to victory. God will sacrifice whatever must come to an end in your life; He will release the works in you that He desires to reward, and He will bless whatever He has purposed. Do not try to resist the work that He is doing in you. Each situation will leave you better prepared for the work He has called you to do.

Think about that woman who was miraculously healed from the issue of blood. Where is that Presence that came from the throne room of God and healed what no man can heal? Why do the vast majority of believers today not experience that level of victory? Why do we lack the presence of God in our lives? Where is the manifestation of the virtue of Christ that rests *upon*, *in*, and *through* us, changing every curse into a blessing, according to the promises of God in His Word? We say that we love God, but we refuse to "think on" His virtues so that we will be *conformable* to His will and character.

Yes, virtue does come from His presence, but many believers are not seeking virtue—we are seeking the anointing. We have been fooled into thinking that God blesses us with His presence because we can experience His anointing in so many different ways. The greatest basketball player in the world is anointed to play basketball with skill and excellence; but that does not mean that he is "thinking on" the virtues of God or living a righteous life.

Let's pause to get a better understanding of the word *anointing*. The Greek word in the New Testament, *"aleipho,"* is a general term used for " 'an anointing' of any kind,"[3] as in applying oil to one's body after bathing. An Old Testament example of a similar usage is in Ruth 3:3, "Wash thyself therefore, and anoint thee, and put thy raiment upon thee...," especially in the Septuagint: "Now bathe and apply oil and put your clothing on your-self...."[4] "Anoint" and "anointing" are also used in a sacred sense when speaking of "anointing" priests, as in Exodus 40:15.[5] Another usage identifies a practice that is still being employed today, "anointing" a building or dwelling to be used in the ministry.[6]

I am using the word "anointing" in the sense that refers to the noun *"chrio"* (or *"chrioo"*), which relates to the sacred and symbolic anointing of Christ in His Messianic office, the "Anointed" of God (see Luke 4:18; Acts 4:27, 10:38).[7] This meaning of the word *anointing* also relates to believers being given gifts of the Holy Spirit. Second Corinthians 1:21 tells us that believers have been anointed by God; this "separates" us into a holy life of purpose.[8]

When God anoints you, He has bestowed upon you a supernatural gift to help you complete your assignment. He has invested a part of Himself into you, which will enable you to accomplish your prophetic purpose. As a victorious thinker you must know that you are anointed. Perhaps you have an anointing to function as a banker. Maybe you are an anointed designer, or a trusted counselor. The area of your passion, that heartfelt desire from God, is where He has blessed you to accomplish your destiny.

God anoints people so that they are equipped to help other people. Many times, believers understand the anointing only in the spiritual sense. The anointing is sacred, but again, it does not have to exist only in the church setting. God can allow anyone who operates within the principles He has already established in the universe to multiply in a specific arena. For example, Jesus told the story in Matthew 25 of a master who gave each of his three servants a certain amount of talents, expecting them to use them wisely.

Allow me to give you my take on this story. Each of the servants received an anointing to multiply by virtue of receiving the talents, but only two of them acted sensibly, while the other one cursed himself. The master had trusted them to bring a return on his investment because the anointing to multiply (from his capabilities) had been transferred to each servant. The master left on a long journey and, upon returning, expected his servants to have yielded a substantial return on his money.

One man did not follow his master's instructions. The servant who buried his talent ended up losing everything, because he did not want to operate in his anointing (see Matt. 25:14–30). Here is a simplified defini-tion of the anointing we can draw from this story and the meanings discussed above: It is a divine endowment from the Master to follow the Master's orders.

Some people think the anointing is operating when they see a whole lot of shaking, quaking, and falling on the floor. This is simply not the truth. Let me go one step further in making it practical. We already learned earlier in this section that the Father anointed Jesus to do what He had sent Him to earth to accomplish (see Isa. 61:1). In turn, Jesus said and did only what the Father had revealed for Him to do. So do not consider that the anointing is something you can only receive and function in at church just because you may sit in the pew and speak in tongues, for instance. From reading Acts 1:8 and Acts 2 in its entirety, we can see that the purpose of the speaking in tongues is to empower us to be a witness for Christ.

When you speak in tongues it gives you a Kingdom-encoded line of communication with heaven through the Holy Spirit. It also strengthens your inner man. It may happen that while you are speaking in tongues as you minister, other people may be able to hear you in their own language like it happened on the Day of Pentecost.

The anointing is with you as you go forth in your assignment. It gives you strategic favor as you go forth achieving the plans and purposes of God. You do not have to be anointed to attend church. It takes discipline to come before the presence of God. Discipline, available in us from the fruit of the Spirit "temperance"[9] (or "self-control" AMP), is birthed out of faith, not the anointing.

God does not anoint you so that you will seek Him. He wants you to seek Him because you *desire* Him—then He will anoint you to fulfill the purpose He has already laid out for you. Too often, we have it backwards. We want to be anointed, but we do not want to commit ourselves to be of any use in God's Kingdom. We do not want to discipline ourselves spiritually or otherwise; we just want to be "anointed." Hear me. In these last days, this "backwards" trend is changing.

God is working His *virtue* in us as we learn to "think on" His virtues: whatsoever is *true, honest, just, pure, lovely,* and of *good report*. In doing so, God is building victorious believers who are well established in *victorious thinking*—not based on the things we see—but on what He has already accomplished, as well as what He has promised that is yet to come.

Internal Intercession

You will never have *virtue* in your life until victorious thinking becomes **Internal Intercession**, which is taken from the second letter of our acronym, "**I**." Let me explain what I mean. You must learn to talk to yourself, and intercede for yourself, or you will never live a victorious life. The woman with the issue of blood knew that Jairus (the ruler of the synagogue) wore a garment that had been sanctified and consecrated, but he did not have *virtue*. He had not been able to help her twelve years before Jesus came, and he still did not have the virtue necessary to heal her.

I believe many people in the church die needlessly because the church has lost its virtue. This is the invariable result when God's people do not maintain victorious thinking; because without it we cannot believe within ourselves that we can have what God has revealed to us—individually or collectively. The woman with the issue of blood knew that Jairus was not able to help her, so when she heard that Jesus was in her city she got out of her bed and went to find Him.

This courageous woman demonstrated that when you start thinking victorious thoughts about who God is and what He is able to do, *anything can happen*. She had heard about Jesus and the miracles that He had performed...and deep in her spirit *she knew* it was her time to be healed. So she began to have *internal intercession*, speaking to herself that it was her time to be delivered, encouraging herself that she could get up and make the journey. *What do you do when everyone around you has problems, but you know it is your time to be delivered?* **Let your victorious thoughts birth internal intercession.** Start speaking to yourself in prayer, declaring that this is what you have been waiting for—*it is your time to be delivered.*

Though he was the ruler of the synagogue, Jairus did not have the virtue to heal the woman with the issue of blood; in fact, he did not even have enough virtue for his own daughter to be healed (remember Luke 8:41–42). Many churches today are full of preachers, pastors, bishops, prophets, ministers, and elders who do not have any virtue. For twelve long years Jairus did not have an anointing to speak healing into this suffering woman's life. Too often, it is the same in the church today. There is no healing within our walls because many of us are caught up in trying to become something we are not, instead of pursuing God and "thinking on" His virtues.

For twelve years this woman's condition had grown steadily worse, and there was no help in sight. So when she heard about Jesus' arrival she began to say within herself, *If I but touch the hem of His garment, I shall be made whole....*[10] She began to make intercession, declaring the faith that no one else could believe or speak on her behalf. Understand this: There are some people around you who could never encourage you in your problems because there is no *virtue* in them. For this reason, you must be careful when you are operating from heartfelt desire in your prophetic purpose that you do not let other people spoil what God is unfolding in your spirit. I am sure as she started on her way to see Jesus, people around her were saying, "Why do you think there is a chance you are going to get healed today? Why would this 'Jesus' even take the time to see you?"

Internal intercession operates according to a vital spiritual code. The virtue being birthed within you is of extremely high value; so you cannot allow anyone who does not comprehend the inestimable worth of this heavenly seed to take it away from you. The value of the virtue that you acknowledge internally is so important that you cannot trust it to a prayer warrior who says he or she might pray for you tomorrow. *You must begin your own intercession inwardly.* And this intercession will establish the thing God already desires to perform on your behalf. It will come to full fruition only because of your faith in God.

Relentless Pursuit of God

You will never have virtue until you have become *Relentless in Your Pursuit of God*, of the fulfilled virtue you are declaring to yourself in prayer. You must determine in your mind that you are going to pursue God *relentlessly* because of your need. If you are not declaring anything in the place of intercessory prayer, you will have nothing to pursue. If you remain quiet in your spirit, failing to declare the promised virtue to yourself, then it will be extremely difficult to get motivated to do whatever God requires to bring it to pass. When you understand there is an ability inside of you to make intercession on your own behalf, you will start pursuing what you desire from God.

Let me teach you a little secret. There are going to be times when God speaks to you, and you will not be able to tell anybody what He said; because if you do, it is going to come back in your spirit contaminated. You need to be silent while God is stirring something deep inside of you, until He brings it out in your life victoriously. When she heard about Jesus' impending arrival, I know that suffering woman said to herself, *I am going to intercede internally [silently] on my own behalf.* That is when she became *relentless in her pursuit.*

When you are awaiting a valued promise from God, you have to be willing to say, "I do not care how many people are crowding around Jesus; I am going to find a way to get into His presence. I do not care if I have to crawl on dirt. I do not care if I am stepped on, kicked, spit on, or pushed around by the crowd." God knows that you want to receive His blessings and deliverance, but there are times that He waits for you to realize that you are ready to pursue Him relentlessly, in order to obtain His desire. Do you have a relentless attitude in your spirit so that you will not let the dream inside of you die, no matter what other people say to you? Is His virtue so engrained in you, so that no one can take your dream away? Then you are set for victory because you have already made up your mind that if God said it, you will not give up pursuing it until you are victorious.

On another note, there are times our "issue" may persist even when we feel that we have been in relentless pursuit. This begs the question of what we consider to be relentless. For example, you cannot set aside two minutes every day for prayer and think that when you go to God He is obligated to answer all of your "micro-prayers" and take care of all of your needs. Luke 8:40 says, "...when Jesus was returned, the people gladly received him: for they were all waiting for him." Many people go to church "gladly" but leave unhappy, because they are trying to "fake" being excited about what God desires to do in their lives. Deep in their spirits they know that they are not pursuing God; they are merely waiting for a gift.

I can just imagine what many in the crowd that day were thinking as they pressed toward Jesus. Clamoring for His attention, some were saying, "Give me something so that I can go back and say I was with You." This is sad, but true. Even today, some go to church simply to go back to their friends and say, "Look what the Lord did for me...." This is not a bad statement; but it definitely is not good when *what He does for you* is more important than *who He is to you.* When you are pursuing His *virtue*, you will be willing to *become* in order to *create* what He has for you.

Remember this: God is not trying to succeed at being God—*He already is God*. He does not need your praise to be God. He desires a people who will pursue Him and say, "I have a need, and I am going to wait until my change comes, no matter how long it takes." How about you? Are you willing to be patient in your *relentless pursuit* of God, until change comes at His appointed time? The words of Job can be a great help to us as we pursue God: "But he knoweth the way that I take: when he hath tried me, I shall come forth as gold" (Job 23:10). God knows exactly where you are in your pursuit of Him…and when you finally "touch the hem of His garment" you will, like that brave woman (and like Job did at the end of his trial), come forth as pure gold.

Trust in the Touch of God

This brings us to the fourth letter of our acronym of *virtue*, "T": **Trust in the Touch of God.** You will never relentlessly pursue God until you know that you can *trust His touch.* If you do not believe that when you reach out to touch Him, that He has already prepared something for you, then you will never pursue what you cannot touch. *You will not reach out to Him until you believe that He has the power to help you.* So many times we gridlock ourselves into a mindset that does not allow us to see beyond our need to the One in whom our victory awaits. Why? We do not trust our ability to *touch Him.* We are waiting for Him to *touch us* at the place of our need.

The woman in Luke 4 was also unique because she was willing to sacrifice anything to *trust His touch.* Is it not amazing that with all the people pushing and shoving, trying to reach Jesus, that He felt *virtue* leave Him when this particular woman touched His garment? So many were trying to touch Him, pull on Him—but the Bible does not record that anyone else was healed at that moment. What was different about this woman? She was willing to trust that touching the Master would heal her.

Reflecting on the account from Luke 8:43–48, it is worth noticing that Peter and the disciples were amazed Jesus would ask, "Who touched Me?" The disciples knew His power and the virtue that flowed from Him; but they still did not understand how He knew that someone had touched Him. This is so much like we are today. We know that Jesus can heal and perform miracles, yet we are still surprised when it happens before our very eyes. How easily we forget that though Jesus may not heal everyone in the crowd, He has a covenant love toward His own. Jesus' focus was never about the multitude (though the multitudes were always following Him); His focus always remained on His Father's mission.

If you want to have heavenly *virtue* in your life, you need to guard *what is on your mind*. If your thinking is not victorious you will not live a virtuous life. If there is no internal intercession, and as a result, no relentless pursuit, you will never *trust the touch* of God. Simply feeling or sensing God's touch is not enough: you have to trust that when He touches you, your change will come.

Understand Your Uniqueness

This leads to our fifth letter in our "virtuous" acronym. The letter "U" reminds you that you must **Understand Your Uniqueness** to receive the touch of God. After the woman was healed she no doubt wondered why Jesus had allowed her to touch Him when so many others—who seemed to be so much stronger, capable, and deserving—were trying to do the same thing. She must have wondered what had made her so *unique*, that Jesus would not only feel, but also acknowledge, her touch. I have gained a bit of understanding. Too many people are trying to pull Jesus their way instead of allowing Him to be God, and entering into *His way*. You will never get the victory you desire until you are willing to go *His way* instead of your own. *God will always be God.* Therefore, you should desire to become like Him, instead of expecting Him to be like you.

Virtue is a gift that God deposits into a believer's spirit because He is willing to trust that individual's uniqueness. Sometimes the very things that make us unique are the "issues" in our lives that we thought we could not survive. It is when we have suffered terrible loss, such as a divorce or the death of a loved one that we grow into our *uniqueness*. God births character in our lives through the things we experience in faith toward Him. Every "issue" causes growth when we trust in His touch for our *unique* situation.

When that woman was willing to crawl on the ground through the feet of a thronging crowd, she proved her uniqueness.

Never let anyone keep you from remembering where God has brought you from. *Celebrate your uniqueness.* Lift your hands and thank Him that He has never left your side. Bless Him because He has walked with you all the way, from victory to victory!

Jesus turned and asked, "Who touched Me?" No one had to tell the Lord that a miracle had taken place...*He had already perceived it.* Then the woman came to Him saying she was the one who had trusted His touch. She knew that twelve years of suffering were over. Her faith made her *unique*, and because of her uniqueness she was made whole. Luke 8:48 records, "And He said to her, Daughter, your faith (your confidence and trust in Me) has made you well! Go (enter) into peace (untroubled, undisturbed well-being)" (Luke 8:48 AMP). When we relentlessly pursue the Lord and ultimately touch Him, we must trust not only in His touch, but also that He recognizes and releases the *uniqueness* of what God has invested in our spirit.

Example of Truth

In this final letter of our acronym, "**E**," we are going to explore the Father's ultimate goal and desire. The woman in our story received virtue from Jesus because, whether she realized it or not, her mind was aligned with the purposes of the Father. God desired for her to become an **Example of Truth**. Hear me. Jesus stopped what He was doing because He wanted this woman to be acknowledged as an example of truth. When He turned to her and said, "Daughter" (a covenant term), He was saying, "I am going to make you an example of truth, so that you not only have a relationship with Me, but more than that, you have a divine responsibility." Most people in church just want to build a relationship and be called "daughter" or "son," but they are not ready to assume the responsibility that goes with that spiritual title. When you receive a touch from the Lord, you have a responsibility to live in the truth that you have been given.

When Jesus called her "Daughter," He was speaking from the realm of the Kingdom. Jesus and the Father are One; so as Jesus spoke to this brave woman He was telling her, "You not only touched Me...when you touched Me you touched the Father." I have been waiting to call you "Daughter" because He has a place for you. The Father has a prophetic purpose for your life."

The Bible says after Jesus was baptized of John there a dove descended upon Him from heaven as a symbol of divine *virtue* being bestowed. The Father opened the windows of heaven and bestowed His own virtue on His Son, "... And lo a voice from heaven, saying, This is my beloved Son, in whom I am well pleased" (Matt. 3:17). The Father authored virtue, and Jesus received it. This gave Him the responsibility to guard that *virtue* and bestow it only upon unique individuals who would willingly become *examples of truth.*

It had taken this woman twelve grueling years to walk through her situation to victory. In biblical terms, twelve is the number of foundation and stability. After she had received her healing, Jesus immediately told her that she was now operating on a new level. "You are going to live undisturbed, untroubled, and in absolute well-being" (paraphrased). We may not know this woman's name (or if she had once had a title) until we get to heaven; but we do know that she was unique enough for Jesus to stop what He was doing to acknowledge that the Father had acted on her behalf. She left that place of destiny knowing that God had healed her, and that she had a testimony God could use to bring untroubled, undisturbed well-being to others.

Our sister's victorious thinking had brought her all the way from beyond hopelessness to internal intercession, and then into relentless pursuit to trust the touch of Jesus. And then He brought her into a new understanding of her uniqueness. Hear me. If you are not operating in the same manner today, then you need to ask God, "Lord, what must I do so that I can be uniquely touched in Your presence?" Because after you have relentlessly pursued Him, after you have trusted His touch, and after He causes you to understand your uniqueness—you will become an *example of truth.*

True restoration of your mind, spirit, and body will come when you become honest enough to say, "God, I have embarrassing issues that I cannot resolve on my own." Until you are willing to admit, "I did some things that were ungodly…God had to reprimand me, rebuke me, and chastise me…" then He will not move on your behalf. *You have to be honest enough to admit that you need His help, or God will not recognize your uniqueness.* When you come to Jesus, be honest with Him about your need. You can trust His healing touch.

The woman who was healed of the issue of blood had nothing else to lose but life itself. So I submit to you: When you come to that place you are finally willing to begin *thinking on* the virtues of God, letting Him deal with your "issues," you will see a mighty transformation in your life. What attracts you to God's presence? Do you feel that He is obligated to give you what you want? Then hear this. *Until you come to God with your "situation," you will never live a victorious life.* You must be willing to get on your hands and knees, press through the crowd, and reach out to touch the hem of His garment. It is only then you will hear Him say, "Your faith has made you whole." You must approach Him in truth to become an *example of truth.*

CHAPTER 8

If There Is Any *Praise*: Letting Your Joy Be the Source of Praise

One of the most famous and intriguing individuals in the Bible was David. As we read through the Psalms we can see that he definitely had an understanding of "thinking on" *whatsoever* was associated with *virtue* and *praise*. Even in David's worst times he still praised the Lord. In Psalm 34:1 he declared, "I will bless the LORD at all times: his praise shall continually be in my mouth." That is a bold declaration, because anything can take place in the process of *continually*.

For example, when David brought the Ark of the Covenant back to Israel, he danced and praised the Lord (2 Sam. 6:12–15). And when his firstborn son with Bathsheba died at birth, David still rose up and blessed God in heaven (2 Sam. 12:18–20). Oh, yes, we can learn a lesson or two about identifying "anything worthy of praise" from David.

We are going to deal with the word *praise* in this chapter, yet I do not want to stray far from *victorious thinking* and *virtue*, because both of these principles are far too important to simply do a quick study on them then move on. God wants to strengthen us and move us to our next level in His Kingdom, so to emphasize the importance of our main text, let's revisit verse 8 once more.

For the rest, brethren, whatever is true, whatever is worthy of reverence and is honorable and seemly [honest], whatever is just, whatever is pure, whatever is lovely and lovable, whatever is kind and winsome and gracious [of good report], if there is any virtue and

excellence, if there is anything worthy of praise, think on and weigh
and take account of these things [fix your minds on them] (v. 8 AMP,
emphasis mine).

Paul tells us that if we are going to have *virtue* and *praise* in our lives we must "think on" the things he listed in the first part of this verse. The logic behind Paul's words is that God gives us *virtues* (covered in detail previously) so that we can pass them on to other people. Think of it this way. When God gives you a gift, it will meet the requirements to achieve the purpose for which He has given it. *Virtue* qualifies as a gift worth giving. *Virtue*, as I said in the last chapter, combines both *moral excellence* and *power*. When we "think on" and operate in God's virtues, He is blessed by seeing His virtues being reflected in us. So if you do not value a gift of virtue when God gives it to you, then you will not realize its true value when you give it to others. That would be sad, indeed.

Praise is a gift that we give directly back to God. It must not be returned to Him as an empty shell or it will have no value to Him; as a result, it will have no value in our lives. Psalm 9:1 says, "I will praise thee, O Lord, with my whole heart; I will shew forth all thy marvelous works." When you come before God in *praise,* you must praise Him with your whole heart. That way, people around you will bear witness of the great works He has done both *in you* and *through you*, which will bring even more praise to His name.

When you are on an assignment for God He will use you as a vessel through which He can pour His blessings in order to pour them out to others. Therefore, you must become a vessel of honor, equipped by God Himself by "thinking on" and living out His virtues. Second Timothy 2:21 tells us, "So whoever cleanses himself [from what is ignoble and unclean, who separates himself from contact with contaminating and corrupting influences] will [then himself] be a vessel set apart and useful for honorable and noble purposes, consecrated and profitable to the Master, fit and ready for any good work."

God releases the power to perform mighty miracles, healings, and deliverance because of the anointing He bestows on the life of His servants—but even more important is the *virtue* that goes out from us. God freely gives us the virtue needed to serve, as well as the strength to complete our prophetic purpose. Because He does this on our behalf, He expects to receive back the praise that is rightfully due to Him. I can confidently say that much of our growth and development as Christians is largely due to our *praise*. However, although most believers know they are to praise God, they do not have a good understanding of *why* we should praise Him.

So let's get to the heart of the matter about *praise*, because it is vital that we understand its true meaning and significance. In doing so, we are going to go beyond what we have been taught and look to the heart of God to see what He requires. Our relationship with Him will grow stronger and more intimate when we know how to *praise* Him. With this in mind, let's go to our acronym:

- **P** rogressive Maturity, *leads to*

- **R** enewed Celebration, *where you come into*

- **A** ggressive Agreement, *the posture through which you receive*

- **I** ntuitive Inspiration, *that internal switch that equips you for*

- **S** ubmission to the Success of God, *which demonstrates that you are*

- **E** ternally Satisfied, *matured, blessed, and thankful in all things*

Progressive Maturity

The first reason we are to *praise* God is for our constant **Progressive Maturity**. If you are not *progressing in maturity,* then your praise will be rendered absolutely null and void. You cannot give God praise until you are maturing in your love for Him. Oh, you can convince yourself (and others) when you believe that you have matured, but unless your *praise* is coming from a heart that is filled with love for Him, your praise is empty. *Maturity is revealed in true praise.* If you praise God only out of emotion, you are not praising from a mature heart. When someone has to "stir up" your emotions before you think about the goodness of the Lord, then you cannot truly say that you are mature. When you are mature you will keep the foundation of your relationship with God in all purity, because you honor and respect who God is in your life.

Mature people respect their parents even when they do not agree with them. Reflecting maturity is not based on always being in total agreement; it is based on the respect and honor we gain through experience. Whenever we think we can put God on the back burner, praising Him only when we feel like it, we are spiritually immature. It is very dishonoring of who God is to dismiss Him as being a secondary part of our life. We must recognize that we are nothing without Him. We must come to the understanding that we are only a breath from eternity...and God controls that breath. I do not know about you, but I have determined to respect His role in my life. It is easy for me to lift my voice in praise to Him, especially when I realize the enormity of His love for me.

This leads to my next point. We must not allow ourselves to be yoked with people who are not progressive. Stagnant people will stop your praise. Let me clarify. Progressiveness is not something that you measure by the things that you possess, such as cars, houses, or college degrees. When I say "progressiveness" I am speaking of you beginning to recognize that your silence allows you to reflect on the level of your praise unto God. It is when you become silent that all distractions fade, and in this reflective state, your heart quietly begins to acknowledge and give praises to God.

Psalm 65:1 says, "To You belongs silence (the submissive wonder of reverence which bursts forth into praise) and praise is due and fitting to You, O God, in Zion; and to You shall the vow be performed" (AMP). Notice that David declares praise to God is "due and fitting." Most of us do not realize that God measures our "praise thermometer." God does not bless something that is dead. If your *praise* is not alive and vibrant you will not receive the blessings that you are hoping to receive from God.

Let's take this a step further. We read in 2 Chronicles 20:18–19, "And Jehoshaphat bowed his head with his face to the ground: and all Judah and the inhabitants of Jerusalem fell before the Lord, worshipping the Lord. And the Levites, of the children of the Kohathites, and of the children of the Korhites, stood up to praise the Lord God of Israel with a loud voice on high."

Notice the process. When Jehoshaphat bowed before the Lord in worship, it encouraged the rest of the people to stand and praise God with a "loud voice." Now, I realize some people do not enjoy loud noises, so they do not understand the concept of a "loud praise." With respect to all forms of praise and worship in the body of Christ, I submit that as believers we must be careful not to get caught up in the kind of praise that comes from those who do not have a relationship with God. When I say "loud praise," I mean the kind of praise that comes from a loving, intimate relationship with Him.

I worship God because He is eternal, and also because He is worthy. I worship Him because of His righteousness, and also because I understand His great love for us. So when I bow my heart in worship and lift my voice in praise unto God, it is coming from my uniqueness in Him. Hear me. No one can praise God exactly like you can—because your praise should be based on your personal, daily experience with Him. Perhaps God did something wonderful for you today, or perhaps you simply realize that His mercies are brand new in your life every morning. How precious are the words of the prophet Jeremiah in Lamentations 3:22–23, which says: "It is of the Lord's mercies that we are not consumed, because his compassions fail not. They are new every morning: great is thy faithfulness."

God does not want you trying to bring yesterday's mercies into today, or trying to store up all of them to carry into tomorrow. If you do not bring full closure to yesterday, you will never get the full benefit of "today." By constantly looking back, you are canceling out His fresh mercies for right now. So here is what you need to do. *Practice thanking Him for your yesterdays, enjoy each new day, and trust Him for your new tomorrows.* If you are not so sure about doing this, just read the beginning of the Book of Genesis. At the close of each day of creation, *God saw that it was good*, and He moved on to a new day and a new focus.

Just like God did in creating the heavens and the earth, you lay the foundation for each new day by what you speak. So when you praise God today you release Him to bless you with "new mercies" tomorrow. We often speak of "the good old days," but we fail to realize that today *will be* our "good old day" when tomorrow comes. *Here is a real mark of maturity: It accepts yesterday, and today, while moving on to tomorrow.*

Now, let's move on. David said in Psalm 119:67–68, "Before I was afflicted I went astray, but now Your word do I keep [hearing, receiving, loving, and obeying it]. You are good and kind and do good; teach me Your statutes" (AMP). Another sign of true *praise* is revealed when you are thankful to God for the "beatings" you have taken. When you are able to thank Him for the times He has chastised you, acknowledging that it was through His correction you became strong, you have come into true *praise*. Just think about it. *It took a great and powerful God to love you through the process of coming to maturity.*

When your maturity becomes progressive it will bring you to a place where you freely give your praises to God *because of your experiences.* On the other hand, when you rely on people to give you the character that only God can build in you through His virtues, then you are immature indeed. Your trust in God must be steadfast, unending, and immovable, because when you do not trust Him you will not *praise* Him. And if you do not praise Him, you will not grow. Do not wait for others to acknowledge your maturity; because in doing so, you are demonstrating to all that you are not mature. Realize this: God sees you as you really are, and also as you will someday be—so your praise to Him should be magnified because He trusts the process of maturity in you. Maturity grows in your spirit because you desire to please God and never fail to praise Him. So as you grow remember David's words in Psalm 42:1, "As the hart panteth after the water brooks, so panteth my soul after thee, O God."

On another note, God is pleased when we come together as believers to *praise* and worship Him in love and unity. The writer of Hebrews reminds us how important this is: "Not forsaking the assembling of ourselves together, as the manner of some is; but exhorting one another: and so much the more, as ye see the day approaching" (Heb. 10:25). It is absolutely true that we gain strength for daily living when we gather regularly with other believers. Our prayer life will be better in our quiet place, and our praise will be even sweeter one-to-one with God, when we are faithful to meet and *praise* God with others.

The bottom line is this: *When you are progressive in maturity you will start operating in a position of understanding concerning the God you serve.* If you become stagnant in your praise, it means that you have become stagnant in your maturity. Whether you realize it or not, something or someone has stopped you from growing in God. Whenever spiritual growth stops or life in *praise* dissipates, progressive maturity ends. Your level of praise will always reflect your relationship and intimacy with God, so stay progressive in relating to Him...and your praise will bring you to maturity.

Renewed Celebration

The next step of praise is always **Renewed Celebration**. Let's go back to Psalm 65:1: "To You belongs silence (the submissive wonder of reverence which bursts forth into praise) and praise is due and fitting to You, O God, in Zion; and to You shall the vow be performed" (AMP).

Once you make a vow to *praise* God you must renew it yourself. God is not going to constantly remind you of it, and He is not going to renew it for you. You have to *renew your own celebration.* That is why Paul says in Philippians 4:4, "Rejoice in the Lord always [delight, gladden yourselves in Him]; again I say, Rejoice!" (AMP). He is telling us in this verse that we should not forget to *praise* our God and live in a constant state of joy. As I said before, all too often we pray to and praise God because we want something from Him; but Paul is telling us to *rejoice* (we covered this a bit previously). It is essential that we remember the joy that God has brought into our life, and praise Him for it. *Let your joy be the source of your praise to the Lord.*

Now, let's take a look at the subject of our vows to God. Vows are not something that we normally celebrate because, once made, they are usually followed by completing a task that we have promised the Lord we will do. There are two types of vows in Scripture: conditional and unconditional. A *conditional* vow is based upon conditions that had to come to pass in order to make the vow valid (Gen. 28:20–22). An *unconditional* vow is performed whether or not an individual receives anything in return (Num. 30:2). Psalm 65:1 speaks of a vow that is *unconditionally* fulfilled in devotion to the Lord.[1] Many today do not understand the power of a vow. When God vows something, He swears by Himself that He will fulfill it. He will not let any human being, angel, or demon change what He has vowed to perform.

In this same vein, it is imperative that you do not let anyone take control of your commitment to God, because people can move you away from the vow that would ultimately bring victory to your life. Others do not understand that God is accomplishing deep things inside you from His desire for your life, all because of your vow. Do not miss out on the final victory that will invariably come from a vow fulfilled. Not only this, your vow has a hidden benefit. It will motivate you to seek a level in God that most people would never strive to reach.

When you accepted Jesus as your Savior you actually made a vow to God. You freely turned your life over to Him. You probably told Him that you were willing to do everything He wanted you to do, and to be whatever He wanted you to be, for the rest of your life. Think about it. Those types of statements, in essence, are vows. God heard it, and He expects you to honor these vows of devotion. Salvation is often thought of as a one-time commitment, but as you can see, it is just the beginning of your journey with God.

The enemy of your soul was not happy about the vow you made to God. Yes, I know you went to the Lord "in secret," but the enemy was aware of the commitment you made to God. This is why the Psalmist said, "For in the time of trouble he shall hide me in his pavilion: in the secret of his tabernacle shall he hide me; he shall set me up upon a rock" (Ps. 27:5). *God will do things in your life that no one, not even the enemy, can see or hear.* Remember 1 Corinthians 2:9, "But as it is written, Eye hath not seen, nor ear heard, neither have entered into the heart of man, the things which God hath prepared for them that love him."

Right now, there are things that God is preparing in you because of your vow to Him that no one else can see or hear. No one can steal what God is secretly doing in you. There is a level of growth in you at times that people do not understand, all the while God is unveiling His secret work in your "secret place" with Him. It is risky to interfere in the life of someone who is meeting with God in his or her secret place. What goes on in that person's secret place is none of your business...it is between that individual and God. This is why we will never fully understand another person's needs, or love and *praise* to God. Each individual's relationship with God is precious.

You may be wondering, *How can it be a secret when that person is speaking to God out loud in my presence?* You may hear that individual praising God or shouting "hallelujah," but in that person's "secret place" it could be a plea for something highly personal. It could also be *praise* for God having wrought a mighty work in this person's heart or life. Remember, we do not have to tell God everything we are holding in our hearts...*He already knows.*

God enjoys our praise because we are His own. Think about *praise* as a "wrapped gift." Usually, we put a bow and card on our gifts to tell the recipient who sent the gift. But have you ever received a gift that had been wrapped so beautifully that you knew exactly where it came from? Details tell it all. You could look at the design of the paper and the color of the ribbon, but you can especially tell who sent it by the care that was put into wrapping the gift. God sees your praise in the same way. Before you even start praising He knows that it is you. He knows how much you long for Him, and He knows your need before you ever call on Him. David described it, as I mentioned before, as a deer that "...panteth after the water brooks..." (Ps. 42:1). God hears the "panting" of your heart when you come to Him with *renewed celebration*.

Jesus made a vow to all of humanity when He went to the Cross; and He will keep His vow. So when you make a vow to Him, He expects no less from you. The Lord "takes it personally" when you tell Him you will "never do it again," or "I promise I will tithe, Lord, if You will just get me out of this problem." When you make such a vow to God do not take it lightly— God takes your vow seriously.

Renewing the celebration of your relationship with God means that you must stay committed, focused, disciplined, and grow in your celebration of praise. There is no place in your *renewed* life for laziness, procrastination, or depression. (Many instances of depression stem from people trying to live a lie instead of embracing the truth of who God created them to be.) When you are partially committed to living at one level, yet are living in a "lower" place spiritually, you will not be able to *renew your celebration* to God...you will be depressed.

Renewed celebration involves "thinking on" the virtues of God, which keeps our attitude and actions right before Him. So renew your vow of praise to the Lord. You will continually be enriched in His presence.

Aggressive Agreement

A renewed celebration of praise leads you into **Aggressive Agreement**. Let's continue reading Psalm 65 in verses two and three, "O You Who hear prayer, to You shall all flesh come. Iniquities and much varied guilt prevail against me; [yet] as for our transgressions, You forgive and purge them away [make atonement for them and cover them out of Your sight]!" (AMP).

When you begin to admit your real issues, you are going to enter into more *aggressive agreement* with God. Many believers stop agreeing with God at a certain place in their growth, so they stop growing in their *praise*. Your maturity level should bring you into renewed celebration. During that renewal God is going to cause you to look more intensely at the truth of your walk with Him, and that is when you will begin to learn about *aggressive agreement*. For example, one of the first areas you will need to face truth is in the time you spend with God in prayer. In the Psalm above David declares that "all flesh" will come to God because He hears prayer. This really made me think: because God is the only wise and true God, even people in false religions pray to Him (from their own understanding). After all, He is the God of prayer and so He is able to hear all prayers—whether they come from a Muslim, a Buddhist, or a Hindu. The question is, "Does He answer all prayers?"

I believe God joyfully answers the prayers of His covenant children, those who love Jesus Christ with all of their heart and have given their lives to Him. I also believe that He can choose to extend mercy to whom He desires (see Ex. 33:19). No, I do not believe God will ignore a believer's prayer based on whether or not he or she speaks in tongues. Again, answered prayer is not based on tongues; it is based on a living relationship with God through Jesus Christ and the ministry of the Holy Spirit. Now, do not get me wrong. I firmly believe that speaking in tongues brings a deeper level of intercession in an individual's prayer life, but God answers prayer whether or not we are Spirit-filled.

In its truest sense, I believe the word *prayer* refers to relationship to a God whom we believe lovingly directs and controls our life. When an unsaved person prays in his or her natural language, God hears the prayer because He has the ability to hear and understand the relationship that individual desires to find with Him. However, when you pray in tongues as a believer your spirit makes intercession in the spiritual dimension. Yes, there are different realms in prayer. Praying audibly is a different manifestation of prayer than intercession that flows in your heavenly language by the Holy Spirit.

My point is, regardless of how bad you may think another person is, God hears all prayer. There are numerous cases recorded of someone who was an atheist lying on a deathbed, crying out to God for salvation. Do you think God did not hear that prayer from a lost person wanting to meet Him? Many testify of crying out to God, "Oh, Lord, if You are really there just show me the truth... I want to know You." *If an atheist can pray in this manner and touch God, then how much more will God respond to you as one of His children?* So as God brings you into *aggressive agreement*, your prayer life will definitely be examined—because as a covenant son or daughter, God will respond to you joyfully.

Prayer brings you into *aggressive agreement*. So if you do not have a prayer life, you can forget about being in agreement with God, because all you are going to do is sit there and argue with Him. Either you are in agreement with God, or you are in disagreement with Him. Let's say that you think simply going to church feeds your relationship with God. On a certain level, yes, but going to church alone will not develop your intimacy with God. For example, you may have been taught that if a person does not go to church he or she cannot have a prayer life. *The fact is: some people have a strong prayer life, even though they do not attend church, because illnesses keep them homebound.*

Oftentimes these individuals live in solitude, so they are silent before Him. They have hours and hours to establish an intimate relationship with God that is based on constant, close communication. Many who are in good health and are able to attend church regularly do not have this level of relationship with the Lord.

Since we must acknowledge that church attendance is not the criteria for determining if we are in *aggressive agreement* with God, then we must closely examine our hearts. If His virtues are not transforming our life, then we will have impure motives. Hear me. An impure heart will not only hinder your ability to have a strong prayer life, but it will send you into a cycle of guilt that could prevent you from seeking God's face altogether.

However, God is a just and loving Father. When you go to Him and ask His forgiveness you re-establish the connection that was lost through sin in your life. God will joyfully forgive you. He will not only wipe away all your iniquities, but He will also wipe away your tears. God never ignores a repentant heart. He also is attentive to the prayers of the righteous, those in whom He is perfecting His virtues. As He works in us, we simply need to *agree*. Psalm 24:5 says, "He that hath clean hands, and a pure heart; who hath not lifted up his soul unto vanity, nor sworn deceitfully, He shall receive the blessing from the Lord, and righteousness from the God of his salvation." Oh, yes, rich blessings will come when you are in *aggressive agreement* with God.

Intuitive Inspiration

Let's continue from the previous section with Psalm 65:4, "Blessed (happy, fortunate, to be envied) is the man whom You choose and cause to come near, that he may dwell in Your courts! We shall be satisfied with the goodness of Your house, Your holy temple" (AMP). This introduces the next point from the third letter in our acronym. If you do not have **Intuitive Inspiration** your *praise* will go flat, because your agreement with God will only be temporary.

Many people agree with God only because they feel like doing so at the moment, in order to get an answer from Him. *Yet, there are others who do not need a word from God before they begin to praise Him.* These believers truly possess *intuitive inspiration*. Let me clarify. The factor that separates people who *praise* from people who do not praise is *intuitive inspiration*. Intuitive "praisers" do not need a praise and worship team to "get them started"—their outward celebration comes from deep within their heart (remember the previous discussion?). People who have *intuitive inspiration* value their relationship with God so much that they live in a continual state of heartfelt praise.

I often say that my intuitiveness is based on the fact that God has put a little switch inside me that He alone controls, *and no one else can turn it off*. Intuitively, I have the inspiration to praise God, because I am not trying to seek the Kingdom; I know God's Kingdom is inside of me. Because it is within me, and I possess a Kingdom mindset, I do not need to ask you what you think God's purpose is or will be for my life. The same is true for you. When you are operating from the vantage point of God's Kingdom within you, nothing can prevent His assignment from coming to pass in your life, because the Kingdom within will always reward you for the *intuitiveness* of how you continually seek the King.

Intuitive inspiration is not stimulated externally; it is deep inside your spirit. You cannot receive this divine endowment because someone sends it to you, or you receive a check in the mail. Think about it and examine yourself: *Have you tapped into the real resource of praise?* When you develop a mature life of praise you will understand that the Kingdom of God lives inside of you. The Bible says in Matthew 6:33, "But seek ye first the kingdom of God, and his righteousness; and all these things shall be added unto you."

Many people seek after the Kingdom as if it is something far removed from them. If this is your understanding, then you should ask God to allow you to know His presence in a more intimate manner. The righteousness of God will work in your heart to direct you to His will for your life. Perhaps you will awake at 2:00 a.m., hearing the voice of God speaking inside of you. The television is turned off and the phone did not ring so you know it is not a voice from outside of your heart. God is well able to give you *intuitive inspirations* with answers for the problems in your life. People do not seem to realize that when you are in relationship with God, He wants to work *in* you to solve the issues that your human mind cannot even conceive.

Let me pose this question: *If God has called you into His Kingdom, does He not have the right to call on you as He wills?* Many want to receive the calling of God, but they do not want to bear the responsibility of that call. God calls you because He recognizes your capacity to *inspire* yourself from within. He makes no mistakes. God intimately knows your abilities and your desire to please Him. So when God wants to use you He calls you—because you are willing to speak to yourself within and stir yourself to action.

Some people do not want to speak to themselves in their inner man. They want to act as if they have it all together, so for all intensive purposes it seems like they have been perfect all of their lives. Their demeanor says, "I do not need to inspire myself inwardly; I know it all anyway." This is a flawed attitude; no one possesses inward inspiration except by virtue of God within. Let us remember David's words to himself in Psalm 42:5: "Why art thou cast down, O my soul? and why art thou disquieted in me? hope thou in God: for I shall yet praise him for the help of his countenance." Stop now, and ask yourself what kind of attitude you have about praise. Are you thankful to God for the help of His countenance, or are you trying to keep it together on your own?

One last thought about speaking to yourself: *your soul will only obey your voice.* No one else can encourage your soul but you. This means when God calls you to a task, no one but you can hear the call or answer the call. As you mature spiritually, you become increasingly aware that your eternal destiny rests on your ability to activate *intuitive inspiration* and speak words of wisdom to your soul.

Submission to the Success of God

Deep inside of you there is a revelation that brings you into **Submission to the Success of God.** Let's briefly refer back to Psalm 65:4, which says, "...blessed is the man whom You choose...." Though God chooses you He often must cause things to press you into the place of submission. Everybody is not easily broken in His presence. Here is a little heads up. While you are going through what you are going through, you must know it is because you have been chosen to carry a cause; and the cause that calls out the *praise* in you will make people envious, because you are so happy in God.

You have to understand the happier you become, the more blessed you look, and the more envy you attract. God is not concerned about envy, because when He chooses you and causes you to come into His presence you cannot be removed from the place of your assignment. Psalm 16:5–6 says, "The LORD *is* the portion of mine inheritance and of my cup: thou maintainest my lot. The lines are fallen unto me in pleasant *places*; yea, I have a goodly heritage."

When you are *submitted to the success of God* you must be assured that promotion does not come from the north, south, east, or west. Promotion comes from God alone (Ps. 75:6–7). Stop right now, lift up your hands, and say, "Lord, I trust You for the next level You are setting me into. I am not going to be upset or distracted by the signals of the enemy, because I know You are going to promote me after my 'flesh' suffers a while." Listen to 1 Peter 5:8–10:

> *"Be well balanced (temperate, sober of mind), be vigilant and cautious at all times; for that enemy of yours, the devil, roams around like a lion roaring [in fierce hunger], seeking someone to seize upon and devour. Withstand him; be firm in faith [against his onset—rooted, established, strong, immovable, and determined], knowing that the same (identical) sufferings are appointed to your brotherhood (the whole body of Christians) throughout the world. And after you have suffered a little while, the God of all grace [Who imparts all blessing and favor], Who has called you to His [own] eternal glory in Christ Jesus, will Himself complete and make you what you ought to be, establish and ground you securely, and strengthen, and settle you"* (AMP, emphasis mine).

Let me encourage you. Some people do not understand why the word *after* is in the Bible. *There is a process to establishing your victorious praise.* God will bring you through situations other people have never experienced so that they can see His favor in your life and desire it. Unfortunately, those who do not seek after God and His virtue often envy what they do not possess. This is why God wants your blessing to show up in your *praise.* He wants people to recognize that you are praising a God you cannot see or touch in the physical realm. You are praising a mighty Father that you cannot hug…yet you are praising Him because He is *in you*, touching and transforming your life. The mighty One in you is tugging at your spirit, and birthing you out.

God gives you virtue, and in return, you are supposed to give Him *praise*. So let me review. If you do not have *progressive maturity* that leads to *renewed celebration*, and ultimately to *aggressive agreement;* you cannot possess *intuitive inspiration*, and as a result, you will not be able to have *submission to godly success*. As a believer, your success does not come from deciding to do things your own way. You will experience success because God chose you and has caused it to happen. If you want to live an empowered life of divine destiny, you have to face this truth.

I was traveling recently and ran into a very well known speaker, someone most people have seen on television. When he sat down next to me on the plane, I acknowledged him and he acknowledged me. During the flight we started talking for a bit, and then he returned to his notes. After writing about four pages of notes he turned to me and said, "My pilot called this morning and said a certain part was missing from my private plane, and that it would be better for me to fly commercially. I was upset because I do not prefer flying commercially. In fact, he said for what God has increased me to do for His Kingdom, if I were to calculate that value for every hour of the day, my time would be worth nine thousand dollars an hour." He continued, "...I can't hang around small-minded folk and produce for the Kingdom...because if I hang around small-minded people in the Kingdom, then I will start producing thirty dollars an hour for God instead of nine thousand dollars an hour for the Kingdom."

That conversation thrust my thought back into progressive maturity. It jump-started something in me. I sat there and added up all the value God has added to me and the things I produce in the Kingdom. I started multiplying and dividing these factors by the hours in a day, which made me reflect on my Tested Thinking. If this man, whom God divinely appointed for me to meet and talk with that day, is mindful of never failing to produce what God desires for His Kingdom, then am I wasting my time when I associate with people that do not understand the value of my praise and my relationship with God; who do not relate to my continual renewal of celebration on an intuitive level, nor to my satisfaction with submitting to His success?

This deeply impacted my spirit, and it can do the same for you. How would you like to be satisfied with the success of the Kingdom to the place that God increases the value of your life to nine thousand dollars every hour? When you "think on" His virtues, God increases the capacity of *what is on your mind*...and no one can take this away from you.

Be honest. Wouldn't you praise God if you knew that whatever you did during the last hour earned you nine thousand dollars? Just think if you spent an hour and a half at that value: that would yield thirteen thousand five hundred dollars into your life. Can you image being on that level with God? When he finished talking I took some notes. As my encounter on the plane continued, he noticed something I was doing on my computer and asked me about it. I responded by showing him a few things. A few moments later he dropped his head back and said, "Come, teach me about that." I shared with him for forty-five minutes and he took four pages of notes. That really hit me. A man whose value to the Kingdom is worth nine thousand dollars an hour saw something *maturing* in me that he perceived was of value.

Later, he looked at me and said, "Here is my personal email address. Only ten people have it in the world. I want you to talk to me. I want you to reveal some things to me that you talked about...." Immediately, I recognized that God was saying, "Son, here is another level of maturity that you must advance toward." God brought this encounter to pass so that I could see another level of maturity He is pressing me toward.

We have to *submit to the success of God*—not increase our capacity according to our own design. Hear me. You will miss God if you think that He operates the same way in everyone. You have to "wake up" to your own praise that is being birthed from the maturity and intuitiveness God has given you. Wake it up and pull it out of you, and then you will start walking close to God. You might not meet someone on an airplane; you may run into somebody at the office, or at a restaurant. But your focus should be unto God. That way, when He brings a divine encounter you will be able to discern beyond the words that are being spoken to hear what "thus saith the Lord."

We need to come into *aggressive agreement*. Pause for a moment and thank God for what He is doing within you. Say, "God, I want to agree for everything that You have said will be working inside of me." Remember this: Sometimes God closes one thing to get you to your next level of experience. Some things in your life, often those you would least expect, must be closed in a timing you did not anticipate. God allows this, so that He can press you to a place of greater expectancy.

As you go about your everyday life, you are going to run into people that have something eternal connected to you. Do not mistake them. *Write some notes and start living the experience.* Do not bypass destiny.

One of the things he said to me really made an impact. He shared, "Three words touched my life...*Decisions decide wealth*." He continued, "If you are broke, it is because of a decision you made that is keeping you broke." Notice that he did not say, "Education decides wealth." He did not say, "Who you know or where you were born decides wealth." Hear me. *Thinking on* and living out the virtues of God is accomplished through your making the right decisions. Applying the wisdom of God in your spiritual disciplines, health, and finances are all governed by your decisions...and the Bible clearly states (from our earlier chapters) that the blessing of the Lord comes upon those who decide to honor and activate His Word on a personal level. *Are you ready to make a decision today that will determine how you receive abundant life?* Again, godly abundance and prosperity touches on much more than just money. You could be wealthy at this moment, but fail to recognize the Source of true riches in your life.

Submit to the success of God in your life. If you really start looking at yourself closely you will see that you possess an abundance of untapped skill and potential. You are already wealthy, even though you may not see or celebrate it right now. One right decision can set the course of your destiny. This may sound a bit hard for you, but let me give you a word of advice: Don't be so "spiritual" that you stop exercising common sense. Too many well-meaning believers try to make common sense spiritual, when God never intended for it to be. Common sense is supposed to be common. If you make some basic, sound decisions, it will add incredible value to your life.

Eternally Satisfied

The last point in our acronym of *praise* is to be **Eternally Satisfied**. I have made up my mind that every day I walk through this life I am going to be *eternally satisfied*. Remember our text from the *King James Version* in Psalm 65:4, "Blessed is the man whom thou choosest, and causest to approach unto thee, that he may dwell in thy courts: we shall be *satisfied* with the goodness of thy house, even of thy holy temple" (*emphasis mine*).

Being *eternally satisfied* means, whether it refers to the natural or spiritual realm, I am going to be satisfied with the "goodness" of my Father's house. I like the word *satisfied,* because to me it means that whatever level I am on, that is the level where I will be satisfied. This does not say that I will automatically be increased; but according to my *aggressive agreement, intuitive inspiration,* and *submission to God's measure of success,* His Word and His plan will unfold for me. Remember this Scripture as you go about your day:

> *Now to Him Who, by (in consequence of) the [action of His] power that is at work within us, is able to [carry out His purpose and] do superabundantly, far over and above all that we [dare] ask or think [infinitely beyond our highest prayers, desires, thoughts, hopes, or dreams], to Him be glory in the church and in Christ Jesus throughout all generations forever and ever. Amen (so be it)" (Eph. 3:20–21 AMP).*

This level of blessing can cause you to be envied! Some people get so angry when they see you being blessed and *eternally satisfied* while they are having all sorts of problems. They wonder why they are not receiving the blessings that seem to come so naturally for you. *Eternal satisfaction* comes only when you submit to or are submissive unto God. This means you have been willing to accept, receive, and activate His calling and purpose in your life. Again, no one can take that away from you.

Anyone can worship God from a religious mindset, because He is the embodiment of eternal truth and righteousness; He is altogether lovely and kind, and He is just. (Let me clarify. This is not *godly worship,* which I discussed in a previous chapter). In its most generic form, worship is simply an acknowledgment of who God really is. As I walk in godly worship I can walk in perfect peace, praising God, because I know that He is able to do exceedingly, abundantly above whatsoever I may ask or think. God revels in knowing that He can cause His blessing in us to overflow.

When we are *eternally satisfied* we can say what Paul said in Philippians 4:12: "I know both how to be abased, and I know how to abound: every where and in all things I am instructed both to be full and to be hungry, both to abound and to suffer need." Hear me. If you never learn how to achieve balance in your life, you will not know how to celebrate the "low days" as well as the "high days." Being *eternally satisfied* means we walk in peace with God regardless of what may be good, bad, or indifferent. So we must learn how to *praise* God for the low days as well as the high days—because God is waiting to see how mature your praise really is. *Do you crash to the basement in your spirit when bad news comes, or are you mature enough to come through every trial with the peace of God in your heart?*

When trials and tests come, believers mistakenly think they have come to destroy us. Not so! These situations come to qualify us for *satisfaction.* I arrived at my best place in God when I finally did not care what other people thought of me. In fact, I recognized that the things other people wanted me to care about were the very things that were keeping them in spiritual immaturity. They wanted me to continue spoon-feeding them when they were mature enough to start feeding themselves. Take a bit of advice: When people want you to carry them (and their issues) to maturity, you will lose your maturity in the process—and your satisfaction in your personal walk with God—because you are not letting them mature.

We become enablers for the enemy when we allow a person to get locked into always trusting in us on a spiritual level. Hear me. We must *trust the touch of God*—totally depending on Him—not rely on a human being to fill that place. The Lord may use us as a point of ministry or inspiration in someone else's life, but when that person's focus shifts from God (his or her ultimate Provider) to us, trouble is just around the corner. I have heard it said that sometimes people are not prayer partners, but instead, progressively lazy partners, or maybe even procrastination partners! I often ask people, "Why don't you take it to God yourself?" Nothing can replace your heartfelt desire for God that is expressed in trusting prayer, praise, and worship.

What is really exciting is when people begin to see the Holy Spirit working on their behalf. That is when I know they are coming into *eternal satisfaction*. God wants to raise you up in His virtues to the level where everyone you touch will experience your spiritual maturity. Once again, I repeat, your maturity begins with *praise*. Satisfaction follows praise. Therefore, your praise to God should be your first level of satisfaction in your relationship with Him. So let the abundance come, and thank God for it. Let the superabundant overflow come.

CHAPTER 9

Practice What You Have Learned

Order: The Means by Which God Works in Your Life

In the first eight chapters we have been examining Paul's list of virtues in Philippians 4:8–9, which leads to our ultimate goal, "…and the God of peace shall be with you" (v. 9). Allow me to summarize what we have learned, so that we can stay grounded in God's intention for establishing His virtues in our lives. When we are saved we receive a comprehensive benefits package from God that gives us the promise of eternal security and an abundant life now, which includes a wealth of blessings that we can find in the "small print" of God's eternal Word.

Among these blessings are healing, deliverance, peace, wisdom, and every virtue that reflects the character of God. Second Corinthians 1:20 says, "For as many as are the promises of God, they all find their Yes [answer] in Him [Christ]. For this reason we also utter the Amen (so be it) to God through Him [in His Person and by His agency] to the glory of God" (AMP). When we are filled with the Holy Spirit we are empowered to be witnesses unto God in the earth (Acts 1:8). This establishes the foundation for applying the six virtues—*true, honest, just, pure, lovely,* and *of good report*—and it also determines the depth and the power of our *praise*.

The Matrix of Thinking

Now, bear with me, because I am about to introduce a new term to encapsulate "thinking on" the virtues of God that we have been studying. It is a term that I call the *matrix of thinking.* By using this term, I am referring to the foundation of our thought life from applying the six virtues. As we mature in Christ, everything we think, say, or do must be built on this foundation. So let me pull this all together. Salvation and the infilling of the Holy Spirit establish the foundation for our new life as sons and daughters of God. This is also the foundation of the *matrix of thinking*.

Whatsoever we "think on" after becoming a new creation begins to come directly from His character virtues, seeds of which were deposited within us at salvation to fulfill our prophetic purpose. As we guard "what's on our mind" we will preserve what God has already ordained to manifest in our life...*and the God of peace will be with us*. If we fail to guard these virtues, trouble, turmoil, and anxiety will be the result...because the God of peace is not with us.

Let's take a moment to consider this principle from another angle. There are six virtues listed in our text: *Six is the biblical number of man*. When we add our discussion of virtue and praise in the last two chapters, it yields a subtotal of eight: *Eight is the biblical number that represents a new day*. When we begin to *practice* the virtues God has planted in our spirits, thus transforming our mind and conforming our lifestyle, the result can be related prophetically to taking that next vital step, which yields an exciting total, the number nine: *Nine is the biblical number that represents birthing*. Do I need to remind you that we are currently in Chapter 9? Watch out! Your new day is coming! When you apply the six principles of virtue by "practicing what you have learned," you are about to give birth to a new life! Go ahead and give God praise for bringing you thus far...because your walk of virtue is about to come to maturity.

Having set this foundation, let's talk about the word *practice*. Once you have activated the seeds of virtue in your thoughts, so that they begin to manifest in your lifestyle, you must *practice* them in order for them to be perfected (brought to fullness or completion). This is why as you grow in Christ, sometimes you get victory in a situation and other times you do not. If you were on a sports team, you would go to practice until it was time for the actual game—and that is when you would pull from everything you had applied during practices to produce your peak performance. So rest assured, as you remain in vital relationship with Christ—receiving wisdom and strength from Him, repenting of your sins, and walking in obedience—you will come to maturity and show forth His character virtues *continually* in the playing field of life.

Now, let's take a look at Philippians 4:9 in the *King James Version*, "Those things, which ye have both learned, and received, and heard, and seen in me, do: and the God of peace shall be with you." The word that seems to "jump off the page" is the tiny word *do*. For such a small word (which encompasses the meaning of practice and model in the *Amplified Bible*), it has a powerful lesson in it that we should learn. Paul is stressing that after we *think on these things,* which we have *learned, received, heard, and seen* in him, we should *do* them. The Philippians probably said to Paul, "But these are hard things that we do not know how to do. How do we learn to do them all?" Paul's answer to them might have been, "Practice what you have learned." I want to offer a few ways for you to do just that.

In the practical sense, practicing refers to, "repeated performance or systematic exercise for the purpose of acquiring proficiency."[1] There is one catch. You cannot practice what you do not have a purpose for—but if there is purpose behind your performance there will definitely be a passion to fulfill it. It also stands true that if you do not have passion you will lose the desire and the power to *practice*. With this in mind, let's learn some key principles from our acronym. I know they will be of help to you in the coming days, if you will earnestly put them to use.

- **P** rojected Goals, *set the groundwork to receive*
- **R** eal Feedback, *which gives you the ability to make*
- **A** ccurate Assessments, *that enable you to make*
- **C** alculated Adjustments, *from which you can perform a*
- **T** entative Review of the Results, *which leads to*
- **I** nvestment Dialogue for Mentorship, *that provides the basis for*
- **C** alculated Growth, *which always produces*

- **E** mpowered **Projected Results**, *maximum yield from your life-style of virtue*

Projected Goals

When you have a passion for the things of God and a desire to *practice* what you have learned you must look for something that you believe is your *purpose* in life. When you are functioning in the area of your passion, you will perform well without having to think too much about it. Whether you teach, work with children, or are skilled at creating with your hands (crocheting, painting, construction work, and so on), your passion will engage you to fulfill whatsoever is in your hands. Perhaps you have an affinity for working with computers, televisions, or cell phones. You could even have a passion for the ministry, whether it be preaching, leading in praise and worship, helping the needy, or a host of other things. The area you have realized is your main interest or *purpose*, the thing you do without effort, becomes the place of your *practice*.

As you begin to understand that the desire inside of you is waiting to come forward, you must apply yourself to setting **Projected Goals**. This is the end result of the three-step process from *purpose*, to *passion,* and finally, to actual *practice* of what you have learned, received, heard, and seen in your walk with God. As you set *projected goals*, you will begin to analyze where your efforts, energy, and time must be utilized. Nothing will ever be accomplished toward God's prophetic purpose for your life unless you begin by setting goals.

What is God asking you to do for Him? How should you go about doing it? What plans do you need to make in order to put them into action? Begin to set some goals now for where you want to be a month, six months, or a year down the road. Go talk to someone who is successfully doing what you would like to do. "Pick his or her brain" and get some insight into what it will require for you to pursue your purpose. There are many practical steps you can take to ensure you get off to a good start, and you can read them all in my recently published mini-book, *The Millionaire's Boot Camp.* I have borrowed from several of the winning principles it contains to help you perfect the virtues God has invested in you. As you progress through this chapter, you will probably want to reap the full benefit by reading the entire mini-book. I highly recommend that you add it to your learning library.

When you understand that your relationship with God and your faith in Him is your foundation to reaching your goals and to experiencing a divinely peaceful life, you will no longer let doubt, fear, or any "weight" of sin that has held you back in the past keep you from pressing forward into victory. The new perspective you have gained will empower you to reach your goals, especially as you become more *practiced* at identifying temptations, trials, and the hidden blessings in every trying circumstance—seeing them as opportunities to embrace the success of God.

Real Feedback

If you are not accustomed to holding a solid set of priorities that bring order into your life, you will most likely struggle as you begin to *practice* what you have learned. As you have seen from Paul's systematic and progressive list of virtues in Philippians 4, order is the means by which God is working in your life. As you embrace divine order, it will bring you to the next level of accountability in your spiritual walk. Without accountability, without being able to review your goals at a glance to confirm that you are on track, then completing the necessary tasks will be a somewhat cumbersome process. That is when you need **Real Feedback** as a checkpoint along the way. Always surround yourself with people who love God and will give you feedback based on real information and truth, not simply offer you emotionally based opinions.

The most significant value of order is that when we do things the way they are supposed to be done in light of God's Kingdom, everything begins to make sense. There will be far less confusion in your life when you begin to do things decently and in order. As you *practice* becoming the virtuous man or woman of God you were created to be (from Paul's list of virtues), everything will begin to fall into place. Remember the old saying, "Practice makes perfect." You may not be perfect in your walk with God, but with *practice* you will become closer to Him and to achieving your goals.

Accurate Assessments

This brings me to the next point, identifying exactly what your next steps will be, and seeking to find that level of interaction with others who have similar goals and desires. If you are going to submit to the success of God on a practical level you must make **Accurate Assessments** of how you are progressing in relation to your opportunities. If starting a business venture is what you desire, then one of your first steps should be to become part of the Chamber of Commerce in your city. If you need to seek counsel or confirmation about where you believe God is leading you spiritually or in ministry, this can many times be accomplished by meeting with your pastor or a friend who can give you wise counsel. You can start with a self-assessment: *How is your prayer life? Are you tithing? Have you found a place of service in your church? What new things are aiding you in your practice of what you have learned?* All of these questions can be answered by accurately assessing your progress.

At times, it can be easier to assess your growth by comparing your spiritual walk today with what it was a year ago. When you look at where you were then, and then compare it with where you are in applying the *virtues* today, you will know if you are really *practicing* what you have learned...or if you have not embraced progressive maturity in your relationship with Him.

Keeping a journal on a daily basis can help you to identify the areas where you are weak. Then when you look back at your notes you will begin to see your growth (or lack of it), and can redirect your *practice* accordingly. You will also see how God has been dealing with you, both in the short- and long-term, which will give you understanding and confirmation of His overall direction for your life. Keeping records, spiritually or otherwise, will demonstrate your ability to keep every aspect of your life in order. It will also reveal the strength of your passion toward your purpose, and your ability to put into *practice* what you have learned. The documentation process invariably results in another powerful benefit: new discipline being birthed in your life to walk in even greater intimacy with the Lord.

The Law of Opportunities

On a practical level, it is very important that you realize the law of opportunities. *Opportunity is not waiting for you to make up your mind; it has already made up its mind about you.* An opportunity of a lifetime may come for a fleeting moment and be gone; therefore, you must be prepared both to recognize it and act upon it. Make *accurate assessments* about what you are doing with the opportunities that come your way.

Let me suggest a few spiritual opportunities that we all overlook. For example, we walk down the street every day, passing people who are hurting, suffering from illnesses or the loss of loved ones, or perhaps are addicted to drugs. They desperately need help to regain their lives. Yet many Christians walk past them without so much as casting a fleeting glance in their direction. Let me remind you: Opportunities are often disguised as challenges or inconveniences. Think about Jesus. Had He not stopped and turned around that day, we could not have read the story about the woman who was healed of the issue of blood. Jesus constantly stopped to take advantage of godly opportunities.

Allow me to pose a question. What would happen if, just once, you stopped to talk to a homeless man or woman on the street? Who would receive the greatest blessing from a brief conversation, a "God bless you," or slipping a ten dollar bill in his pocket to allow him to go to a restaurant and eat a meal? I suggest you might be the one who would walk away with a heart blessed by the love of God. *Practice* "thinking on" what Paul said would bring you the peace of God: whatsoever is *true, honest, just, pure, lovely,* and *of good report.* And as much as you can, share these thoughts with those around you who desperately need a "cup of cold water." You are not on this earth simply for your enjoyment, but to fulfill the assignment God has given you.

Calculated Adjustments

Making **Calculated Adjustments** is essential, because it will allow you to recapture the momentum of your original enthusiasm, by adjusting your plans to seize more opportunities. To make the proper *adjustments* you must have the right information. If not, you will be trapped into making short-sighted decisions based solely on what you can see *right now*. The most useful information is that which has been tracked—because it provides a historical overview.

Now, of course, you know where I am heading—the Word of God is the best source of historical information ever known to man. When you are not certain if you are *practicing* what you thought Paul said in Philippians 4:8–9, you can go right back to the Bible and realize that he did not say (in so many words, "think about what you feel is worthy of your thoughts." He said, "think on what is worthy of your reverence." There is a monumental difference. That is when an adjustment in your application of the Word becomes necessary. Just pick up, right where you went off the road a little, and get back on course.

I have begun to develop and release a line of books…and by making adjustments I am capturing the momentum. I have many brainstorms for my books and products, yet it is often necessary to adjust because of timing or some other factor that may not initially have been in place. After establishing momentum, whether in business or in your spiritual disciplines, you can always revisit your original goals and make needed adjustments. For instance, I made an adjustment not too long ago and began developing a sequel to my first book along with a companion resource, because the original book has continued to perform well in the marketplace.

Your perspective or attitude in making life or business adjustments is vital. If you have a positive attitude you will be able to make adjustments with ease. If you are upset, downhearted, and generally frustrated, you will lose perspective and valuable focus. Failing to remain centered in your area of passion will cause major setbacks and delays in making *adjustments*. Again, Jesus is an excellent example. He handled an amazing daily schedule with constant interruptions, spiritual warfare, and the needs of His disciples ever before Him. But Philippians 2:6–7 tells us that He willingly relinquished His position with the Father to take on the form of a servant. Jesus is the Perfect Example of grace in motion; nothing distracted His resolve to achieve the goal set for Him by the Father.

Think about the process we have covered thus far. You seek the right kind of purpose, apply order and organization to your life, are careful not to waste any opportunity, and are consistent in making adjustments to capture and maintain momentum in your spiritual and practical disciplines. Therefore, you must maintain a positive attitude to continue making adjustments as needed and maintain your focus. You have to stay on top of things—track information, get regular feedback, and always be prepared to adjust your plan when necessary.

This leads to a final thought about making *calculated adjustments*— they must always be made cleanly and efficiently. In other words, as you adjust your attitude and disposition (the essence of your character), you will be able to guard what matters most as you relate to others. The difference could rest in the fact that when you speak to someone you say, "Yes," instead of saying, "Uh, huh." Instead of saying, "Right," you say, "Absolutely." It could mean that you stand and raise your hands while worshipping God instead of sitting in your seat worried about what other people might be thinking about you during praise and worship. As you advance in *practicing* God's virtues, small upward shifts will make all the difference in how soon you reach your next level.

Bear in mind, adjustments do not just happen. They do not materialize at the push of a button. Positive adjustments are the product of a strong inner resolve—which is one of the many benefits of a strong prayer life.

Stop and reflect right now. Ask yourself, *What do I need to adjust in order to release even greater momentum in my life?* Trust God to answer, and then write down what He reveals to your spirit. Now, create a plan, adjusting when necessary, and you will reap rich benefits in the days and years to come.

Tentative Review of the Results

Let's take a moment to review. What is your passion? Does it come from God's *heartfelt desire* for your life? Are you walking in your prophetic purpose, seizing every opportunity to *put into practice* the things you have learned? Here is a word to the wise: If you start something you need to carry it through to the end. At times, that may require a lot of energy, but it is crucial to achieving godly success. This is part of making accurate assessments; only now I am applying it to making a **Tentative Review of the Results**. Paul gave us a good example of this when he said, "I have fought the good (worthy, honorable, and noble) fight, I have finished the race, I have kept (firmly held) the faith" (2 Tim. 4:7 AMP). He knew that he had achieved the results God desired because he had run the race set before him with obedience and patience. Paul knew that he had achieved every goal the Lord had given him.

Here is another lesson we can learn from Paul. When you are filled with passion for what God has given you to accomplish, you will not avoid dealing with the hard issues in life. You will follow through to the end. Let me encourage you with a reality check. When you commit to living a life that is pleasing to God, you might as well be prepared to put your own needs on hold. God will keep you so busy that you will not think of yourself until everyone else has been cared for and the work has been completed. The road to accomplishment is often not an easy one, but the rewards are great. It will be worth all the sacrifices we have made when we stand before the Lord and hear, "…Well done, thou good and faithful servant: thou hast been faithful over a few things, I will make thee ruler over many things: enter thou into the joy of thy lord" (Matt. 2:21).

Investment Dialogue for Mentorship

Without training or the discipline to excel you will become stagnant, and anything stagnant eventually loses its potential and dies. That is why there must be what I call **Investment Dialogue for Mentorship**. Training is always an important key because it allows you to open doors to new areas of business and/or ministry. For example, you must make time to read and study the Word, while on the practical side you are seeking out those who are more experienced in the area you have chosen for service or vocation. Remember Proverbs 11:1: "A false balance *is* abomination to the LORD: but a just weight *is* his delight." The proper *investment dialogue* in the right setting—in the classroom, in the church, or the corporate arena—will keep you balanced and advancing in both your calling and your occupation.

Train yourself to read about principles, patterns, and strategies that will define areas to expand the knowledge you already possess. If there is group training or individual mentoring available where you can learn with others in a one- or two-day seminar, train yourself to take advantage of these opportunities. The same is true in your spiritual development. Know your Bible, use Bible resources to deepen your understanding, and read all of the books you can muster. Take advantage of spiritual development opportunities like Bible training in your church, or perhaps enrolling in a seminary course or two; attend prophetic conferences, Christian industry events for networking, and more. Practice taking advantage of the many *investment dialogue for mentorship* opportunities God makes available to you.

In any area of training it is essential that you remain consistent in your perspective and practice of utilizing your new knowledge and abilities. For example, any knowledge gained is yours; it will start by empowering your life, but then through this empowerment you should generously share this *investment dialogue* with others. Be willing to let God use you as an anointed and capable mentor. As you take on this role, *practice* learning to respect your own abilities and those of others, through instruction and inspiration. God will mentor you in order to help you empower others, to the degree you will allow it. As He drops thoughts and bits of truth down into your spirit, be willing to receive and activate His wisdom, and put into *practice* that new knowledge for the benefit of someone else.

When you stop learning, you have stopped being empowered. Hear me. Once you feel that you have "arrived" in accomplishing your goals, you are putting yourself in danger of losing what I call the "momentum of success." In Philippians 3:12–16 Paul wisely said, "Not that I have now attained [this ideal], or have already been made perfect, but I press on to lay hold of (grasp) and make my own, that for which Christ Jesus (the Messiah) has laid hold of me and made me His own. I do not consider, brethren, that I have captured and made it my own [yet]; but one thing I do [it is my one aspiration]: forgetting what lies behind and straining forward to what lies ahead, I press on toward the goal to win the [supreme and heavenly] prize to which God in Christ Jesus is calling us upward. So let those [of us] who are spiritually mature and full-grown have this mind and hold these convictions; and if in any respect you have a different attitude of mind, God will make that clear to you also. Only let us hold true to what we have already attained and walk and order our lives by that" (AMP).

Keep pressing forward! And, like Paul, in everything you do remember that you are a virtuous son or daughter of God. Above all, you have a prophetic purpose, a passion, and a desire to *practice* what you have learned.

Calculated Growth

You should know by now that whatever you "think on" is what will ultimately manifest in your life…and you can tell *what's on your mind* by what you think about when you're *not thinking*. Let me clarify. Unless you have a focused image of the results you desire (in any area), it will be difficult to proactively expand to a new level. In other words, you must learn how to apply principles of **Calculated Growth** in your life. Think about the extravagant images you see on certain magazines—such as one-of-a-kind homes and condos that are located in remote, lush locations, incredible boats, watches, golf courses, spas, resorts, and more. If you were to keep these images before your eyes, you would elevate your desire and passion to produce those same quality experiences. The same holds true in your walk with the Lord. You must *see* in your mind that God has already enabled you to accomplish the very thing you are seeking Him about. Keep focused on the goal. Then you will be able to project when, where, and how that growth will be realized.

If your passion and purpose is to build an orphanage for AIDS orphans in Africa, you must see in your mind those children playing on their swingset out in the front yard. Picture a little girl named Zawadi smiling shyly as she is led into her new home...perhaps the first one she has ever known. Picture the little boy with the sad eyes looking at you, wondering if you, too, will go away. Begin to see yourself holding those children, singing them to sleep, giving them the love they so deeply miss from their mothers and fathers who are no longer with them.

What will you do with the vision that has birthed *heartfelt desire* in you? Will you let it die or will you leave no stone unturned until the money is raised, the building has become a reality, and those children are safely in the orphanage that was built by your passion, your purpose, and your desire to *practice* what you have learned?

Empowered Projected Results

The final way you can release your spiritual potential is by protecting and projecting your resources to achieve **Empowered Projected Results**. Your arsenal of resources begins, of course, with the Word of God. As you walk with Christ, you must store God's unchanging principles and virtues in your heart, and keep open, intimate, and consistent communication with Him through prayer. You must guard these resources by *practicing* these disciplines continually, because your enemy, the devil, will try to steal them away from you. "The thief cometh not, but for to steal, and to kill, and to destroy: I am come that they might have life, and that they might have it more abundantly" (John 10:10).

As you come into a full appreciation of what God has given you, the first thing you must do is to protect it from people that would abuse it. Having dealt with the first level of abuse, that which would come from yourself, you must now make sure that the same principle does not carry over to others. You must guard yourself from living the type of lifestyle that will cause certain people to want to use you for their own selfish gain. Keep your heart pure; be true to yourself and others. As God brings you into abundance, it is extremely important for you to let everyone in your life know how much you value your resources, your stewardship to God, and the purpose He has given you.

Here are three rules of thumb. First, always manage your life in a way that allows you to develop a deep level of respect for the Source of your provision, the One who gives you the power to gain wealth—God Himself. "But thou shalt remember the Lord thy God: for it is he that giveth thee power to get wealth..." (Deut. 8:18).

Second, manage your life in a way that allows you to establish a powerful line of communication with God. You have invested much time and energy in building a relationship with Him, so you must maintain a consistent level of effort to manage your time, so that you are available to Him at any time. Third, manage your life so effectively that it provides a resource to others who are in need, hurting people who may have no one but you whom they can call a friend. Be available! God blesses those who make themselves available in this way.

Let me illustrate. I personally give God a tithe and offerings for everything that I am able to produce by the power that He gives me to accomplish my goals. He is my Source, and I am a vessel He uses to pour out onto other people what He has given to me.

To *project* the purpose you have in your life you must understand the power of the untapped resources within you. God will use these yet to be realized resources to multiply the works and projects you have created. As you continue *practicing* the virtues you have learned, remember Philippians 1:6: "Being confident of this very thing, that he which hath begun a good work in you will perform it until the day of Jesus Christ." So keep *practicing,* confident in knowing that God is leading you into all truth.

"And let the peace (soul harmony which comes) from Christ rule (act as umpire continually) in your hearts [deciding and settling with finality all questions that arise in your minds, in that peaceful state] to which as [members of Christ's] one body you were also called [to live]. And be thankful (appreciative), [giving praise to God always]" (Col. 3:15 AMP).

Practice What You Have Learned, Received, Heard, and Seen in Me

Now, I would like to touch a little on a few of the final words we read in Philippians 4:9 before we enter into the amazing peace of God. "Practice

PRACTICE WHAT YOU HAVE LEARNED

what you have *learned* and *received* and *heard* and *seen* in me, and model
your way of living on it, and the God of peace (of untroubled, undisturbed
well-being) will be with you" (AMP, *emphasis mine*). Let's quickly take a
closer look at these words.

In order to **learn** you must be "teachable." In studying the meaning
from the original Greek word, I discovered this word relates to a fact: something that really occurred, is occurring, or will occur. We are "to learn by
use and practice,"[2] inquiry, and observation. Many who desire to learn a
certain thing have great difficulty doing so, because their mind is not really
on the subject. Proverbs 1:5 puts it this way: "A wise man will hear, and will
increase learning; and a man of understanding shall attain unto wise counsels...." In order to learn, you have to stay *in the moment*. Be fully invested
in right now, whether you are in prayer, at work, or singing in the choir at
church. Maximize every moment and you will maximize what you are able
to learn. I have heard it said that we never stop learning—*we learn something new every day.*

When I know that I am lacking wisdom in a certain area, I exercise the
due diligence to initiate an *investment dialogue of mentorship* and *learn*
about that thing. Upon making that commitment, something begins to break
in me that I refer to as the "law of capacity." Capacity gives me the ability
to receive and manage impartation, increase, overflow, and abundance. It is
of no use to give someone facts or information that they do not know how
to appreciate, especially if he or she is not teachable.

Let's go a little further by taking a look at Proverbs 1:2–4, "That people
may know skillful and godly Wisdom and instruction, discern and comprehend the words of understanding and insight, Receive instruction in wise
dealing and the discipline of wise thoughtfulness, righteousness, justice, and
integrity, That prudence may be given to the simple, and knowledge, discre-
tion, and discernment to the youth" (AMP).

If I possess wisdom, the first thing I should check is my godliness.
Then I should question if I am skillful in the manner in which I use the
wisdom. This is very important. When I have godly wisdom I should be

living a lifestyle that is wise according to God's Word. How can you determine if you are using the wisdom skillfully? The writer's next word is *instruction*. Are you teachable? Are you willing to seek instruction in the things you have not learned? Because after instruction will come *practice,* which will lead to your anticipated results.

When you develop skill in a certain area, performing whatever may be required becomes instinctive, because you have *practiced* it so many times. An example is the mother who has been cooking for so many years that she never uses a timer when cooking or baking. She puts a cake in the oven, and almost to the minute that it is ready she is there checking to see if it is done. That is skill.

That same level of skill applies to anything we do in the spiritual realm. When you first came to Christ you did not have the level of discernment that you now possess. Someone had to instruct you in what to study, how to pray, or how to hear God's voice. As time went on you became more skilled, and by assumption more godly (by practicing the virtues), until one day you will look back and realize how much you have grown.

As you continue your journey with God you become more skilled in spiritual things, just by virtue of walking with Him. You begin to discern what is right and wrong, even before someone tells you or you read it in the Word. Understand that when God gives you discernment He is giving you a little peek into your future walk with Him. It takes wisdom for you to comprehend what His will is for your life.

Moving along in our text in Proverbs 1, we must learn how to discern the difference between knowledge and understanding. *Understanding is an ability that we are born with, while knowledge must be learned.* Some people have knowledge of the principles of God, but they do not have the understanding that would allow them to apply them. However, as we grow in the knowledge of Christ, our understanding grows as well. And again, a good part of that growth can be attributed to *practicing* what we have *learned.*

Here is another benefit of spiritual *learning.* Using godly wisdom you can look at the world's system and discern everything it has to offer, but the world is unable to look at what you have achieved through God's system and interpret the wisdom and understanding you have gained. My question to you is this: Do you want to stay stuck, trying to learn a system that will never appreciate your wisdom, or do you want to be part of a system that you can live and grow in continually because it was designed for you. Wisdom goes hand in hand with knowledge and godly skill to give you the tools you need to not only live on your present level, but to constantly be moving higher. *Wisdom operates in the place where God wants you to grow.*

Bill Gates is a good example of a man who had the desire to be great, and availed himself of all the knowledge he could gather. He had passion for the purpose he felt in life, and kept on *practicing* it until he developed something that has made him the richest man in the world. Another good example is Moses. Have you ever wondered why God chose Moses to lead His people out of Egypt? Even though Moses had a problem with stuttering he *learned* enough in Pharaoh's house to lead millions of people for forty years. Moses not only had knowledge, but God also gave him wisdom and the skill needed to apply it.

Finally, do not ever dismiss the need for imparting wisdom, skills, and knowledge in your children (if you have any), younger family members and friends, or youth in your church (or elsewhere for that matter). Train them how to discern truth. Teach them how to keep an area of their heart free to store godly wisdom. Knowledge is not just for the mature; it is never too early to start teaching children right from wrong, especially when you consider that children learn more quickly than adults; so as you learn, do not neglect teaching the younger generation about God's virtues and other important things they should know.

Follow the principle of the "matrix of thinking." Remember, a matrix sets the foundation for the next thing to follow, which in turn, sets another foundation for another level, and so on. In the movie entitled *The Matrix,* the wisest or oldest person always represented this "matrix"; the most experienced person who was tied to all knowledge. The one who was the most experienced ended up being the most powerful. In the end, the only one (Neo) who could surpass "Mr. Smith" in knowledge and power ultimately gained all of his power. We often see the same scenario playing out in the church. Look at the spiritual side of matrix. When you know you have power to tread upon serpents and scorpions, and have been given power over the enemy, you can simply take the enemy's authority and begin to live in a new revelation on a new level. When you are able to take everything you have learned from God and do this, you have entered another realm of spiritual growth, measurement, and empowerment.

In review, you must *practice* what you have learned. Learning to think on the six virtues of Philippians 4:8 that are centered on knowing the God of peace that will bring you into living from the place of peace He has for you is the key. Continuing to learn is the key because if you allow your ability to learn to drop to a low level, you cannot receive the truth or be invested into in order to reach a higher level than your current one. Using the "matrix" principle, if you are on a low level in learning, then you will receive at a lower level, and the opportunities of investment into your life will likely remain on the ground floor. So continue to seek God and you will keep yourself in the learning mode. *Practicing* His virtues will yield maximum results in your life.

Receiving involves what we allow entrance into our minds through teachers or others God uses to impart truth, wisdom, or knowledge. It is the vehicle through which we learn and hear. *The Strong's Greek & Hebrew Dictionary* describes the word "received" (as used in Phil. 4:9) as, "to take to, to take with oneself, to join to oneself...to receive something transmitted."[3] Notice that when you *receive*, you are taking something to yourself and making it your own. That is a powerful part of the *practicing* process.

Hearing is different from learning. It has more to do with perception than with practice, though in order to *practice* we must have the empowered ability to perceive. Hearing speaks of the ability to catch what inspires you to learn. You may hear something, but does that mean you want to learn it? Not necessarily. Hearing must stimulate your ability to learn more, and in biblical terms this can be described as having *an ear to hear*. "He that hath an ear, let him hear what the Spirit saith unto the churches" (Rev. 2:29). Many people are motivated by what the gossip says, but I am eternally motivated by what the Spirit has to say. What about you? The Spirit understands what the mind of the Father is; therefore He speaks to you the will of God. And when He speaks, He does not simply give you the spiritual side of a matter.

In the natural realm, there is an innate ability for you to grow when you learn to appreciate hearing good information. That is often a challenge because disciplining yourself to *hear* can be more difficult than training yourself to learn. Why? Ego will tell you that you know it all *now*, so as a result, you shut down your *hearing*. Watch out for the "saints" in church who feel like because they are "something to somebody" they have arrived in the Kingdom. If there is nothing more than levels one or two in hearing, there cannot be much opportunity to receive *investment dialogue for mentorship*. And if there is minimal investment then you are not going to learn. A person who has *learned* sees the value of an investment and *wants to hear* more, because they are investment minded. The learned know how to expand themselves in God's economy to maximize their capacity. When Paul told the Philippians to *practice* what they **saw** in him, he was demonstrating the power of creating capacity.

In the Old Testament, David had men following him who were in debt, discontented, and in distress. Let me show you something. Whenever you are in debt, it is because you do not have enough knowledge to produce more of what you lack in learning. Whatever you lack in your life is because your learning is at the level of your lack. That causes discontent with your perceived "lot" in life, and distress because you feel powerless to change it. But Philippians 4:8–9 and a host of other Bible passages tell us that when we apply ourselves to learning the Word of God and doing what it instructs us to do, the superabundant blessings of God will begin to rain down upon our lives.

Now, here is a balance to this equation. Watch out for people who could destroy the potential of your destiny. What do I mean by this? One of the greatest travesties we have in the church is that we too often let another person stop our growth in God, because he or she makes you feel like you are great—you have "arrived." Hear me. When an individual feels like he or she is great (as mentioned before), spiritual growth stops. As a result, this person will feel great within the immediate circle, but if you take them to a "larger" atmosphere they become like an eon in a pond.

The question is not who you are to the people immediately around you, but who you can become when you meet new people, because you are always judged on the content of your mind. That is why God urges us to "think on" things that can be attributed to His character. Yale University will pay for you to attend there if you can prove that your mind has the capacity to learn. The struggle with the matrix of thought is, people try to live what they have not learned, so then they lose what they can never gain—because they never invested in what God had purposed for them to obtain.

What happens is they end up getting mad at people that do obtain what has been destined for their lives. Unfortunately, the only value that remains for them is to struggle against people that are doing what they should have already done. No one taught them that if they failed to learn, it would shut down their ability to receive the investment dialogue of mentorship. As a result, their ability to receive is shut down, and thus, they will never hear. Their ears are closed. All they can hear is a destructive interior dialogue about the people they hate, because these "privileged few" are already doing what they should have learned.

As a believer in Christ, you can live from one or two vantage points. Either you will be hearing what the Spirit is saying, or you hate what the enemy baits you to embrace. Again, you must remember Paul's words about "thinking on" Christ's virtues and follow His example. Because Jesus did nothing except that which He had seen the Father do, He demonstrated that He was willing to be *learned*…and that is why the Father was able to invest in Him rich virtues and power. The choice is yours.

God only invests in that which is eternal, because one day He is going to destroy the earth. Let me review. In the beginning God formed the first human body from the most viable, flexible, movable, tangible substance He could find…the dust of the earth. After doing so, He blew into this prized creation what He could not put in the earth. One day you will trade your earthly body for a heavenly one, and the earth we know is going to be replaced with a brand-new, perfect creation. So whatever you do, "think on" whatsoever is *true, honest, just, pure, lovely,* and *of good report*—because as these virtues "mature" the Christ in you is coming to completion.

God is saying to us today, "I will give you the capacity to download My Kingdom because I have put My Son, Jesus Christ, in you. I have put His Spirit in you so that you can reference what I am doing in heaven and learn of Me."

Let me ask you a question. Where does God hide when you cannot find him? Why do the Scriptures tell us we must seek the Lord *while He may be found?* (see Isa. 55:6). God is omnipotent—He is everywhere all at the same time, so where can He hide when it seems you cannot find Him? Here is the answer: *God hides where your mind cannot think where He is.* Whenever God does not want you to know where He is, He moves to a place where your thinking could never exist.

I am sorry to say, there are many people in the body of Christ who still cannot find Him. This is the reason why there are so many depressed Christians and also why suicidal believers are on the rise. There are so many disenchanted people, who come to church only when they feel like it once a month, because they have not found it within themselves to find God.

Once you find the Lord you will become like a deer that "…panteth after the water brooks" (Ps. 42:1). That is when your soul will begin to long after Him. Your soul is the beacon to know where your investment opportunity is awaiting you. Taste and see that the Lord is good; reach toward your next level of understanding. Rejoice that you have been saved, but realize: Heaven is not a place you should be waiting to die for; instead, make a decision to live for your eternal reward. Switch this perspective and say, "I am not living to get to heaven. I am living eternally because heaven is coming to me."

The voice of the Lord is not only calling you; He is speaking to you right now. If you are reading this book, you are not oblivious to hearing His voice. God has already been working in your life. If you tap into God and begin to "learn of Him," on an ever-increasing level you will begin to manage the Kingdom within you from the virtues that are already planted deep in your inner man. Start "thinking on" them right now. Better yet, activate them in your life by *practicing* what you have *learned, received, heard,* and *seen* in Christ. A whole new life is awaiting you.

CHAPTER 10

Model Your Way of Living on It: The Result of Practice

As you actively practice the six virtues listed in Philippians 4:8–9, God reshapes your life into a form (or model) that others can see and follow. Practicing and modeling are closely related. Just as the virtues—whatsoever is *true, honest, just, pure, lovely,* and *of good report*—are all interrelated and work progressively in your life, such are practicing and modeling. In some ways, however, they are different.

As we covered in the last chapter, when you *practice* you are acquiring a skill or discipline that you will call upon later to its fullest capacity. The process of *modeling,* on the other hand, is the result of conditioning yourself during practice: much like developing toned and defined muscles by virtue of running three miles a day, five days a week. The more you practice, the more you become a "model" for others to follow.

Here is another way to look at it. As God increases your spiritual strength through "thinking on" His virtues, you will be able to tap into that strength to run a consistent race—and everyone who is watching will imagine themselves running…and winning the prize.

Do you not know that in a race all the runners compete, but [only] one receives the prize? So run [your race] that you may lay hold [of the prize] and make it yours.

Now every athlete who goes into training conducts himself temperately and restricts himself in all things. They do it to win a wreath that will soon wither, but we [do it to receive a crown of eternal blessedness] that cannot wither.

Therefore I do not run uncertainly (without definite aim). I do not box like one beating the air and striking without an adversary.

But [like a boxer] I buffet my body [handle it roughly, discipline it by hardships] and subdue it, for fear that after proclaiming to others the Gospel and things pertaining to it, I myself should become unfit [not stand the test, be unapproved and rejected as a counterfeit] (1 Cor. 9:24–27 AMP).

Let's take a look at the "forerunner" of our spiritual race, Jesus Christ. He is the ultimate Model for us to follow. Philippians 2:5–7 reveals the process, "Let this mind be in you, which was also in Christ Jesus: Who, being in the **form** of God, thought it not robbery to be equal with God: But made himself of no reputation, and took upon him the **form** of a servant, and was made in the likeness of men..." (*emphasis mine*). Because He was in every way the perfect, sinless expression of the Father in the earth, Jesus did not have to practice. The strength and virtue of the Father was already fully vested in Him. Jesus simply exercised discipline to model the "form" of God (that was intangible) while taking on the "form" of men (a temporary physical body)—thus creating a pattern for us to run a *perfected* race.

God knew that by creating a model, He would establish the perfect pattern for all who *receive* (i.e., join to one's self) *the form* of Christ to be saved and delivered from the curse of Adam, thus completing His plan of redemption.

So remember, as you obey Paul's instruction in Philippians 4:9 to "...model your way of living..." by the virtues of God, you are following a pattern that revolutionized the lives of eleven men (the original disciples, less Judas, who ultimately betrayed Jesus), and subsequently reshaped the lives of multiplied millions throughout the world. With this in mind, let's go to our acronym:

- **M** anifesting Personal Authenticity, *is the first step to*
- **O** pen Layers of Authenticity, *that reveal your*

- **D** istinctive Attributes, *as*

- **E** ...He Empowers Your Strength, Giving, and Partnership, *affirming that you*

- **L** et God Supply Your Need, *as a model of His sufficiency*

Manifesting Personal Authenticity

As you begin to model your way by the virtues you "think on" in Philippians 4:8–9, it is important that you do not try to reshape your life someone else's way. The "shaping" will come by the Holy Spirit in a way that is perfectly tailored to who you are, thus **Manifesting Personal Authenticity** in your walk with God. During the process of modeling, God will cause you to focus on what you are doing and why you are doing it, regardless of what anyone else thinks about your ability to model your way. If we were to use Hollywood as an example, it is difficult, once a celebrity has been labeled as a comedian, for that individual to move into playing serious roles. Will Smith is an exception. He transitioned easily from "BelAir" to starring in major roles on the big screen. If you were to look closely at his career you would find that he has claimed success because he created his own model. No matter what part he may be playing he is still Will Smith.

As you are formed into the image of Christ you must *manifest personal authenticity*, because if you try to "copycat" someone else's anointing it will come out sooner or later. When you take on someone's old information, old jokes, and whatever else he or she used to build a successful life, the cat will one day "come out of the bag"...and once it is discovered that you are an imitation, you will no longer be credible.

Some years ago there was a popular group that, as it turned out, had lip-synched all of their songs. Everyone thought they were great until one day they were asked to perform, and they could not sing a note. Soon after that, it was discovered that all of their songs were "fakes"—they had hired another group to sing their songs for them. In the end result, they had portrayed an image of authenticity, but it was not truly their talent. In one day their career was gone.

Whenever you try to be what God has not ordained for you to become, you will eventually be found out...and soon after will find that you are alone. You will have ceased being "real" and will be labeled as a "fake." Think about it. One little misrepresentation can wipe out a lifetime of godly success.

If you have ever been shopping for a new home you are familiar with the "models" that the real estate agent shows you. These homes will be approximately the same size, with the same quality carpet and wood trim as the homes they will ultimately build for their clients. Of course, the builders try to put their best foot forward in the model, adding lots of special cabinetry, perhaps a sub-zero refrigerator, and many other "extras" to entice you to make a long-term investment. Having owned several homes I have learned that the best way to know what kind of community you will be moving into, is to find out the quality and price of the most expensive house that has been built in that area. Usually, it was once a model home.

On the average, a builder usually constructs five or six "models" to display what the subsequent homes will be like when they are ready for sale. The models could range, for example, from $300,000 to $700,000. Each home, on its scale of reference, represents the authenticity of the builder.

Every home will have "bells and whistles" corresponding to the cost. Since it is the builder's purpose to add credibility to their homes, they build a model for each style and cost range to show to prospective buyers. It is one thing for them to tell you they build homes, but when you can actually walk through a model you immediately know their ability and capacity to build. *The model displays the authenticity of the builder.* It is the proof that he has gone far beyond merely putting his design on paper; he has actually built the home.

One of the things that hurts the church today, is that we have too many people who are talking about things that they have not yet "put to paper." They have not produced anything that models the characteristics of the Kingdom. They have not gained the results of practicing God's virtues to serve as a "model" to those who would follow after them. Now listen closely. *It is imperative that you do not follow someone who has not accomplished the level of purpose God has put in you.* When God sends a mentor into your life, someone you can model your life after, he or she will be someone who can bring out in you the real potential of your purpose.

How does this play out in your spiritual life? Sylvester Stallone is another good example. He achieved such a great level of success in the *Rambo* movies that everyone related to him as an action hero. So when he tried to become a serious actor most people found it difficult to see him in that light. The same thing can happen in the spiritual realm. You can become so "churchy" that you will never be seen as anything more. There is more to the Christian life than sitting in a church pew, thinking about going to heaven, but never identifying that there may be other levels where God is waiting to take you.

Who or what inspires you to become more like Christ? If you do not have a realistic understanding of Christ and your relationship with Him (a model), then your experience with God will be ritualistic. You would be practicing principles from a design you have seen on paper, rather than having a tangible experience with God that shapes your life. Even God knew that He had to put what He had established on tablets (i.e., the law of Moses) into "living form" in order to advance His plan of redemption to the next level (see Ezek. 36:26–27). That is why John 1:14 tells us, "And the Word (Christ) became flesh (human, incarnate) and tabernacled (fixed His tent of flesh, lived awhile) among us; and we [actually] saw His glory (His honor, His majesty), such glory as an only begotten son receives from his father, full of grace (favor, loving-kindness) and truth" (AMP). When Christ came, we actually saw everything the Father had put on paper before the foundation of the world.

Think about Abraham, who was destined to become the father of our faith:

> *By faith Abraham, when he was called to go out into a place which he should after receive for an inheritance, obeyed; and he went out, not knowing whither he went.*

By faith he sojourned in the land of promise, as in a strange country, dwelling in tabernacles with Isaac and Jacob, the heirs with him of the same promise.

For he looked for a city which hath foundations, whose builder and maker is God (Heb. 11:8–10).

When you are destined to become a "father of faith" you will go out by faith, seeking authenticity in your future dwelling place. Abraham wanted to find a house that could not be built with human hands. "For we know that if our earthly house of this tabernacle were dissolved, we have a building of God, an house not made with hands, eternal in the heavens" (2 Cor. 5:2). Let me present to you that the greatest part of "you" is the "you" that no one has seen. I am not contradicting the principle of modeling or minimizing the importance of when a person may walk up to you and say, "I see God working in your life." That is great news, but truth be told, *the real you has not shown up yet.* It is still forming within you to take shape as you practice. Again, I refer to 2 Corinthians 2:9, which declares: "...Eye hath not seen, nor ear heard, neither have entered into the heart of man, the things which God hath prepared for them that love him."

The person you are displaying to others right now is really an "old model" that is about to die—*because the real you is about to show up.* There is another "model" of you taking shape that is about to create the authenticity of who you are *becoming* in Christ. As His virtues are established in your life, you will discover who you really are and conform to new paradigms. God wants those who are Kingdom bound to continually produce a renewed image that empowers the model of the Kingdom. If you cannot produce or manifest personal authenticity, then you do not have an authentic relationship with the King.

Picture with me, if you would, a scene in Nazareth over 2,000 years ago. The young man, Jesus (the son of the carpenter), walked into the home where He had lived with His mother and "step-father" until after His baptism by John in the Jordan River. "Mother, please sit down," I can hear Him say. "I have something to tell you. I am leaving Nazareth to follow the will of My Father in heaven. I love and appreciate you. I will always honor you, but I can no longer use you as My model in My next level. For Me to become who God has created Me to be, I must pattern My life after My Heavenly Father."

There came a day when Jesus asked His disciples, "Whom do men say that I am?" (Mark 8:27). This communicated the imperative that people around you should be able to see your authenticity, and as a result, do not try to qualify who you are by any other means. If you are waiting for people to confirm why your mentor is in your life, you will miss the benefit of that person's mentorship. You need to get that fact down in your spirit, because too many people have missed the person that was sent by God to be their mentor.

The disciples answered Jesus' question, "And they answered, John the Baptist: but some say, Elias; and others, One of the prophets. And he saith unto them, But whom say ye that I am? And Peter answereth and saith unto him, Thou art the Christ" (Mark 8:28–29).

When you understand the authenticity of God He will speak to your spirit, reveal your prophetic purpose, and give you understanding about that call. Do not let anyone try to rule your life who does not know who you really are. For this reason, you must be able to clarify and clear up relationships immediately. Do not let people stay around you who do not know the authenticity of your Kingdom relationship. You may be in church, clapping with the praise and worship, worshipping, or cheering on the preacher, but if nobody in your church understands your assignment, then do not settle for pleasing those who accept you simply because you are "churchy."

When Paul was called to be an Apostle he was knocked off his horse and blinded for three days (Acts 9:1–9). After being baptized, he remained with the disciples in Damascus for a certain period of time and then went for seventeen years up to the northern part of Arabia to find Jesus for himself. The thing I like most about Paul's testimony is that it encourages all who receive Jesus, especially if we feel completely alone, that we do not need anyone to confirm the authenticity of who Christ is in us.

Here is a nugget of wisdom. A best friend is one who desires nothing from you, except to be your friend. He or she does not desire a relationship with you to have access to your money or talent…everything is centered on your relationship. If you are not in the position to freely receive from someone, but you have to give before you receive, that may be a relationship you really do not want. There are others who will understand who you are, and it will be a blessing for them to give of themselves to you. Like Paul, you must dwell with people who see you as a blessing and not as a curse. Never stay where your authenticity is not recognized.

Not everyone is meant to be in your inner circle. Jesus knew that when He picked out twelve disciples, yet only allowed three to become truly close to Him. You have to watch out for people that try to get into "one of the three" positions, yet they are not supposed to be there. You have to be very sure that your authenticity is based on what the Father says to you, and not on what people are trying to convince you of.

If your friends are trying to promote your career and your passion, and that is the reason you are doing what you do, then you might as well put a hold on everything until you discover the will of God for your life. Because once your friends give up on you (and they will as soon as you step outside of the pattern with which they are comfortable), then you will be in a world of hurt trying to pursue a purpose that was not authentically yours in the first place. Take this word of advice: *Find your purpose and then open up your circle of friends.*

When David arrived in the devastation of Ziklag (see 1 Sam. 30) and all of his "friends" were picking up stones to kill him, he said (and I am paraphrasing), "Wait a minute, I am not here because of you. I am here because of what God has anointed me to do."

You will not have to act like you are someone special when God has already anointed you. When *He anoints you*, you will become who are you meant to be *in Him*, regardless of what other people's opinions might be. The fact that they want to "stone you" when troubles come will reveal they do not understand your authenticity.

Open Layers of Authenticity

When I speak of **Open Layers of Authenticity**, I am communicating that God will always lead you to the next "layer" of your authenticity. As His virtues manifest within you, new "layers" (depths) of who you are in Christ are revealed. *Do you know that God is building something inside of you? Do you have a two-year or five-year plan by which you are working, that is also working for you?* I am not referring to goals that you speak of; I am talking about actually having the goals written on paper (as mentioned in the last chapter), including a time line, a chronological map, and references.

How many of those goals have you seen come to pass in the last five years? The authenticity of knowing what God can do is to have the ability to pull up a track record of what He has already done in your life. I am certain this is one of the reasons why Revelation 12:11 says, "And they have overcome (conquered) him by means of the blood of the Lamb and by the utterance of their testimony…" (AMP). Your testimony is the time line, chronological map, and point of reference to God's completed work in your life—and this enables you to gain victory over the enemy both *right now* and *in the future.*

For generations the church has been teaching the lost how to miss going to hell, to the detriment of demonstrating to them how to make sure they are going to heaven. Most people come to the altar to receive Jesus because they want a guarantee they are not going to hell. This puts a mindset within them that they never want to qualify themselves for heaven, meaning growing closer to God and walking in His abundance now. On the other hand, when you let God qualify you for heaven, meaning justifying you, but also by working His virtues in your life, you will not even think of waiting to die before reaping eternal rewards.

You would never take a job where the employer told you, "This is going to be your minimum base pay…I am going to meet your all of your needs, but you will not get promoted to abundance, increase, prosperity, or success until you die. If you work for me, only your basic needs will be taken care of now, and when you die you will get all of the benefits."

On the other hand, you would gladly choose an employer that says, "We are going to give you a good salary, and the necessary increases to enable you to live in a new home; and, by the way, here is your benefits package. You will choose how long it takes for you to arrive at the professional level you desire, and here are the plans for you to consider. If you earn a Master's degree you will get a $45,000 increase. If you take ten years to get it, then you will hold up that additional earning potential for that period of time." By then, $45,000 could have devalued to $25,000. If you do not choose correctly, you could lose a possible immediate benefit and minimize the greater benefit down the road.

What I just described in the last scenario is referred to as *incentive*. Every viable corporation has incentives. In the spiritual realm, one of the greatest incentives of the Kingdom is authenticity. If you are authentic, you will begin to operate in your incentives and you will reap the benefits as you *practice*. For example, I know that I am called to preach, and I also know that my wife is called to be a Prophetess and a voice to the nations. We both grew up in the church; we were in the pews when we were babies. For the level of our calling, it was very important to God that He raised each of us up from a lineage of people who had been called before us into His prophetic purpose.

About a month ago, I was preaching when I accidentally hit the pulpit and cracked the amethyst on my Bishop's ring. While I was in the process of sending it out for repair and giving instructions that I had to get it back soon, the Lord said, "I need to break the mold of your being 'churchy.' What I am about to do for you in the next three years means that you cannot go on national television, or in any venue, as the person who is wearing a familiar cross around his neck and a ring on his hand, but as the person that I am getting ready to make you. In short, God was telling me that I have to open up another layer of authenticity.

He had to break off my habit of wearing the cross and the Bishop's ring, unless there was official business that required me to wear these items, such as an ordination night. Now, God only allows me to bring out these items at the appropriate time. I said, "Yes, Lord." For me, that constituted a major change.

Then God started intimating with me, "I have to open you up to another layer. People will be coming, looking for you to fulfill ministry opportunities." Trust me, these new associations will pass me by if I do not look like *what He wants me to be*. That means I had to submit to the success of God in *becoming* what He was revealing in my spirit, even as He was speaking it...because again, people only see the "you" that is about to change, because the new you is yet to come. Bearing this in mind, it is vital for you to be in your place, knowing, understanding, and practicing in the area of your prophetic purpose before an authentic "model" of Christ in you can be seen by the world.

This takes me back to the first virtue listed in Philippians 4:8, because the entire process of what God is forming in your life begins with *whatsoever is true*. When you embrace the truth about your authenticity, it completes the cycle of your current level, because that is where the Father connects with you...in truth. From this birthing place, He empowers you with the ability to inundate yourself with passion and purpose for your next level of virtue. In its simplest form, *layers of authenticity* means that something new has taken place in your life. Authenticity declares that which is yet to be revealed, like Peter did in Mark 8:29: "...Thou art the Christ." After Jesus' resurrection they did not immediately perceive who He was. He had to reveal Himself to them on a new level. No more could they view Him as just being Jesus, the Son of God. They had to acknowledge Him as *the Christ*—the Resurrected Son of God, King of kings and Lord of lords.

That is why Jesus said in John 20:27 (and again I am paraphrasing), "Look, Thomas I want you to put your hand into My side, because I want you to *touch* authenticity. I want you to experience the form of My next level of authenticity."

When God moves you to a new level, you have to let the people who need to grow with you to that level, see you in your new level. You cannot hide what God is doing in your life and expect anyone else to appreciate it.

Jesus could have risen from death and gone directly to His Father, and His disciples would never have seen anything more than an empty tomb—but that is not God's pattern. He always creates a model of what had already been established. The disciples never would have never known the authenticity of what Jesus had become unless He allowed His new "form" to be seen and experienced by them.

I was in prayer recently when the Lord stopped me, and then told me to not ask Him for my next level until I could believe Him for it. He told me to not ask for it if I could not "think" it, because if you cannot "think" your next level, then you are not ready to receive it—and He will not move you into it. People who ask for the "next level" are those who become attached to purpose. Purpose always leads you into a *progression*. When you have purpose, your focus should always be looking toward where that purpose is leading you. I said that to establish this point: When you are trying to find authenticity, but you have no sense of prophetic purpose, you will always be trying to identify your level. Jesus said that He had no other purpose but to do His Father's will. He did not concern Himself with identifying His next level; He was busy "doing" what the Father identified for Him to do.

Do yourself a favor. Stop asking God to show you the next level. Now, bear in mind there are some who still need to ask because they need to find their purpose. But the real key for you, if you have already started walking in God's path of purpose for your life, is to embrace the fact that you are becoming a model for those who are to follow. If by "thinking on" the virtues, and they are already being displayed in your life, you should already have received instruction from God about your prophetic purpose, because the will of the Father is being played out in you already.

Before you choose another friend, have your plan ready, to see if he or she can connect with it. Before you let anybody connect with your "next day," have at least a three and one-half year plan and see if they can pick up something that connects with it. If they do not have a plan, they will not know why they are supposed to be with you. You have authenticity because of what Jesus endured on the Cross, and because you keep your flesh on "the cross" by virtue of maintaining an ongoing relationship with the Lord.

When you "pick up" people around you that do not understand the mission of your assignment, they will never allow you to reach another open layer of your authenticity. The bottom line is this: As you allow God to continue the "modeling" process—even if he breaks a mold to bring you into a new one—you will continually rise to new levels of skillfulness and fruitfulness in His Kingdom.

Distinctive Attributes

I want to review a little right here. First, you must *manifest personal authenticity*. Then you must *be open to new layers of authenticity*. Next, you must be willing to display your **Distinctive Attributes**. The value of who you are comes from what you have mastered. Are you considered to be "average" by your peers? Do you have some difficulties in your life that, try as you may, you have not been able to overcome? Have you been dealing with the consequences of unusual situations, like perhaps dropping out of school or not being able to finish college? Have you been through a divorce and now you are a single parent with two or three small children? If so, understand this. God is a loving Father who will take *distinctive attributes* about your personality and your difficulties in life, and make them work *in your favor* when people see that your struggle has formed you even more richly into your Father's image.

Let's return to the illustration about model homes. The thing that attracts you to a particular model is its *distinctiveness*. There is a specific area—like the oversized bathroom in the master bedroom, the skylights in the kitchen, specialty staircases, an office with a tremendous outside view, the circular drive-way, the type of brick being used, or perhaps even a specialty swimming pool or Jacuzzi. What keeps you sold on investing in a particular home is its *distinctiveness*.

Distinctiveness will always cause you to celebrate why you invested in something in the first place. Generic items have less perceived value. You would not be satisfied about investing in something that has no *distinguishing* characteristics. This is why Philippians 4:9 (as quoted from the *Amplified Bible*) speaks in terms of "modeling your way." Do you think

Christ would have been satisfied relinquishing His heavenly role, taking on the "form" of men, and living a life of obedience and devotion until He was ultimately crucified, resurrected, and glorified, if He thought you would receive the gift of salvation only to remain exactly as you were when you first encountered Him? I do not think so.

God wants you to be a model for others, so He wants you to display your *distinctive attributes*. *Distinctive attributes* are the characteristics that God puts in you that are absolutely mandatory to shape the model to which other people can relate. Your *distinctive attributes* also create the criteria and the qualities in you that enable you to begin moving into your next level of assignment with God and man. *Have you ever wondered why God has moved friends out of your life that were no longer supposed to be around you?* It was because they could not appreciate *new distinctions*. God moves people away from you, because they will not add to or celebrate new levels of distinction in your life. Your new friends will testify of and prophesy true *distinctiveness*.

Nicodemus (one of the chief Pharisees) went to Jesus privately one night and said, "...no man can do these miracles that thou doest, except God be with him" (John 3:2). Nicodemus was seeking answers to questions he had probably been asking for years. Jesus got right to the point, "Verily, verily...Except a man be born again, he cannot see the kingdom of God" (v. 3). Why did Jesus mention the Kingdom? He was emphasizing to Nicodemus that he needed to understand the process of salvation in order to enter the Kingdom.

Everything that has been written in the Bible leads us to an understanding of how to live from a Kingdom perspective. Salvation will save you from the penalty of death; but it is only through living a virtue-directed life that God will teach you, over time, about the Kingdom. Many who have been in church for years do not yet appreciate the true value of the Kingdom of Heaven. We do not appreciate or acknowledge the Kingdom that is within us.

Instead, the body of Christ is filled with people who have found the model that grandma left them. No one has peeked into the supernatural realm to find a new model for the Kingdom that can only be found in Jesus. We still "sweat" the old issues.

Another aspect of *distinctive attributes* that we have missed is that when we discover a distinguishing attribute, we apply more attention to it than to the God who modeled it. This is extremely dangerous. Let me explain why. Let's say you suddenly discover that you have started walking in the authority of God. You get so excited about it that everyone around you starts trying to find out why. Then they start trying to imitate you...*but they cannot imitate authenticity.* If you are not authentic in God, you might as well stop trying to "copycat" someone else and start looking inside of you, asking God to show you who you really are.

When I lift up my hands to God, He immediately recognizes and opens up my spirit. He knows my voice. When I bend my knees, God knows my prayer before I start praying. When I open my mouth, He knows my heart-felt desire before the words are released into the atmosphere. When I speak blessing to Him, He sees my passion. That is authentic.

You must appreciate and celebrate the unique works God has performed in your life, because those things are what identify you as being authentic. One of the families in our church just had a baby boy. The baby was born several months premature. After I got the news that they were admitting the mother in the hospital, I knew while I was praying this was a sign that their son was going to be distinctive. The mother's water had broken prematurely, and the baby was not supposed to live, so they had to take him early.

Just recently, the father brought me pictures. Looking at that blessed little boy you can see the spirit of enlightenment that is already on his life. When he grows up, knowing and appreciating the circumstances surrounding his birth, he will understand that he has a distinctive call. If you do not celebrate anything else, celebrate the things that no one knows about you, but you. These things celebrate who you are, because whether you realize it or not, God has already modeled them in your character.

While sharing recently with a well-known Christian minister, he shared something with me that was powerful. Through this, I saw a model of what was unfolding in my life. I had not known that he had already experienced some of the things I was going through. Later, while I was sitting with another Christian leader at dinner he just stopped, turned to me, and said, "I need to tell you this story...." What he told me was profound, something that I never would have imagined he had been through. The experience he shared with me was so compelling, I listened as if I were paralyzed in my chair. I could not move for about ten minutes, at the shock of hearing what he had gone through. That was an unequivocally authentic experience...as he openly shared with me about a season when he had faced the greatest struggle of his life.

I, too, had gone through a gut-wrenching season where everybody laughed at me, the wise Bishop. People talked terribly about me while I was going through the throes of change. And though other people may never understand why God let me go through it all, in His mercy God allowed me to recognize the reason. *No one will understand the transition that gives you the depth to be able to hear from God on a new level.* Hear me. Your distinction comes through the difficulties you overcome. It was not fun while I was going through the process, still sitting alone asking God, "Why?" There were many days when I asked God why I had invested all I had to that point. That is when He reminded me—He had already told me to get rid of the "old things."

You cannot hold on to "old things" and walk into a *new level* with God. Recently He told me again, "I am going to take everything that represents where you began, because I am going to start you in an entirely new place." That is why I knew, sitting at the restaurant with a father of ministry today, that when he stopped (yielding to the prophet inside of him), and said, "I don't know why I am telling you this, but I just need to say it..." he began to share details about his life that related so powerfully to what God had walked me through. This confirmed deep in my spirit that I had walked through an authentic experience.

I would never have known today that this internationally known pastor had once lived in a garage. You never know what God is going to take you through, so that one day when you open your mouth and tell somebody about it, that person will be able to say, "Oh, God, now I know you are really in my life; because if he survived I know that I can, too."

He began to mentor me and give me words of wisdom from a heart that had been prepared by having gone through the same thing I experienced. With such a heart of compassion he invited me to share some time with him, "...I want to just sit down with you and tell you some things." I often wonder why God has blessed me with friends in ministry all over the country. But instinctively, I know. He took me through a test that determined I could handle *distinction*. Unless you are tested for *distinction*, people who look at you think you are just "churchy"—but it is through what you survive and overcome that enables people to recognize the favor God has added to the "form" of your walk with Him. Now, I can confidently say I am a man of distinction, because God has brought me through the process.

No one can hinder your destiny. Because no individual can put up his or her hand and stop the wind (see John 3:8). No man can build a wall that is big enough to stop the wind. No weapon that has been formed against your life will stop God's pre-planned, *authentic* destiny that has been ordained for your life. That is why, as Jesus counseled Nicodemus, you must also get a revelation about the Spirit realm. When you begin to praise the Spirit of the Living God, you are saying, "Continue to blow on me." The Lord recently spoke to me while I was waking up, saying, "This is the 10th day of the month and you are 30 days away from your conference. I am about to send people." That is when I started seeing people register from Texas and Jacksonville.

He said, "I am blowing a wind. I am going to blow a wind around the world. People are going to show up because you are getting ready to be a place of birthing." I asked, "Lord, why are You reminding me?" He said, "I want to birth some things early." God wants to take some things that are about to happen (in another season) and get them started early. Hear me! He is going to start setting some things in motion earlier than the enemy anticipates.

After you manifest personal authenticity, are open to layers of authenticity, you have to grow and be challenged to drop old things to embrace *distinctive attributes*. God is always going to challenge you to greater depths in Him because there are always new things on the horizon. He is in the process of defining you with *distinction*. Listen to me, now. He is in the process of re-qualifying you so that people, 1) Are not put off by your "churchiness," or 2) Do not want to trust your distinctiveness. Philippians 4:13 says, "I have strength for all things in Christ Who empowers me [I am ready for anything and equal to anything through Him Who infuses inner strength into me; I am self-sufficient in Christ's sufficiency]" (AMP).

If I had never experienced need, I would never reach out to tap into His sufficiency. Because God is sufficient, He keeps a need before you so that He can show you how much He is willing to be sufficiently Christ in your life. He allows the need to be there so that He can sufficiently supply it. And because He supplies it, my trust in Him grows far greater as He models His virtues in my life—because as I embrace *distinctiveness* I have ceased to rely on my own sufficiency or self-righteousness. I trust in Him who is the Christ.

E...He Empowers Your Strength, Giving, and Partnership

Philippians 4:14–15 continues, "But it was right and commendable of you to contribute for my needs and to share my difficulties with me. And you Philippians yourselves well know that in the early days of the Gospel ministry, when I left Macedonia, no church (assembly) entered into partnership with me and opened up [a debit and credit] account in giving and receiving except you only" (AMP). The individuals in this passage were so mature that they decided to sow into Paul's ministry because they were *Empowered by Christ's Strength in Giving and Partnership*. If you want your giving to go to another level, start trusting God for what He wants to supply in your life.

Paul was teaching the people to appreciate the strength that God gives, which enabled them to do what He had called them to do. When Christ is dwelling in your heart you should not struggle with need. Your need should be met because of His sufficiency; because He is the authority of your life and wants to live virtuously in you, He does not want to live in a vessel who is stressing over physical need. If you are stressed in this area, hear me— you will never have a relationship with Him, as it should be. You will always look first to what has met your need (in the natural realm) or what looks like it can meet the need, instead of acknowledging the Source who can retire the need...permanently.

When you trust in your own sufficiency instead of Christ's sufficiency, you are in trouble. Because, again, the reason you are experiencing need is to make you activate His sufficiency *in you*. This represents yet another level of modeling. Because you trust in Him, and because you love Him, you are willing to make the sacrifices needed—because you are assured that He is able to produce *whatsoever is needed* in your life. In other words, your countenance begins to become a model of trusting Christ in you.

Paul was showing the believers in Philippi how much they had grown in trusting Christ's sufficiency. I can almost hear him saying, "Of all the churches I have visited, you were the only ones that thought about my well-being in such a tangible way. You were the only ones that were so strengthened in Christ that you could think about giving and partnership. You are so strengthened that you are willing to give and partner with me like no other church has ever done." That was a powerful commendation.

In this short, four-chapter book to the church at Philippi, Paul shares intimately about how he is able to model his life because of his sufficiency in Christ. Paul had stated earlier in his letter (paraphrased), "I have learned how to be abased. I have learned how to abound. I have learned how to suffer need, and I have learned how to have abundance." Think about these timeless words of truth. There will always be times when you do not have as much as you think you will have, and there will always be something that you will not have enough of, but do not let that distract your focus. These are the very reasons why you need Christ in your life. He will meet every need with all sufficiency. But beware, if you try to fill the "need" yourself and fail you will suffer from depression and unbelief, because you will feel that He has not supplied to you as He had promised.

Most of us consider our job to be our source of supply until a need comes that it is not able to meet. When you are content to live only from the proceeds of a nine-to-five job, I dare say that you are not letting Christ be your sufficiency. You have not discovered the joy of knowing that He is your Source. He is your all in all. See this as a necessary step in the modeling process, because unless people can see not only His virtues, but also His blessings, modeled in and through your life, they will not be able to believe that Christ will do the same for them.

Jesus did not perform the miracle of healing as His first miracle, because the first miracle of Christ is creativity. Let me explain. The first work of Christ in your life is your salvation. The first miracle of Christ takes place when He *causes you to create* what other people need. If you do not have the capacity to create what other people need, you will have no value here on earth. Christ put you exactly where you are, not simply for you to attend church once a week and call yourself saved. He called you so you could be part of the need-meeting "model" that we know to be the Kingdom of God on earth.

Christ's sufficiency in you will never allow you to look at lack and call it lack. What may be low is not lack when you have Christ's sufficiency. I am sure that President Bush does not have to carry money, because of the sufficiency of his office. If he identifies a need, his office gives him the sufficiency to satisfy it.

There are two dynamics that must come into play. Christ gives you His Spirit so that you can start modeling His sufficiency, but you cannot activate the sufficiency until you have received (joined to yourself) the mind of Christ. If Christ is in you, then He is going to meet all of your needs. There is no question about it. When you have a need, He cannot ignore that need when your mind acknowledges Him in everything you do. If the Spirit of Christ lives inside of you, and you have a need (having already "put on" the mind of Christ through "thinking on" His virtues), He cannot ignore giving you the potential to access the sufficiency of His office.

The real value of an image or model is that it gives you sufficiency. You cannot walk as though you do not have a relationship with Christ and expect to have sufficiency. Why? Christ is not going to give value to somebody who is not willing to expand his or her capacity to receive it. Therefore, some things in you will have to change. You can own a plastic watch for a season; however, you must realize there are some things that must grow with you in with authenticity.

One of the hardest things for people to understand is the process. Jesus wore a robe that had been made from one piece of thread. Three years later, when His disciples were with Him in the Garden of Gethsemane, Judas had to identify Jesus because His disciples had started modeling His sufficiency. At the beginning of His ministry they could have walked right up to Jesus and said, "That is Jesus, right there." By the time He prayed in the garden before His crucifixion, the disciples looked so much like Him that sufficiency was all over them. *Wouldn't it be wonderful if we really started believing what Christ has already "vested" in us to achieve?* Remember, what you model yourself after is the "image" you have been taught is your level and limit. So, again, watch for your God-appointed mentors carefully—make sure they have been where you are going.

I was sitting in Phoenix, Arizona, at a book signing. While I was signing books, the Lord had reminded me that He had already prompted me to write the book *Even as Your Soul Prospers*. It was already in my spirit. I already had the chapters written...but then He taught me something new right there in Family Christian Bookstore. He told me to go ask the salesperson to print a list of every book that had the word *soul* in the title. He brought me a printout, and it only had three titles on it...and they did not carry any of the three choices. That taught me it is not enough to do something; you must do something *that is needed*.

The Lord confirmed to me on a piece of paper that no one was writing about the soul. No one was marrying prosperity to the image within according to 3 John 1:2: "Beloved, I wish above all things that thou mayest prosper and be in health, even as thy soul prospereth." Do not join a church that is prospering if your soul is not going to prosper. If you cannot grow

WHAT'S ON YOUR MIND?

and become *distinctive* within yourself, three years from now you will still be in as much debt as you were when you first walked through the door. Your soul must prosper first. It must be transformed by the virtues of God.

Check out the person you are modeling your life after, either directly or indirectly. Check out his or her prayer life. See if it would be worthwhile modeling after them. Does this person get results from God? Paul told the Philippian church (paraphrased), "You celebrated me, and because you celebrated me, we are in partnership. What you have sowed unto me, I am now going to partner with you. I am going to open up my life so that you can see what is in me. You sowed with all sufficiency, so you can get the results of becoming what you have never seen in anybody else—because you will know how to value your substance." Hear me. When you start modeling your life after the Kingdom, you will start getting results.

When I heard God say, "Let Me supply the need," I knew that I no longer had to carry the burden. He is providing marvelously for our church daily; we are expanding our television ministry, and people all over the world are being saved because of our website. Because of the enormity of the vision, we are letting God supply that need.

Let God Supply Your Need

Philippians 4:19 says, "But my God shall supply all your need according to his riches in glory by Christ Jesus." This brings us to the last point, **Let God Supply Your Need**. In Matthew 17, when Peter approached Jesus about paying a tribute to Caesar, He said (and I am paraphrasing), "I need you to do something, Peter. I need you to go and become a prophetic pipe for Me. I need you to catch the very first fish. I need you to look in its mouth and pull out the coin. Peter, go to a place that is familiar to you. Pull out the first fish; *pull out the first thing the Spirit says to you* (see Matt. 17:24–27). When Christ wants to get His sufficiency to you, He always sends you to a familiar place to produce the wealth you need.

Jesus needs you to catch what the Spirit has in His mouth for you. This means you need to speak only what the Spirit says to you. Notice inside of the fish's mouth was a coin that was sufficient to pay the taxes. A fish cannot eat a coin of that size. The fish picked up something that someone else had lost. It could not walk up to somebody's house, and go into his or her wallet, and pull out a coin. When you begin to model your way after God, He will allow things that you are familiar with to come into contact with resources that somebody else either forgot or lost. Paraphrasing, it is like Jesus was saying to Peter, "If you catch the spirit of why God wants you to obey My order of going about it this way, you will receive the reward of the Spirit." I am blessed because the Lord has chosen to favor me. I decided that whenever the Spirit of the Lord ministers to me about doing something that is powerful, I would not miss expanding my capacity to be obedient.

Take this challenge. Who have you looked at that has set the limitations of why you have become who you are today? Who told you that all you can handle is being a clerical worker, a cook, or a stay-at-home housewife? Who has limited all that you have modeled your way after? Who told you that all you could do is simple accounting or teaching elementary school? Now, if this is something you feel called to, that's different. But if you are doing something only because you feel your abilities limit you to doing only that, who sets the limits for you?

Consider what Christ has done for you and begin to "model your way of living on it," because you will never appreciate another level of living until you walk into a new experience with God. If He does not have the authority in your mind (because you have not "put on" the mind of Christ by "thinking on" His virtues), then how can He model Christ's sufficiency in your life? Let God meet your needs, and you will become a "model" of excellence.

CHAPTER 11

And the God of Peace Will Be With You: Staying Close to Move With God

Before listing the virtues of God, Paul established the founding principle governing all that would follow:

> *Do not fret or have any anxiety about anything, but in every circumstance and in everything, by prayer and petition (definite requests), with thanksgiving, continue to make your wants known to God. And God's peace [shall be yours, that tranquil state of a soul assured of its salvation through Christ, and so fearing nothing from God and being content with its earthly lot of whatever sort that is, that peace] which transcends all understanding shall garrison and mount guard over your hearts and minds in Christ Jesus (Phil 4:6–7 AMP).*

In other words, before you can even set your mind's focus to "thinking on" the six virtues of God in the two verses that follow, inclining your heart to virtue and praise, practicing and modeling what you have learned, you have to put away every troubling anxiety by making your wants known to God. And here is the good part...*His peace* that puts your soul into a state of tranquility, because you are eternally secure and satisfied, will flood your inner man and give you an unexplainable sense of well-being. Though you may be looking at trouble on every side, it cannot come near you—because

God is guarding your heart and mind with His unmistakable peace. How can this level of peace be possible? Let's go to Psalm 91:

> *He who dwells in the secret place of the Most High shall remain stable and fixed under the shadow of the Almighty [Whose power no foe can withstand]. I will say of the Lord, He is my Refuge and my Fortress, my God; on Him I lean and rely, and in Him I [confidently] trust! For [then] He will deliver you from the snare of the fowler and from the deadly pestilence. [Then] He will cover you with His pinions, and under His wings shall you trust and find refuge; His truth and His faithfulness are a shield and a buckler.*
>
> *You shall not be afraid of the terror of the night, nor of the arrow (the evil plots and slanders of the wicked) that flies by day, nor of the pestilence that stalks in darkness, nor of the destruction and sudden death that surprise and lay waste at noonday. A thousand may fall at your side, and ten thousand at your right hand, but it shall not come near you. Only a spectator shall you be [yourself inaccessible in the secret place of the Most High] as you witness the reward of the wicked. Because you have made the Lord your refuge, and the Most High your dwelling place...(vv. 1–9 AMP).*

Do you hear this promise? If you stay in God's "secret place," you will remain stable and fixed under His shadow, leaning, relying, and confidently trusting in Him! When you start every day "saying" the Lord is your refuge, your steadfast confession will release you to walk in a continual state of deliverance, having no fear of the enemy! As you learn to dwell in His "secret place," you will only be a spectator of the calamity that befalls those who trust in their own strength and abilities, refusing the grace that Jesus died and rose again to give them so freely. But it shall not be so with you and your house! You are eternally blessed in His presence.

Oh, yes, when you set the "secret place of the Most High" as your "starting block" each day, you will not struggle with applying His virtues in your life. By simply staying under His shadow, you are close enough to just "breathe them in." You are close enough to feel how God moves in every situation, so that you can instinctively do what you see your Father doing. When you make the Most High your dwelling place, you will walk differently, talk differently, love your family more excellently, take care of business more thoroughly, worship with more integrity, and serve with more fervency. God's virtues are better "caught" than "taught." You can expedite your destiny by resting under His wings. Now, let's look at what you can look forward to by dwelling there:

> *The LORD is my Shepherd [to feed, guide, and shield me], I shall not lack. He makes me lie down in [fresh, tender] green pastures; He leads me beside the still and restful waters. He refreshes and restores my life (my self); He leads me in the paths of righteousness [uprightness and right standing with Him—not for my earning it, but] for His name's sake.*
>
> *Yes, though I walk through the [deep, sunless] valley of the shadow of death, I will fear or dread no evil, for You are with me; Your rod [to protect] and Your staff [to guide], they comfort me. You prepare a table before me in the presence of my enemies. You anoint my head with oil; my [brimming] cup runs over. Surely or only goodness, mercy, and unfailing love shall follow me all the days of my life, and through the length of my days the house of the Lord [and His presence] shall be my dwelling place" (Ps. 23:1–6, emphasis mine).*

Praise God Almighty! No wonder Paul starts with God, and then ends with God, with respect to applying His virtues in Philippians 4:6–9! As I said before, the thought that "the God of peace" will be with me is the loveliest thought of all. There is nothing better than being in the presence of the Lord. He is the Alpha and the Omega, the First and Last; He is the King of kings and Lord of Lords; He is the bright Morning Star…Wonderful, Counselor, Mighty God, Everlasting Father, Prince of Peace. What could possibly be better? What could even compare?

Now, before I move on, I want you to think about this: In order to become a model, God must shape you by causing you to lie still in a "mold" that He has fashioned just for you. So I submit to you—when you stay under the shadow of the Almighty, you are already inside of His "form." *As you rest "in" His form you "take on" His form.* And the longer you lie still in His presence, the better *His form* will be set *in you.* So in applying godly virtues we must begin with prayer, being careful to jealously guard the time we spend with God in His "secret place"—for it is God that *works in us* both to will and to do of His good pleasure (see Phil. 2:12–13).

This is also why Jesus made this promise in Matthew 11:28–30:

> **Come to Me, all you who labor and are heavy-laden and over-burdened, and I will cause you to rest. [I will ease and relieve and refresh your souls.] Take My yoke upon you and learn of Me, for I am gentle (meek) and humble (lowly) in heart, and you will find rest (relief and ease and refreshment and recreation and blessed quiet) for your souls. For My yoke is wholesome (useful, good—not harsh, hard, sharp, or pressing, but comfortable, gracious, and pleasant), and My burden is light and easy to be borne.**

Jesus was not saying we would never have to expend any effort; "taking" His teachings (yoke) upon ourselves implies action. Jesus was promising that when we come to Him, a supernatural rest would refresh our souls as we go about applying His virtues in our daily lives.

With that said, I would like to give you an acronym just for "good measure," but I am not breaking down the text as I have before…because by now I hope you agree: *the peace of God cannot be measured.* When you are walking with "the God of peace" you are:

- **P** urposed, *you are no longer struggling to find meaning in your life*
- **E** lected, *you understand that you have been specially chosen by God*
- **A** ssured, *you are confident of Christ's finished work in your life*
- **C** alled by God, *you understand God's purpose and assignment for you*
- **E** ternally Justified, *you are eternally innocent in the Father's eyes*

Starting on the Path of Peace...

It was Friday, June 13th. Superstitious people say that is a day you should not do much of anything, but for me it will always be a day to remember. Pastor Rufus Saunders was in town preaching about "Heartbreak Hotel." I was sitting in church watching people coming out of the Holy Spirit receiving room, one after another. That is when the Holy Spirit spoke to me and said, "Tonight is your night."

I walked into the receiving room, and sat down as a woman opened her Bible. She said, "I want to read two Scriptures to you. Close your eyes, lift your hands, and speak." I had been baptized in water when I was five, so I had been tarrying for eight years to receive this heavenly gift. Truth be told, you can lose hope after eight years—you can lose a whole lot of hope. Eventually your spirit can become retarded to the things of the Spirit. If a child is seven or eight years old and cannot say "Mommy" or "Daddy," some vital developmental function has been retarded in its growth. Yet, as I lifted my hands and closed my eyes, I instantly began speaking in tongues.

I came out of the room, practicing speaking in tongues all the way down the hall. I wanted to make sure I had it! I realized that as I was speaking, I could not stop. So I went into the sanctuary, still speaking in tongues. I went into the bathroom and tried to close my mouth so the words would stop coming out, but I was still speaking in tongues! My eight-year-old brother was so impressed he decided that he wanted to receive the Holy Ghost...so he got up, went into the receiving room, and received the Holy Ghost that very night.

When I reflect on that special night, I am so thankful for this precious heavenly gift God has provided for His church. Our children need to receive the gift of the Holy Spirit. If we take them to the house of the Lord, and teach them about the Holy Spirit, they will receive...even if they are just four or five years old. Children can receive the gift more quickly than adults, because their desire to receive it is pure. There is nothing like seeing your children experience the presence *and peace* of God at an early age.

Now, let's go back to our foundational text in Philippians 4 and read Paul's instructions again on how to live a life of "...untroubled, undisturbed well-being..."—a life that is only made possible by walking with the *God of peace* and dwelling in His "secret place."

Practice what you have learned and received and heard and seen in me, and model your way of living on it, and the God of peace (of untroubled, undisturbed well-being) will be with you (v. 9 AMP).

Growing in Grace...

To explore this text in a different light, I would like to take you to the book of Romans, because I love Paul's attention to detail. He does not leave out anything that is necessary for our growth. Paul is so straightforward that by the time he gets to the seventh chapter, he is openly talking about his own issues. The Book of Romans reveals that God, our heavenly Father, gives us the power of salvation through His Word, yet He also challenges us to deal with real day-to-day situations.

Paul says, "For I am not ashamed of the gospel of Christ: for it is the power of God unto salvation to every one that believeth; to the Jew first, and also to the Greek" (Rom. 1:16). If you really love God you cannot be ashamed of the gospel that He is calling you to live...because your salvation is a "gospel" to someone else. Your testimony or "distinctiveness" (as we discovered so richly in a previous chapter) is a living "model" that tells the world about the God you serve. If no one can see God in your life, then the "gospel" is hidden.

This is why we must take upon ourselves the "yoke" of Christ and deal with our issues, because the gospel can easily be hidden by our weaknesses. The Word will become of no effect. As Paul progresses to the eighth chapter he begins to open up some things to us. He says, "O wretched man that I am! Who shall deliver me from the body of this death?" (see Rom. 7:24). Then he asks an important question, "Where is my deliverance?" "Who can deliver me from the 'me' no one knows?" We already know our answer from Psalm 91, but let's bring this spiritual reality to a practical level. People around you know the "you" that you show them, but you must know who delivers you from the "you" no one knows.

Paul answers the question, "There is therefore now no condemnation to them which are in Christ Jesus, who walk not after the flesh, but after the Spirit" (Rom. 8:1). You will not walk in condemnation when you are "in" Christ Jesus—abiding in the shadow of the Almighty and walking after the Spirit. Think about it. If you had never recognized you were dying, you would never have sought true life. Paul recognized that he was at the point of a miserable death. He was asking, "How do I get delivered from this body that is constantly tempting me to sin?" In Romans 8:2 Paul continues, "For the law of the Spirit of life in Christ Jesus hath made me free from the law of sin and death."

No matter how much you love your pastor and trust his prayers for you, it is the Holy Spirit that must take up intercession for you in some situations. Paul makes it clear that it is only through the mind of the Spirit that you can know the will of the Father for your life. God alone is able to produce that which is the mantra and the mandate of His glory.

I want to encourage you before I go any further. God's glory cannot be hindered when the Holy Spirit is making intercession on your behalf. Jesus told Peter, even before Peter denied Him, that He had prayed for him and his faith would not fail (Luke 22:31–32). I do not know about you, but it encourages me greatly to know that the Lord cares for me so much that He is praying for me, even though He sees all of my weaknesses and failures. Oh, yes, I have discovered that when I am in my weakest state, I find my greatest strength in Him (see 2 Cor. 12:9).

Blessed Assurance...

So far, we have learned how to receive His peace and have looked at the process God uses to impart it to us—*but do you understand how to recognize when you are walking with the God of Peace?* We all want to experience the "abundant life" that Jesus came to give us, but how do we know when we are living in that life? Before you can live abundantly you must understand His peace; this state of "...untroubled, undisturbed well-being ..." Romans 8:28 tells us, "We are assured and know that [God being a partner in their labor] all things work together and are [fitting into a plan] for good to and for those who love God and are called according to [His] design and purpose" (AMP).

Before you can walk with the God of Peace, and live a life of peace, you must have the assurance that you are His child, one of His own. If you do not understand your purpose, and do not have the assurance He is in control of your life, there is no way you will have peace. If you lack eternal assurance you will struggle with coming to rest under His wings.

Peace starts with the assurance that God knew you before the foundation of the world: "For those whom He foreknew [of whom He was aware and loved beforehand], He also destined from the beginning [foreordaining them] to be molded into the image of His Son [and share inwardly His likeness], that He might become the firstborn among many brethren" (Rom. 8:29 AMP). *Do you see that?* From the beginning of time God ordained that He would put you into the "mold" of His Son, Jesus Christ. And as long as we are in this human form, we will undergo a consistent "molding" process. Just listen to 2 Corinthians 3:17–18:

> *Now the Lord is the Spirit, and where the Spirit of the Lord is, there is liberty (emancipation from bondage, freedom). And all of us, as with unveiled face, [because we] continued to behold [in the Word of God] as in a mirror the glory of the Lord, are constantly being transfigured into His very own image in ever increasing splendor and from one degree of glory to another; [for this comes] from the Lord [Who is] the Spirit (AMP).*

Is this chapter helping you to gain assurance in God? I certainly hope so, because if you do not have assurance you will not have peace. Think about it in natural terms. The reason you are able to sleep at night is that you have the assurance you are safe—because you either have locks on your doors, have an alarm system, or both. You most likely have smoke detectors in every room. You have the assurance that the dangers which could be lurking around you are being buffered by the "protection" you have set in place... which prevents worry and anxiety from interfering with your sleep.

Have you ever had a "bug night"? That is when you are settling down to go to bed and you spot a bug across the room. You hate bugs, so you pay someone to come in periodically and make sure there are never any bugs in your home. But now there is a bug! Worst of all, you cannot identify what kind of bug it is, so you wonder if there are more where *that one* came from. I had that experience recently and I could not sleep. I had to leave the light on so I would be able to see if there was another bug in the room. I could not sleep until I had the assurance there were no more bugs coming in my room. I finally got up and got a can of bug spray. That little can of bug spray gave me the assurance that I had the situation under control. Now, *in the spiritual realm we cannot sleep or be at peace if we do not have assurance that God has it all in control.* Therefore, we must have the assurance that our relationship with Him is what it should be; and through our relationship with Him we can gain the assurance that we are living in our purpose, the one thing we were created for and our reason for being on this earth.

Not everyone lives with assurance. This is one of the reasons I am careful who I associate with in my walk with God. A person with no assurance has many worries, and these worries can get mixed with your worship and cause your faith to waver. Wavering faith leads to waning worship. It is a good idea to check the level of your assurance from time to time. Ask yourself if you are trusting God as you should. The same Word that brought you to salvation has the power to strengthen your assurance. Remember that if Christ lives in you (*which He does*) and His likeness is in you (*which it is*), God is still in control and you can walk in His peace.

Entering Into Purpose...

Read once more Romans 8:29:

> *For those whom He foreknew [of whom He was aware and loved beforehand], He also destined from the beginning [foreordaining*

them] to be molded into the image of His Son [and share inwardly His likeness], that He might become the firstborn among many brethren (AMP).

Paul says that God *foreknew* us…He destined us, from the beginning, to be molded into the image of His Son. If you do not know what God knew about you from the start, especially concerning what He has purposed for your life, then you are not going to have peace. You must have assurance in the meaning of your existence. If you are living without purpose, then you can have no peace, because you have no assurance of what your purpose is. This may seem elementary, but if you were to ask a lot of people what their purpose is in life, most of them would just shrug their shoulders, look at you, and say, "I don't know."

Let me give you God's first and foremost purpose for your life. Your first purpose is that Christ may be glorified in you. God created every one of us, and He created His likeness in those He foreknew would be His. He foreknew that you would first pursue the fleshly nature that you inherited from Adam, living "after the flesh" with no desire for the spiritual side of your being. So He vested *in you* the desire to want to know Him, thus insuring that you would one day turn to Him in total trust and faith.

It is your choice either to turn to the Lord in faith, or to follow the flesh to your destruction. For example, there is a difference between those who go to church because it is the "right thing" to do, and those who want to *experience God* in worship and truth. Some people reject Him, not obeying the truth they have been given. God knew these people before the foundation of the world; He knew the decisions they would make, just as He knew what your decision would be *before you even knew it.*

God looked down into time and *saw you.* He knew you before you were ever born. Read Psalm 139 in its entirety if you want to gain a clearer understanding of how great God's love is for you. *God searches deep inside of you, looking for that spark of desire for Him.* He sees your obedience (or your disobedience), and is intimately acquainted with your every thought.

There is no place you can run to escape Him. His love will pursue you all the days of your life.

I have heard some ask why God does not punish various people for the horrendous sins they have committed. Others ask why God is delaying His coming for the saints. God is a God of mercy. Second Peter 3:9 tells us: "The Lord is not slack concerning his promise, as some men count slackness; but is longsuffering to us-ward, not willing that any should perish, but that all should come to repentance." Brother or sister, you may be the one that He is waiting for, waiting for you to turn to Him in faith, desiring to spend eternity with Him. He longs for that moment.

Now think with me on this thought: God never puts purpose in someone who will not obey Him. If you are willing to follow Him in obedience, you can be certain that your purpose is sure and secure. You may be thinking, *Well, I love Him. Isn't that enough?* Many people love God, but to love Him does not necessarily mean that you are willing to obey Him. *Obedience is the truest part of love* (see John 14:15, 23). It is a sure fact that when I obey someone love is there. You do not obey someone whom you do not love and trust.

If you know that you are not living in complete obedience to God at this moment, I would suggest that you put this book down, bow your head, and get things cleared up between you and God. Many people run to the altar every Sunday. Altar calls do not automatically break curses off of you, but hear me, *obedience will.* Many people run to a counselor to find the answers they are desperately seeking. Even good counsel will not break a curse off of you, but again, *turning to God in obedience will.*

There are two groups of people in the world. Those who are lost and do not know God, and those who have placed their trust in Him. Within these groups there are the *obedient* and the *disobedient.* You may have sought a "word" from a prophet of God. That "word" is only as effective as your obedience. When God gives you His instructions, either through the Word of God, or a Rhema word from a prophet, they will not do you any good unless you pay attention to the instruction and line up with what it requires. Let me add this: When God speaks a word, the virtue to walk in it is already there...just like when God said, "Let there be light..." at the beginning of creation, and it was so. Creation did not have any choice in the matter, but you do.

You can choose whether or not to act on a word you have received, obeying what God has given for your edification, or you can turn away from the word in disobedience. Think about what you would think or feel if you gave your child instructions concerning something specific and he or she disobeyed. Remember, God is a Father who loves His children, but how long do you really want to remain in disobedience to Him?

Are You Letting God Mold You?

Let me go deeper in Romans 8, because verse 29 is loaded with truth. Look again at what it says, "For those whom He foreknew [of whom He was aware and loved beforehand], He also **destined** from the beginning [foreordaining them] to be molded into the image of His Son [and share inwardly His likeness], that He might become the firstborn among many brethren" (AMP).

This reveals a profound truth...you have been *created,* but perhaps you have not yet submitted to the *molding* process I talked about earlier. God has created you in His image, but because you have not learned how to "dwell" with God, you have not been "molded" into His likeness. Molding is a process that grows with obedience. Let me illustrate. You are not the same person you were at six years old. Even though your overall image is most likely still intact, still, you are not the same. If you do not believe me, look at your teeth. You would look pretty funny if you still had your baby teeth, because the structure and size of your jaw has changed.

I know whereof I speak when it comes to teeth. I went through all of the agony of correcting my teeth. Trips to the orthodontist...pulling teeth to correct the spacing...braces, and several years of teasing that go with wearing braces. Now, my daughter Sydney does not need orthodontic work, but if I had looked at her mouth when she was a baby and put braces on her when she was four, five, or six, it would have been a waste of time, because those baby teeth are going to fall out.

Now here is the spiritual application. The reason why God did not save some people when they were much younger is because they still had some growing to do. He had to wait until you got through with all of the "stuff" that was tied to your "baby issues," before He started molding you and "putting braces" on your spirit. You could relate pulling teeth to make space, to fighting the enemy in the spiritual realm. If God had not pulled some things out of your life you would not be able to stand against the enemy today. God cannot mold you until you become mature enough to endure the process. But take heart in the fact that God is "still working on you." Just keep coming to Him in the "secret place" and He'll lead you the rest of the way.

Let us go back to the principles I have covered so far. Number one: God has *purposed* to foreknow you. Number two: He *elected* to foreordain you. Number three: *He calls you son or daughter* when you submit to Him in obedience. We are not all called to the same purpose, but we each have to determine what His purpose for us really is. We each have to find our own place in worship and in prayer. You should thank God every day for making you the unique individual you are. There is no one else in the world just like you. He purposed it that way.

I know that I am one of God's own. I have found favor with God...*my favor*, not yours.

Do you want to experience undeniable favor with God? You must go to Him in prayer and praise. John 4:24 says, "God is a Spirit: and they that worship him must worship him in spirit and in truth." You must ask Him for *your favor* because you are made in His likeness and He has favor just for you.

Like I shared before, I know that my praise is authentic and original because I know my purpose. I know that I am called of God, ordained, justified, and glorified. I may be walking on this earth, but I am seated with Him in heavenly places (see Eph. 2:6). *Are you sensing His peace yet?*

When you offer something to God, He does not return it to you by giving you something that is counterfeit. He gives back what you give to Him. He will give back the same measure you have given Him.

Why Did God Choose You?

This brings us to the question that many people ask, "Why did God choose me?" God does not have a referral system in heaven. No one sent in a letter of recommendation for you. God *chose* you because He *knew* you before the foundation of the world. Again, He knew the choice *you* would make. He saw your heart, your desire to know Him. He knew the mistakes you would make, and the times you would disappoint yourself. You could not disappoint God, because in order for Him to be disappointed, He had to have expectations that you would not fall. God expected nothing from you. He already knew, in His wisdom, who you were and who you would become; and knowing this He simply loved you, and chose you to fulfill His purpose. That is awesome! No other word can better describe the joy we should feel when we think of God's great love for us. *He saw us, He knew us, and He chose us anyway.*

I am quite confident that your next question might be, "Why did God choose me, and not someone else?" There are a lot of philosophies and theological discussions on that subject. For years people have debated the matter of "free will" versus "predestination." Let me "toss out" my understanding on the matter in the best way I can. When God looked at you, long before He even created the world, He looked at you *in the spirit*, because He does not deal in the flesh. He looked out through time and space and *He saw you*. He saw, far in the future, what your response to His tender, loving call would be.

Now, there is a difference between foreknowledge and foreordination. God knew from eons past what your choice would be...*He ordained that choice.* You may be wondering what your purpose is and how to determine God's choice for you. The simplest way to determine your purpose is to ask yourself, *What is it that I must do? What is it that I cannot be happy without doing?* **That is your purpose**, the one thing that you know deep in your inner man God desires for you to accomplish. Never give up on that purpose; never throw away that special thing God has "vested" in your heart.

Be careful not to confuse your purpose with your assignment. Your purpose is what God has called you to fulfill, and it is yours for a lifetime. An assignment can be for a season. You may have many assignments in your life that are connected to your purpose, but do not confuse the two. You will have a *knowing* or an *assurance* tied to your purpose, but you will often feel that an assignment is not contributing to anything, or that it is not fulfilling your life.

Most of us want to experience the anointing. Your anointing does not come with your purpose; it comes with your assignment. Your anointing will not always be consistent, because your assignment is seasonal. Your purpose births the favor of God in your life. Favor gives you relationship with God in intimate ways, giving you the ability to accomplish tasks that could otherwise not be done.

When you enter a new season of your life you will need a fresh anointing. That is no problem because God renews our anointing every day. "It is of the Lord's mercies that we are not consumed, because his compassions fail not. They are new every morning: great is thy faithfulness" (Lam. 3:22–23). Now let me ask: *Do you really know your purpose, and are you living from your assignment?* When you know your purpose you will not always be shifting from one goal to another. Your purpose is as near as your heartbeat. In other words, it is extremely hard to miss it.

On the other hand, you will generally not see a look of peace on a person's face who does not have a purpose. Living and walking in the peace of God requires that you know for certain why God put you on this earth, why He called and ordained you, and why He justified you for all eternity. People who know that God not only foreknew them, but destined them to be among the called and the justified, will not struggle in prayer every time trials and testing are taking place. You rarely hear the question, "Why?"

from a person with purpose—because it no longer matters *why.* This individual knows God holds the reason in His hands. "Why?" is no longer a human responsibility or concern.

Your purpose brings you into a deeper covenant relationship with God. Others may try to destroy your assignment, but they will never be able to destroy your purpose. When Jesus was baptized, the heavens opened up and a voice of confirmation was heard. "And there came a voice from heaven, saying, Thou art my beloved Son, in whom I am well pleased" (Mark 1:11).

Why was the Father "well pleased" with Jesus? It was because of His obedience. Many have understood that they have a purpose, but they do not show any willingness to obey or operate in their purpose. It is because they have not learned to submit in obedience to authority. Jesus understood this. Even though He was God in the flesh, He could not do the will of His Father until He submitted Himself to John in baptism. People who learn how to submit to the spirit of a leader will eventually become the leader.

When God called you He released your authenticity in heaven, but there is a time for it to be released on the earth. There is a season when people will realize that you are "real" and that God has called you for a purpose, but first you must learn to submit to authority.

My natural father is my spiritual father and I submit to him. I have also found a spiritual father in Rod Parsley and Bishop T. D. Jakes. In addition, other spiritual men have been added to my life as spiritual fathers, and I submit to them because they are the authorities in my life. It does not do any good to talk to them and get their spiritual input, if I am not willing to listen and do the thing they tell me is best for my life.

Remember this: You will never have empowerment in your life until you learn to submit to earthly authority, just as you will never fulfill your purpose until you submit in obedience to your Heavenly Father.

Your obedience to authority will give you an *open heaven.* So if you do not know how to obey God you will never have an *open heaven.* As you learn to obey God, He hears your voice and opens up heaven, calls out your assignment, and then begins to speak to you. *When God calls you, it will be to another level of authority.* Jesus was only twelve years old when He knew that He was called for a purpose. He did not operate in His ministry until He was thirty-three, because what had been called or purposed in heaven had not yet been called out on earth.

Your calling is important, because when He calls you He will make it known in front of people. If He calls you in secret, people would not acknowledge your calling; but when God calls you in front of the masses no one will doubt your call or the favor God bestows on you to be equal to the task. Do not misunderstand me here. God is not going to speak to you about how many bags of corn chips to buy, or at which market. Wisdom and common sense will tell you that. The reason some people get confused about the will of God for their life is because their will is so much *their will* that they make *their* will *their* voice. Never mistake your voice for the voice of God. Your call will come clearly through circumstances, the Word of God, and/or His voice speaking to your heart in the "secret place."

Look again at Romans 8:30, "Moreover whom he did predestinate, them he also called: and whom he called, them he also justified: and whom he justified, them he also glorified." Notice that *justified* comes directly after *called.* God does not justify those whom He has not called. However, rest assured: If you are saved—anyone who receives Jesus—you have an eternal call. God called you before you were born, and He would not know you or call you if He was not willing to justify you. If He justifies you, that means He has to protect what He has already called *just.*

Why do you think Psalm 23 says that *goodness and mercy will follow you all the days of your life?* If God justifies you, He has ordained you, because if He has ordained it, then it must stand. Does this mean you can frustrate the grace of God? Does it mean you can keep on continuing in that sin concerning that issue? Absolutely not! I keep an open dialogue with God saying, "God, I need You to deal with this." I am completely justified. No matter what you know about my past, it is okay. God has already cleared that from the slate, because I celebrate Him in everything I do. (I think sometimes that is why we need some enemies around us, who keep on telling you who you are, just to keep you running back to God. That way, you can stay in the posture of giving Him thanks for changing and justifying you.)

Notice in the last part of Romans 8:30 Paul says that we are *glorified*. You might still be having problems, but you have dignity in heaven. You cannot know your purpose without having a passion to fulfill the Father's will.

Let's continue reading verse 30:

And those whom He thus foreordained, He also called; and those whom He called, He also justified (acquitted, made righteous, putting them into right standing with Himself). And those whom He justified, He also glorified [raising them to a heavenly dignity and condition or state of being].

Now I get excited about that... God gives us "right standing" with Him, even knowing our weaknesses. God would never justify you if He did not know the purpose of you overcoming your weaknesses.

Let me share with you about your "situational thorn," the thing inside of your flesh right now that you need to submit to the Lord. God often gives us a "thorn" to help us remember His grace and mercy when He takes it away. So when you notice the thorn, call out to God to remove it, and wait for His deliverance. Remember Romans 8:31–33:

What then shall we say to [all] this? If God is for us, who [can be] against us? [Who can be our foe, if God is on our side?] He who did not withhold or spare [even] His own Son but gave Him up for us all, will He not also with Him freely and graciously give us all [other] things? Who shall bring any charge against God's elect [when it is] God Who justifies [that is, Who puts us in right relation to Himself? Who shall come forward and accuse or impeach those whom God has chosen? Will God, Who acquits us?] (AMP).

These verses give us a perfect reason to live a life that is undisturbed and untroubled. He has given His Son, and has graciously given us all things freely. There is no one who can accuse us or bring a charge against us. We are forgiven, called, and justified. God has chosen us before the foundation of the world. *What more could we ask?* God has acquitted us, even before our enemies. Once that is done, no man can reverse it. No demon in hell can accuse us.

Romans 8:37–38 continues:

> *Yet amid all these things we are more than conquerors and gain a surpassing victory through Him Who loved us. For I am persuaded beyond doubt (am sure) that neither death nor life, nor angels nor principalities, nor things impending and threatening nor things to come nor powers, Nor height nor depth, nor anything else in all creation will be able to separate us from the love of God which is in Christ Jesus our Lord (AMP).*

The Spirit of the Lord is speaking here of *well-being.* We are more than conquerors; we have the victory through Him who loves us. *Look at our heavenly benefit!* Nothing can separate us from the love of God which is in Christ Jesus our Lord! *Therefore, our peace begins with the assurance that He knows us.* We can know our purpose because He foreknew us, ordained us, called us, justified us, and glorified us. Now, that is peace!

In Deuteronomy 28:1–2 we read:

> *If you will listen diligently to the voice of the Lord your God, being watchful to do all His commandments which I command you this day, the Lord your God will set you high above all the nations of the earth. And all these blessings shall come upon you and overtake you if you heed the voice of the Lord your God (AMP).*

Remember this statement: *My obedience determines my overflow.* Whatever area I am obedient in, that determines my overflow. The theme of Global Destiny 2005 was "Birthing Out the Order of the Vision." You have to set a vision of order in your life; an order of obedience to God's prophetic directives. Obey everything God requires of you without question. Again, God will not give an overflow to people that He cannot trust to faithfully manage it, spiritually or otherwise.

If you cannot be trusted with the tithe, 10 percent of your increase, do not expect God to bless your life. When you have it and then choose not to give it, you are being disobedient, and God is not the first priority in your life. You cannot give God an offering until you first give God what rightfully belongs only to Him…the first 10 percent of all your increase (see Mal. 3:7–12).

No one can stop your overflow when you are obedient. They cannot hinder your miracle, your assignment, or your increase. God's favor on your life *is yours*. It belongs to no one else. What a blessing it is to serve a God who pours out His favor on us! Just think of it. When you have completed your calling and God has finished this work inside of you, you want to be able to say (like Paul did), "I finished the course God wanted me to run."

So let me review. Peace enters your life when you understand that you have been **foreknown** before you were formed in your mother's womb. From before time began, God knew your **purpose**, and because of that fore-knowing He **foreordained** you. He **elected** you to be foreordained. He has **authentically** called and **justified** you. Once you have been completely jus-tified, He **glorifies** you. You are **more than a conqueror** and no one can separate you from the love of God. Are you fully assured now of God's unmistakable, unfathomable peace? Do yourself a favor—take everything you have just read to God's "secret place." Let Him give you understanding of your true position in Him as He "makes you lie down" into your next "mold" of glory! As you rest in His presence, remember Paul's timeless instruction: "Those things, which ye have both **learned**, and **received**, and **heard**, and **seen** in me, **do**: and the **God of peace shall be with you**" (Phil. 4:9).

As you submit to the success of God from your *virtue-empowered* life, no weapon that has been formed against you shall be able to prosper!

CHAPTER 12

21 Power Principles to Become a Unique Thinker: Tapping Into the Mind of Christ

God's "protocol of prosperity" is tried and true. It will bless your life abundantly as you learn to "think on" the virtues of God that are listed in Philippians 4:8–9:

- Whatsoever is *True*
- Whatsoever is *Honest*
- Whatsoever is *Just*
- Whatsoever is *Pure*
- Whatsoever is *Lovely*
- Whatsoever is *of Good Report*

The *Amplified Bible* tells us that if we *practice what we have learned* of these virtues and *model our way of living on it,* that the God of peace (of untroubled, undisturbed well-being) will be with us. We also know that we will prosper and be in health even as our soul prospers. As a result, the victorious life God has promised to believers who take the time to prosper their soul can be released in them—in *you,* if you are a believer—in its fullest measure.

Do you believe that you can enjoy a meaningful and abundant life in Christ? Do you want the best that God desires for you? Then make sure to use this supplement as a handy spiritual arsenal of life-changing tips that can keep you on the path of *true prosperity*—not one of merely meeting your own financial needs, but a life of true abundance and satisfaction where you are genuinely blessed: spiritually, physically, emotionally, financially—in every area—and will bless and empower others!

Included in this chapter are 21 major "Power Principles" that, if applied properly, you will "renew your mind" and become "transformed" into a unique thinker for God. This means you are vitally tapped into the mind of Christ, yet are *uniquely you* in activating His wisdom in your daily life.

These 21 Power Principles are specifically designed to yield a balanced life of devotion and discipline that will empower your every success and make you an excellent witness, as well. In each chapter, I present one major "Devotion" principle, with two devotion points beneath it, and one major "Discipline" principle, with five practical discipline points listed underneath for you to follow. All in all, you have 77 anointed and practical "nuggets of wisdom" from the virtues you have obtained by reading the first eleven chapters. When applied, you will move into the full empowerment of whatsoever is *true, honest, just, pure, lovely,* and *of good report...* and the greatest blessing of all, *the God of peace will be with you.*

One final note. I am sure you have noticed the number "7" is a predominant theme in this chapter, because 7 is the number of divine completion in the symbolism of biblical numerology. Just to be clear, the 21 Power Principles can break down to 7 multiplied by 3, and of course, the number 77 is self-explanatory! Five consecutive sevens in all symbolize the number of grace, which reflects what God extends *to us,* as well as how He works *through us.* I anticipate hearing many exciting testimonies about how God begins working in people's lives as they apply the truths contained in this book. I believe you will want to use this handy reference section again and again for your daily devotional time with the Lord, or as a quick guide, when needed, to make sure God's virtues are being fully revealed and manifested in you.

So...take a few moments a day and start *thinking on these things.* As your mind is transformed, your life will be conformed into the image of our Lord and Savior, the one and only, Jesus Christ. Enjoy.

Whatsoever Is True

Thomas saith unto him, Lord, we know not whither thou goest; and how can we know the way? Jesus saith unto him, I am the way, the truth, and the life: no man cometh unto the Father, but by me (John 14:5–6).

1. **Make sure you are His. Are you saved?**
   - Put your trust in Jesus, and ask Him to be your Savior and Lord. Repeat this prayer:
   - *Dear Jesus, come into my heart and change me. I believe You are the Son of God, that You died for my sin, and that You rose from the grave to give me a victorious, abundant life—both now and in eternity. Fill me with Your Holy Spirit, Lord, so that I can become a witness for You. Thank You, Jesus, for saving, healing, and delivering me. I will serve You from this day forward. Amen.*

2. **Develop keen discernment of** *whatsoever is true.* **Facts can change; truth endures forever. To walk in truth you must:**
   - Spend time with God, in the Word and in prayer, daily.
   - Thank God that you are one of His sheep and that you can hear His voice (John 10:1–5).
   - Be obedient to His voice as He leads you out of emotional thinking into a virtue-directed life (John 10:3; Phil. 4:8–9).
   - Understand that God knows what is best for you.
   - Begin to align your thoughts with "the protocol of prosperity"—by thinking on *whatsoever is true.*

   Then said Jesus to those Jews which believed on him, if ye continue in my word, then are ye my disciples indeed; and ye shall know the truth, and the truth shall make you free (John 8:31–32).

Whatsoever Is Honest

Now I pray to God that ye do no evil; not that we should appear approved, but that ye should do that which is honest, though we be as reprobates. For we can do nothing against the truth, but for the truth (2 Cor. 13:7–8).

3. **Maintain an intimate relationship with Jesus Christ through the leadership of the Holy Spirit.**

   • Understand that developing a close relationship with the Lord takes time. You will become more and more comfortable relating and responding to Him.

   • Develop a dialogue with Jesus. Bring your requests to Him, and then be silent, so that you can hear what the Lord speaks in your spirit.

4. **Develop discipline in demonstrating *whatsoever is honest*:**

   • Learn to measure your thoughts and actions against the Word. If they do not line up with Scripture, repent to God, ask Him to help you change, and then obey what He leads you to do.

   • Stay God-centered as you go about your day. When He speaks in your heart, pause and listen. When you do not know what to do in a situation, pause and ask Him for wisdom. Then do what He reveals to your heart.

   • Say what you mean, and mean what you say. Do not tell half-truths to get your own way, or play passive-aggressive games in order to manipulate others. When you say you are going to do something, do it, unless it does not line up with the Word (Matt. 5:37).

   • Be willing to admit to others when you are wrong, and ask for their forgiveness. Do whatever is needed to make the situation right before God. You are God's representative; therefore, you must be honest in all that you do.

   • Handle all of your business and personal affairs with God in mind. Be honest, fair, and upright in your dealings with others. Do not allow your emotions (what you want or desire) to cloud your thinking.

Be of the same mind one toward another. Mind not high things, but condescend to men of low estate. Be not wise in your own conceits. Recompense to no man evil for evil. Provide things honest in the sight of all men. If it be possible, as much as lieth in you, live peaceably with all men (Rom. 12:16–18).

Whatsoever Is Just

For I am not ashamed of the gospel of Christ: for it is the power of God unto salvation to every one that believeth; to the Jew first, and also to the Greek. For therein is the righteousness of God revealed from faith to faith: as it is written, The just shall live by faith (Rom. 1:16–17).

5. **Manifest His righteousness, by trusting in God's unchanging love and obeying His commands.**

   - Trust God's ability to bring change in your heart and life.
   - Pour out your heart to God, good, bad, and indifferent, and leave your burdens at the Cross.

6. **Develop unwavering faith in the word of the Lord by doing** *whatsoever is just*:

   - Learn to trust what you are learning in the Word by acting on your faith.
   - Learn to respond immediately when you hear His voice, regardless of what you are doing or where you may be.
   - Be fair to all. Do not impose your desires on others, and never take advantage of other people (at home, in business, or otherwise) for your own benefit.
   - Be willing to do what is right, even when it hurts.
   - Strive to maintain balance between God, family, work, church, and ministry.

   Now the just shall live by faith: but if any man draw back, my soul shall have no pleasure in him. But we are not of them who draw back unto perdition; but of them that believe to the saving of the soul (Heb. 10:38–39).

Whatsoever Is Pure

Blessed are the pure in heart: for they shall see God (Matt 5:8).

7. **Make sure that ungodly behavior or entanglements do not hinder your prayers.**

   - Walk in purity. Avoid anything that even appears to be ungodly, including watching inappropriate programs on television or at the movie theater, reading suggestive magazines, visiting questionable Internet sites, wearing immodest clothing, and the like. Think of it this way: Can others see a reflection of Christ in you? Can you see His reflection in yourself?

   - Keep your thought life pure. Do not let your mind lead you into "secret sins." Maintain an attitude of repentance, and keep short accounts with God.

8. **Develop self-discipline to walk in *whatsoever is pure*:**

   - Determine that you will not lead, or be led by anyone, into a conversation or situation that is of questionable moral standards.

   - Be willing to give up any perceived "benefit" that is associated with anything that is impure (this includes possible financial benefit from an illicit business venture).

   - Learn how to keep all of your relationships pure before the Lord. Identify and respect spiritual boundaries (i.e., conduct yourself in a worthy manner in male/female relationships; be careful to guard the integrity of friendships with individuals who are married; and so on).

   - Learn to pray more, and talk less.

   - Be an example of Christ.

For the grace of God that bringeth salvation hath appeared to all men, teaching us that, denying ungodliness and worldly lusts, we should live soberly, righteously, and godly, in this present world; looking for that blessed hope, and the glorious appearing of the great God and our Saviour Jesus Christ; Who gave himself for us, that he might redeem us from all iniquity, and purify unto himself a peculiar people, zealous of good works (Titus 2:11–14).

Whatsoever Is Lovely

One thing have I desired of the LORD, that will I seek after; that I may dwell in the house of the LORD all the days of my life, to behold the beauty of the LORD, and to enquire in his temple (Ps. 27:4).

9. **Maintain an attitude of humility before the Lord. Willingly surrender all in obedience to Him.**

   • Let go of it all—especially what you think you have *done right*—and then let God fill you with His thoughts about your prophetic purpose.

   • Follow His path for the rest of your life.

10. **Develop a mindset that is tailored to your divine purpose, as you pursue *whatsoever is lovely*:**

    • Become a servant to God and others. Learn how to put the needs of those around you first. Discipline yourself to do things for the benefit of all; not to advance or support your personal, professional, or spiritual reputation.

    • Do everything as unto the Lord. Do not let pride motivate you to conform to what other people think you should be doing. Stay focused on your vision, mission, and goals.

    • Consider others—both small and great, experienced and inexperienced, strong and weak—to be as valuable to God as you are. Empower them to achieve excellence.

    • Bless, pray for, and do good to your enemies.

    • Give glory to God in all you do.

And let the beauty of the LORD our God be upon us: and estab-lish thou the work of our hands upon us; yea, the work of our hands establish thou it (Ps. 90:17).

Whatsoever Is of Good Report

Now faith is the substance of things hoped for, the evidence of things not seen. For by it the elders obtained a good report (Heb. 11:1–2).

11. **Maximize your testimony through expressing your faith in God.**

   - Believe His report (the Bible), instead of your own.
   - Act on what you believe.

12. **Demonstrate every virtue you have received from Christ as you focus on *whatsoever is of good report*:**

   - Worship God in spirit and in truth, not from your emotions. Other people will see your devotion and discipline, and know that God is real.
   - Maintain an attitude of gratitude. It will be contagious.
   - Focus on the promise, not on the problem. Deal with everyday issues with a mindset of victory.
   - Have more confidence in what you can achieve with God, than in what you can accomplish on your own. Refuse to be distracted by what you *assume* should be rightfully yours. Depend only on God's grace and favor in your life.
   - Keep focused on your eternal assignment, and let God strengthen you for the task. Do not let anything hinder your intimacy with Him. Conform yourself completely to His will and let all things *become new.*

   The light of the eyes rejoiceth the heart: and a good report maketh the bones fat (Prov. 15:30).

If There Is Any Virtue

Grace and peace be multiplied unto you through the knowledge of God, and of Jesus our Lord, according as his divine power hath given unto us all things that pertain unto life and godliness, through the knowledge of him that hath called us to glory and virtue... (2 Peter 1:2–3).

13. **Measure your progress in receiving and incorporating God's virtues in your life.**

    - Examine your prayer life. Is it the same today as it has always been, or is God leading you in new and progressive ways? Are you seeing more results from prayer?

    - Are you still committed to applying His virtues, received through prayer, in every area of your life? What about those areas that are extra sensitive? Are you willing to surrender these negative behaviors to Him?

14. **Do everything with excellence as you uphold the *virtues of God*:**

    - Think victoriously, even when circumstances seem to be against you. Learn to believe God beyond hope in your outward condition. Do not look to other people to solve your problems. Embrace your divine potential.

    - Ask God to reveal your assignment, and then pursue it. Let the touch of God transform your life. Be willing to "press through" every hindrance to reach your goal.

    - Flow in the anointing God has bestowed upon you to achieve your prophetic purpose. You can do far more, spiritually and otherwise, when you submit to the anointing in your area of business or ministry.

    - Hold your seed of promise in prayer, encouraging yourself in the Lord, until the Holy Spirit releases you to perform it. When it is time, speak the promise...and watch your destiny unfold.

- Celebrate your uniqueness by allowing God's virtues to heal your "issues." Be honest with yourself and God. Take responsibility to become an example of what Christ has performed in your life.

And beside this, giving all diligence, add to your faith virtue; and to virtue knowledge; and to knowledge temperance; and to temperance patience; and to patience godliness; and to godliness brotherly kindness; and to brotherly kindness charity. For if these things be in you, and abound, they make you that ye shall neither be barren nor unfruitful in the knowledge of our Lord Jesus Christ (2 Peter 1:5–8).

If There Is Any Praise

I will bless the LORD at all times: his praise shall continually be in my mouth (Ps. 34:1).

15. Make a joyful noise unto the Lord for bringing you this far.

- Always return the praise to Him, for who He is and for what He has done.
- Praise Him at all times, not just when you feel like it.

16. Distinguish who you are becoming in Christ by your *lifestyle of praise*:

- Keep God as the foundation of everything you do, recognizing that you are nothing without Him. Others will see the integrity of your praise.
- Refrain from forming associations with people whose eternal thinking is not as progressive as yours. Instead, let your praise be an example for them to follow.
- Fulfill your vow of praise to the Lord. Be thankful when times are good or bad. Trust the process of divine maturity that God is working in you.

- Praise God 24/7. Do not make your praise exclusive to the church setting.

- Trust God to promote you in your occupation or spiritual assignment. Be aware and prepared to seize each divine opportunity... then give God the praise for releasing it to you.

I will praise thee, O Lord, with my whole heart; I will shew forth all thy marvellous works (Ps. 9:1).

Practice What You Have Learned

For if any be a hearer of the word, and not a doer, he is like unto a man beholding his natural face in a glass: For he beholdeth himself, and goeth his way, and straightway forgetteth what manner of man he was. But whoso looketh into the perfect law of liberty, and continueth therein, he being not a forgetful hearer, but a doer of the work, this man shall be blessed in his deed (James 1:23–25).

17. **Make consistent progress in "thinking on" the virtues of God. Let His character attributes transform your life.**

- Renew your mind daily by reading and meditating on God's Word.
- Maintain an attitude of repentance. Ask God to restore you if you fall, and obediently respond to Him as He redirects your steps. Obediently continue building on the principles you have learned.

18. **Dare to "practice what you have learned" by stepping out through faith in God and DOING what God has called you to do:**

- Set measurable goals, spiritually and otherwise, to monitor your progress. Be accountable to God and others, and support your goals by making timely and accurate assessments.
- Seize every opportunity that comes from God, whether it be in your home, in the workplace, at church, or in your area of ministry.
- Be flexible to adjust your goals, if needed, to address needs as they present themselves.

- Review the results of your focused efforts, and know that you cannot accomplish anything of value without God. Invest in yourself through training to continue developing in the practical disciplines of your prophetic purpose.
- Handle the increase God provides with wisdom to maximize your fruitfulness for the Kingdom.

And whosoever doth not bear his cross, and come after me, cannot be my disciple. For which of you, intending to build a tower, sitteth not down first, and counteth the cost, whether he have sufficient to finish it? Lest haply, after he hath laid the foundation, and is not able to finish it, all that behold it begin to mock him, saying, This man began to build, and was not able to finish (Luke 14:27–30).

Model Your Way of Living On It

Let this mind be in you, which was also in Christ Jesus: Who, being in the form of God, thought it not robbery to be equal with God: but made himself of no reputation, and took upon him the form of a servant, and was made in the likeness of men... (Phil. 2:5–7).

19. **Manifest the authenticity of who you are by becoming who God has destined you to be.**

- Press deeper into God through consistent prayer and instant obedience.
- Live, move, and have your entire being in Him.

20. **Dedicate yourself to "modeling" His virtues continually to establish your renewed lifestyle:**

- Never try to "copycat" another person's anointing. Be who God created you to be.
- Understand that God has expansive plans for you. Take the limits off. Be a model of Christ wherever you go.

- Choose people of like vision and purpose to be in your inner circle. Never remain where your authenticity is not recognized.

- Be willing to let everything go when and if God chooses to "break a mold" in your life. If required, change your habits, associations, or anything that cannot come with you into a new level of virtue-directed living.

- Acknowledge the struggles you have overcome that have pressed you to this new level in Christ. Be transparent and willing to share your testimony as God directs so that others can see Christ in you—the hope of glory.

Being confident of this very thing, that he which hath begun a good work in you will perform it until the day of Jesus Christ... (Phil. 1:6).

And the God of Peace Will Be With You

Do not fret or have any anxiety about anything, but in every circumstance and in everything, by prayer and petition (definite requests), with thanksgiving, continue to make your wants known to God. And God's peace [shall be yours, that tranquil state of a soul assured of its salvation through Christ, and so fearing nothing from God and being content with its earthly lot of whatever sort that is, that peace] which transcends all understanding shall garrison and mount guard over your hearts and minds in Christ Jesus (Phil. 4:6–7 AMP).

21. **More than anything, remain in His presence and rest in His "secret place," where you will be free from every fear and anxiety, overcoming your flesh and every troubling circumstance, fully assured that you have a safe refuge from every demonic attack—*because the God of peace is with you.***

- Stay under the shadow of the Almighty by dwelling with Him in prayer. Do not just pay the Lord a visit every now and then. Learn to linger.

- Be still and know that He is God. Let Him mold you. Be prepared to move from "glory to glory" as you are transformed into the ever increasing stature of the image of Christ.

- Know who you are in Christ. *Firstly*, you are *purposed.* You have found the meaning of your life, so be bold and move forward to possess everything God has for you!

- *Secondly*, you have been *elected.* You have been hand picked by God to become His very own son or daughter. Walk like a child of the King.

- *Thirdly*, you are *eternally assured* of your salvation, healing, and deliverance. Go and impart these free eternal gifts to others.

- *Fourth*, you have been *called by God* to fulfill His purpose and each of your earthly assignments. Know the difference and BE the difference, everywhere you go.

- *Last, but definitely not least*, you have been *eternally justified*, "just as if" you had never sinned and fallen out of fellowship with God. Never let the enemy deceive you into thinking there is no hope for you if you fall. A righteous man falls seven times (God's number of completion), yet rises again each time. Remember this as you go forth carrying God's love, mercy, and forgiveness.

- For the rest, brethren, whatever is true, whatever is worthy of reverence and is honorable and seemly, whatever is just, whatever is pure, whatever is lovely and lovable, whatever is kind and winsome and gracious, if there is any virtue and excellence, if there is anything worthy of praise, think on and weigh and take account of these things [fix your minds on them].

Practice what you have learned and received and heard and seen in me, and model your way of living on it, and the God of peace (of untroubled, undisturbed well-being) will be with you (Phil. 4:8–9 AMP).

Endnotes

Introduction

¹ Albert E. Brumley, *"I'll Fly Away,"* (words and music A. E. Brumley, 1932; Albert E. Brumley and Sons, 1960).

² James Strong, "Hebrew and Chaldee Dictionary" in *Strong's Exhaustive Concordance of the Bible* (Nashville: Abingdon, 1890), s.v. "heart," Prov. 4:23, #3820; *Brown-Driver-Briggs Hebrew and English Lexicon*, Unabridged (coded to Strong's), Electronic Database, copyright © 2002, 2003 by Biblesoft, Inc. All rights reserved.

Chapter 2

¹ Sol Steinmetz, Editor-in-Chief, *Webster's American Family Dictionary* (New York: Random House, 1998), s.v. "honest." All rights reserved.

² Joseph Henry Thayer, *Thayer's Greek-English Lexicon of the New Testament*: coded with the numbering system *from Strong's Exhaustive Concordance of the Bible* (Peabody: Hendrickson, 1996), Strong's "Greek Dictionary"), s.v. "honest," Phil. 4:8, #4586.

³ Webster's Family, s.v. "dishonest."

⁴ William Shakespeare, *Hamlet*, Act 1, Scene 3.

Chapter 3

¹ Strong, Hebrew Dictionary, s.v. "just," Isa. 45:21, #6662; *Brown-Driver-Briggs* (coded with Strong's numbering).

² "For whom the LORD loveth he correcteth; even as a father the son in whom he delighteth" (Prov. 3:12).

³ Romans 3:24, *emphasis mine*; Ephesians 2:8, respectively.

⁴ Strong, Greek Dictionary, s.v. "justified," Rom. 3:42, #1344 from #1342; Thayer, coded with Strong's numbering.

⁵ Ephesians 2:8.

⁶ 2 Corinthians 4:4.

⁷ Hebrews 1:3.

⁸ 2 Corinthians 3:18 AMP.

⁹ Bill Gaither, Gloria Gaither, and Richard Smallwood, "Center of My Joy," (Gaither Music Company, Century Oak & Richwood Music, 1997).

¹⁰ See Romans 8:28.

[11] "The Lord your God is in the midst of you, a Mighty One, a Savior [Who saves]! He will rejoice over you with joy; He will rest [in silent satisfaction] and in His love He will be silent and make no mention [of past sins, or even recall them]; He will exult over you with singing" (Zeph. 3:17 AMP).

[12] For the Lord takes pleasure in His people; He will beautify the humble with salvation and adorn the wretched with victory" (Ps. 149:4 AMP).

[13] Romans 8:28.

Chapter 4

[1] Strong, Greek Dictionary, s.v. "pure," Phil. 4:8, #53, "from the same as *40*...."; s.v. "holy," i.e., Rom. 12:1, Eph. 1:4, #40.

[2] See Philippians 3:8-11.

[3] See Proverbs 18:24.

[4] See John 1:29.

[5] See Romans 8:34; Hebrews 12:2.

[6] See John 15:15,17; Luke 6:27-28,35; Romans 12:14; Proverbs 25:21; Matthew 5:44 (paraphrased).

Chapter 5

[1] Strong, Greek Dictionary, s.v. "peace," Phil. 4:9, #1515; also Thayer, coded with Strong's numbering.

[2] See 1 Corinthians 2:16.

[3] See Lamentations 3:22-23.

[4] Philippians 2:5.

Chapter 6

[1] Exodus 17:6.

[2] See 1 Timothy 2:8.

Chapter 7

[1] Webster's Family, s.v. "virtue."

[2] Strong, Greek Dictionary, s.v. "virtue," Luke 6:19, #1411; Thayer, coded with Strong's numbering.

[3] W. E. Vine, "An Expository Dictionary of New Testament Words," in *Vine's Complete Expository Dictionary of Old and New Testament Words* (Nashville: Thomas Nelson Inc., 1984), s.v. "anoint, anointing," "A. Verbs," p. 28.

[4] Frederick W. Knobloch, trans., *"Routh* Provisional Edition" in *A New English Translation of the Septuagint*, The International Organization for Septuagint and Cognate Studies, Inc. © 2004; used by permission of Oxford University Press; all rights reserved.

[5] Strong, Hebrew Dictionary, s.v. "anoint," Exod. 40:15, #4886; *Brown-Driver-Briggs* (coded with Strong's numbering).

[6] See Exodus 40:9.

[7] Strong, Greek Dictionary, s.v. "hath anointed," "hast anointed," "anointed," Luke 4:18; Acts 4:27; 10:38; respectively; #5548; Thayer coded with Strong's numbering.

[8] Strong, Greek Dictionary, s.v. "hath anointed," 2 Cor. 1:21, #5548, Thayer coded with Strong's numbering.

[9] Galatians 5:22-23.

[10] Matthew 9:20.

Chapter 8

[1] See the discussion in Vine, "Nelson's Expository Dictionary of the Old Testament," in *Vine's Complete Expository Dictionary of Old and New Testament Words*, s.v. "vow," "B. Noun," pp. 278,279.

Chapter 9

[1] Webster's Family, s.v. "practice."

[2] Strong, Greek Dictionary, s.v. "learned," Phil. 4:9, #3129, Thayer coded with Strong's numbering.

[3] Strong, Greek Dictionary, s.v. "received," Phil. 4:9, #3880, Thayer coded with Strong's numbering.

Prayer of Salvation

God loves you—no matter who you are, no matter what your past. God loves you so much that He gave His one and only begotten Son for you. The Bible tells us that "...whoever believes in him shall not perish but have eternal life" (John 3:16 NIV). Jesus laid down His life and rose again so that we could spend eternity with Him in heaven and experience His absolute best on earth. If you would like to receive Jesus into your life, say the following prayer out loud and mean it from your heart.

Heavenly Father, I come to You admitting that I am a sinner. Right now, I choose to turn away from sin, and I ask You to cleanse me of all unrighteousness. I believe that Your Son, Jesus, died on the cross to take away my sins. I also believe that He rose again from the dead so that I might be forgiven of my sins and made righteous through faith in Him. I call upon the name of Jesus Christ to be the Savior and Lord of my life. Jesus, I choose to follow You and ask that You fill me with the power of the Holy Spirit. I declare that right now I am a child of God. I am free from sin and full of the righteousness of God. I am saved in Jesus' name. Amen.

If you prayed this prayer to receive Jesus Christ as your Savior for the first time, please contact us on the Web at www.harrisonhouse.com to receive a free book.

Or you may write to us at:

Harrison House

P.O. Box 35035

Tulsa, Oklahoma 74153

About the Author

Thomas Weeks, III is a bishop, a prophet, a highly sought after motivational speaker, as well as conference and television host. He is co-founder, along with his wife Dr. Juanita Bynum Weeks, and Bishop of Global Destiny Ministries, with dual locations in Washington, D.C., and Atlanta, Georgia, metropolitan areas. Upon accepting his calling as a third generation pastor, he furthered his studies and garnered an AA in Biblical Studies and a BA in Theology. He later pursued advanced studies toward an MA in Christian Counseling at the Christian International College of Theology and, in Spring 2006, received an Honorary Doctorate of Divinity Degree from Truth Bible College in Jacksonville, Florida.

Thomas Weeks, III has a global vision for prophetic and revelatory impartation to the nation. Bishop Weeks' ministry focuses on empowering believers of Jesus Christ worldwide for the manifestation of the Kingdom of God in the earth. Through Bishop Weeks' divinely inspired multicultural vision, God releases a powerful anointing in the atmosphere as Bishop Weeks delivers life applicable biblical principles and truths to empower and transform countless lives and effectuate spiritual maturity.

Thomas Weeks, III is a prolific and profound orator and author who moves the soul of those listening or reading to a whole new dimension with his words of wisdom. Prepare yourself to shift from both poverty and self-doubt to prosperity and self-confidence as you discover the keys to unlock the doors of wealth and success that already reside within you, if you have opened the Door to the Source of all abundance and all things good through receiving Jesus Christ. After reading Bishop Weeks' books, even with just one encounter, your life will never be the same.

CONTACT INFORMATION
For more information regarding church services
or upcoming events, visit: www.bishopweeks.com

Mailing address:
BTWIII Ministries • P.O. Box 60866 • Washington, DC 20039

Or call: (877) 4BTWIII (877-428-9444)

Or e-mail: info@bishopweeks.com

*Please include your prayer requests
and comments when you write.*

Additional copies of this book
are available from your local bookstore.

EVEN as YOUR SOUL PROSPERS

Written by Thomas Weeks III

Home   Itinerary   About The Author   Sample Chapter   Video Clips   Testimonies   News

GOD HAS PROMISED YOU AN ABUNDANT LIFE.

Why then does it seem so many people are struggling to find purpose, financial peace, and lasting relationships? Are these areas where you feel you are lacking? Does it seem as if God's Word is not working? You could be missing God's best!

Bishop Thomas Weeks, III reveals that God's promise of an abundant life is directly tied into fulfilling your purpose. And your purpose cannot be attained until you train your soul. A prosperous soul causes prosperity in every area of your life. Your "soul"—your mind, will, and emotions—can be taught, trained, and changed for your benefit and for the glory of God.

These divine principles of "soul prosperity" are hidden in the types and shadows of the Torah—the first five books of the Bible. As you journey through the amazing stories and examples in the Old Testament, your life will be changed forever. You will learn how to train your soul and unlock the blessings of God's abundant life!

READ A CHAPTER
Acrobat Reader required

BUY THIS BOOK

TESTIMONIES
READ THE BOOK? SHARE A TESTIMONY WITH US!

Overwhelmed with joy

Just wanted to express again how much I am blessed by the teaching by Bishop Weeks this past Friday Evening. I am taking every principle to heart and am vowing to not be just a hearer of the Word but a doer.

I'm just so excited and overwhelmed with joy...still knowing that there is a lot of tough work ahead...And I know hanging on to every word and putting the teachings from Bishop Weeks in to action will help on this journey. Thanks so much for the prayers of this ministry....for this opportunity to partner and be a blessing so that others lives can be changed as well.
Submitted by C. Longs Houston, TX

I was so encouraged

I was so encouraged by Even As Your Soul Prospers that I wanted to sow into this kingdom. Thank you for blessing me w/ revelation knowledge & life changing mindset of to effectively prosper.
Submitted by C. Longs Houston, TX

...such an "on point" word for this hour! As you read this book, you'll be enlightened and brought to a new level of understanding concerning the necessity for soul growth. ...If you walk according to the prophetic code of God, you cannot and will not be denied. Like me, you'll wholeheartedly embrace Revelation 3:18: "...to purchase from Me gold refined and tested by fire, that you may be [truly] wealthy..." (amp).

- Dr. Juanita B. Weeks

WANT TO INVITE BISHOP WEEKS TO YOUR CHURCH?

Interested in booking Bishop Weeks for a speaking engagement? _____ to complete a request form.

MORE PRODUCTS
FROM BISHOP THOMAS WEEKS, III

40 Days to Prosperous Soul Devotional
When you know your purpose, it's time to unlock your abundance.

MORE INFORMATION

What's on Your Mind?
The level of your success begins with your thinking.

MORE INFORMATION

WHERE TO BUY
FIND A BOOKSTORE

www.harrisonhouse.com
www.amazon.com
www.familychristian.com
www.berean.com
www.mardel.com
www.christianbook.com

NEWS/PRESS
MORE NEWS

Realize Your Purpose, Release Your Blessings
Bishop Thomas Weeks, III offers a fresh interpretation on the theme of prosperity that has proven to be extremely popular among many denominations.
[more...]

Realize Your Purpose, Release Your Blessings
Bishop Thomas Weeks, III offers a fresh interpretation on the theme of prosperity that has proven to be extremely popular among many denominations.
[more...]

Even As Your Soul Prospers

by Thomas Weeks, III

ISBN # 1-57794-710-X

Release the Power to Prosper!

Bestselling author, Bishop Thomas Weeks, III, reveals that God's promise of an abundant life is directly tied into fulfilling your purpose. And your purpose cannot be attained until you train your soul, bringing soul prosperity. A prosperous soul causes prosperity in every area of your life. Your "soul"—your mind, will, and emotions—can be taught, trained, and changed for your benefit and for the glory of God!

You can begin today to train your soul and unlock the blessings of God's abundant life!

This is such an "on point" word for this hour! As you read this book, you'll be enlightened and brought to a new level of understanding concerning the necessity for soul growth....

— Dr. Juanita Bynum Weeks

For more information log onto www.evenasyoursoulprospers.com.

Even as Your Soul Prospers
Thomas Weeks, III

Available at fine bookstores everywhere.

Harrison House Publishers
Books That Bring Hope, Books That Bring Change
www.harrisonhouse.com

40 Days to a Prosperous Soul

by Thomas Weeks, III

ISBN # 1-57794-739-8

Take 40 Days and Turn Your Life Around!

The struggles of life—financial, emotional distress, family challenges, health, and others— can overwhelm you and leave you without hope. You may even feel that God has let you down or His Word does not work. But difficult challenges *can* be overcome and it starts inside—by discovering your divine purpose and developing your soul.

In 40 short devotions, Thomas Weeks, III can put you on the path to training your soul (your mind, will, and emotions). These divine principles of "soul prosperity" are hidden in the types and shadows of the Torah—the first five books of the Old Testament in the Bible. They point to the redemptive work of Jesus Christ, disclosed later in the New Testament, and reveal how your purpose in God ties directly into living a prosperous life.

Don't wait any longer. You can begin today to make a lasting change and unlock the door to an abundant life!

Available at fine bookstores everywhere.

Harrison House Publishers
Books That Bring Hope, Books That Bring Change
www.harrisonhouse.com

EMPOWER YOUR LIFE
WITH SUCCESS FOR DUMMIES

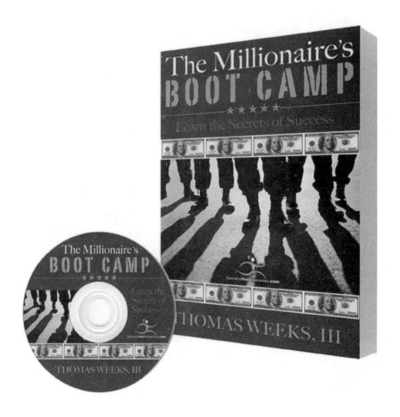

www.harrisonhouse.com

Fast. Easy. Convenient!

- ◆ New Book Information
- ◆ Look Inside the Book
- ◆ Press Releases
- ◆ Bestsellers
- ◆ Free E-News
- ◆ Author Biographies

- ◆ Upcoming Books
- ◆ Share Your Testimony
- ◆ Online Product Availability
- ◆ Product Specials
- ◆ Order Online

For the latest in book news and author information, please visit us on the Web at www.harrisonhouse.com. Get up-to-date pictures and details on all our powerful and life-changing products. Sign up for our e-mail newsletter, *Friends of the House,* and receive free monthly information on our authors and products including testimonials, author announcements, and more!

Harrison House—
Books That Bring Hope, Books That Bring Change

THE HARRISON HOUSE VISION

Proclaiming the truth and the power
Of the Gospel of Jesus Christ
With excellence;

Challenging Christians to
Live victoriously,
Grow spiritually,
Know God intimately.